The Fortean Influence
on Science Fiction

CRITICAL EXPLORATIONS IN SCIENCE FICTION AND FANTASY
(a series edited by Donald E. Palumbo and C.W. Sullivan III)

Earlier Works: www.mcfarlandpub.com

Recent Works: 52 *Michael Moorcock: Fiction, Fantasy and the World's Pain* (Mark Scroggins, 2016)

53 *The Last Midnight: Essays on Apocalyptic Narratives in Millennial Media* (ed. Leisa A. Clark, Amanda Firestone, Mary F. Pharr, 2016)

54 *The Science Fiction Mythmakers: Religion, Science and Philosophy in Wells, Clarke, Dick and Herbert* (Jennifer Simkins, 2016)

55 *Gender and the Quest in British Science Fiction Television: An Analysis of* Doctor Who, Blake's 7, Red Dwarf *and* Torchwood (Tom Powers, 2016)

56 *Saving the World Through Science Fiction: James Gunn, Writer, Teacher and Scholar* (Michael R. Page, 2017)

57 *Wells Meets Deleuze: The Scientific Romances Reconsidered* (Michael Starr, 2017)

58 *Science Fiction and Futurism: Their Terms and Ideas* (Ace G. Pilkington, 2017)

59 *Science Fiction in Classic Rock: Musical Explorations of Space, Technology and the Imagination, 1967–1982* (Robert McParland, 2017)

60 *Patricia A. McKillip and the Art of Fantasy World-Building* (Audrey Isabel Taylor, 2017)

61 *The Fabulous Journeys of Alice and Pinocchio: Exploring Their Parallel Worlds* (Laura Tosi with Peter Hunt, 2018)

62 *A* Dune *Companion: Characters, Places and Terms in Frank Herbert's Original Six Novels* (Donald E. Palumbo, 2018)

63 *Fantasy Literature and Christianity: A Study of the Mistborn, Coldfire, Fionavar Tapestry and Chronicles of Thomas Covenant Series* (Weronika Łaszkiewicz, 2018)

64 *The British Comic Invasion: Alan Moore, Warren Ellis, Grant Morrison and the Evolution of the American Style* (Jochen Ecke, 2019)

65 *The Archive Incarnate: The Embodiment and Transmission of Knowledge in Science Fiction* (Joseph Hurtgen, 2018)

66 *Women's Space: Essays on Female Characters in the 21st Century Science Fiction Western* (ed. Melanie A. Marotta, 2019)

67 *"Hailing frequencies open": Communication in* Star Trek: The Next Generation (Thomas D. Parham III, 2019)

68 *The Global Vampire: Essays on the Undead in Popular Culture Around the World* (ed. Cait Coker, 2019)

69 *Philip K. Dick: Essays of the Here and Now* (ed. David Sandner, 2019)

70 *Michael Bishop and the Persistence of Wonder: A Critical Study of the Writings* (Joe Sanders, 2020)

71 *Caitlín R. Kiernan: A Critical Study of Her Dark Fiction* (James Goho, 2020)

72 *In* Frankenstein's *Wake: Mary Shelley, Morality and Science Fiction* (Alison Bedford, 2020)

73 *The Fortean Influence on Science Fiction: Charles Fort and the Evolution of the Genre* (Tanner F. Boyle, 2020)

74 *Arab and Muslim Science Fiction* (Hosan Elzembely and Emad El-Din Aysha, 2020)

The Fortean Influence on Science Fiction
Charles Fort and the Evolution of the Genre

TANNER F. BOYLE

CRITICAL EXPLORATIONS IN
SCIENCE FICTION AND FANTASY, 73
Series Editors Donald E. Palumbo *and* C.W. Sullivan III

McFarland & Company, Inc., Publishers
Jefferson, North Carolina

This book has undergone peer review.

LIBRARY OF CONGRESS CATALOGUING-IN-PUBLICATION DATA

Names: Boyle, Tanner F., author.
Title: The Fortean influence on science fiction : Charles Fort
and the evolution of the genre / Tanner F. Boyle.
Description: Jefferson, North Carolina : McFarland & Company, Inc.,
Publishers, 2021 | Series: Critical explorations in science fiction and fantasy ; 73 |
Includes bibliographical references and index.
Identifiers: LCCN 2020047543| ISBN 9781476677408 (paperback : acid free paper) ∞
ISBN 9781476641904 (ebook)
Subjects: LCSH: Fort, Charles, 1874-1932—Influence. | Fort, Charles,
1874-1932—Criticism and interpretation. | Science fiction—History and criticism.
Classification: LCC PS3511.O63 Z55 2021 | DDC 813/.52—dc23
LC record available at https://lccn.loc.gov/2020047543

BRITISH LIBRARY CATALOGUING DATA ARE AVAILABLE

ISBN (print) 978-1-4766-7740-8
ISBN (ebook) 978-1-4766-4190-4

© 2021 Tanner F. Boyle. All rights reserved

*No part of this book may be reproduced or transmitted in any form
or by any means, electronic or mechanical, including photocopying
or recording, or by any information storage and retrieval system,
without permission in writing from the publisher.*

Front cover art by Harold Winfield Scott from
Unknown magazine, March 1939

Printed in the United States of America

*McFarland & Company, Inc., Publishers
Box 611, Jefferson, North Carolina 28640
www.mcfarlandpub.com*

Table of Contents

Key Abbreviations — vii
Preface — 1
Introduction: The Damned Facts — 5

1. A Fortean Emergence: The Early SF/Forteana Relationship — 9
2. Defining Maybe-fiction — 18
3. Lo! Forteana! Early Fortean SF Authors — 59
4. Fort's Further Pulpy History: The Editors and the Historians — 78
5. Continuation of Cosmic Dread: A Fortean Analysis of Arthur C. Clarke — 97
6. Forteana and Religious Experience: A Fortean Analysis of Philip K. Dick — 111
7. A Hard-Headed, Commonsensical Fortean: A Fortean Analysis of Robert A. Heinlein — 120
8. Conspiracy and Forteana: A Fortean Analysis of Robert Anton Wilson — 131
9. A Procession of the Damned: Fortean Footnotes — 139
10. Afterthoughts — 147

Chapter Notes — 155
Bibliography — 171
Index — 179

Key Abbreviations

Fortean Times—FT
International Fortean Organization—INFO
Philip K. Dick—PKD
Robert Anton Wilson—RAW
Science fiction—SF

"Do you trust the book you're reading?"
—Boston Spaceships, "UFO Love Letters"

"Chicken that lays an egg with the face of Christ imprinted on the shell, inhuman voices whispering through the static on an empty radio waveband. Don't these things **fascinate** you, Joshua?"
—Grant Morrison, Doom Patrol Volume 2 #19

Preface

The field of science always has a bone to pick with the paranormal and the genre of science fiction is no different. This work began as an English thesis, so I soon found that literary studies, too, has a similar blind spot for the paranormal, unless it is relegated to fiction. This is to say that not much has been written about "true" paranormal stories from a literary standpoint. Because of this, Charles Fort, who was amongst numerous big names in New York's 1920s literary scene, is often unacknowledged. Fort's best friend, Theodore Dreiser, has been subject to abundant scholarship. But the hermit of the Bronx, the foe of science, the prophet of the unexplained has very little scholarship written about him. This book hopes to change that.

My true passion in literature is what many consider to be the bottom of the barrel, alternatively called occult or paranormal non-fiction. I scoured my local library for books about UFOs, aliens, and ghosts and read them with vigor. The works shaped how I viewed the world, especially as young as I was, and made the world seem more fantastic, mysterious, and even terrifying. As I grew older, the less I took these works seriously. Many of them were pieces of sensationalist literature aimed at shocking the reader as opposed to giving a factual account of mysterious events. Urban legends were equated with true reports; none of it was believable any longer. Rediscovering Charles Fort after being only briefly acquainted with him in a young adult novel was what reignited my love of the strange. Fort's works capture the reasons why the paranormal fascinates some of us and frightens others. He made these often-ridiculed subjects matter again to me; he made me more comfortable with the fact that they *did* matter to me.

SF too fought a lengthy battle to gain credibility in the literary community, but it has slowly risen in status over the past half-century—far from its lowly origins in the pulps. "Paranormal non-fiction" continues to live in the dregs, a fate that seems wildly unfair given how codependent the genre and SF have been throughout the last century. When I was first fully introduced to SF, I was already fully aware of Fort and his works. After reading several of these SF classics, such as *2001: A Space Odyssey*, I could not help but notice that the stories were often Fortean. This realization is how this research truly began. I could find numerous references to Charles Fort by SF authors, editors, and historians, but these were never collated. Many SF community members opined that you could fill a book with all the SF writers that Charles Fort has influenced, but no one had done so. This book is an honest attempt to highlight those numerous authors with Fortean ties; it also hopes to explain just why his influence has been so far-reaching. My research led me to interact with several figures in SF and Forteana I never dreamed I would correspond with. It led me down paths sometimes frustrating, sometimes rewarding, but almost always delightfully strange.

I wish to give special thanks to Prof. Gary Wihl for initiating me into SF studies and advising this work from its fetal stage to its present form. I want to further thank Prof. Guinn Batten for advising how this work should progress and giving endlessly helpful feedback. Lastly, I am forever grateful to Prof. Jeffrey J. Kripal for being the premier source of paranormal/SF research and giving me early advice on how to proceed with this work. His writings have not only inspired facets of this book this book, they have also been immensely important resources for contextualizing the relationship between SF and Fortean topics.

The Heinlein Archives, Tessa B. Dick, Ben Rock, Jennifer Reibenspies, and Kristine Helbling have all been immensely helpful in my research regarding the fictional side of things. Tessa B. Dick was especially helpful to give me information about her late husband's interest in Charles Fort. In terms of Fortean research, I would like to thank the ever-helpful Forteans in the email chain; you all know who you are. First and foremost, there is the INFO member Richard Leshuk, who immediately initiated a search for the INFO letters to SF greats. Then there is the SF great in the flesh, David Drake, who gave immensely helpful background information about the organization and its relationship to SF. Former editor of INFO Michael Shoemaker gave similarly helpful information, contextualizing a group about which facts seem hard to come by. Mr. X, the Consulting Resologist, gave me important contacts in this research and numerous other leads that were a joy to follow. Lastly, amongst the Forteans, there is Patrick Huyghe and Anomalist Books for releasing highly readable and groundbreaking works on Fortean topics and pointing me in the direction of the wonderful people at McFarland.

I will forever appreciate Claire Ma whose abundant support and feedback was unending despite my weird interests. Stephen Steinbacher has been an excellent creative sounding board and our horror movie podcast always provides a perfect break from the hours of hard work. Fellow literature scholars Catherine Evans and Bethie Wang provided amazing feedback on the manuscript at multiple stages in the revision process. Catherine gave comprehensive notes and feedback on the full manuscript and Bethie focused on Chapter 2.

And lastly, I want to thank the subject of this book, Charles Hoy Fort, the prophet of the unexplained. As this book intends to illustrate, Fort provides an eccentric yet innovative worldview to his readers. While he introduced me and others to the world of unexplained phenomena, he also provides a beautiful philosophy through which literature, SF especially, can be further appreciated. In casual terms, I hope that I have done him proud.

Introduction: The Damned Facts

> *The datum is so important to us, because it enforces, in another field, our acceptance that dark bodies of planetary size traverse this solar system. Our position: That the things have been seen: Also that their shadows have been seen. Vast black thing poised like a crow over the moon.*
> —Charles Fort[1]

The literary genre name "science fiction" is a slight misnomer. While there is a preoccupation with scientific discoveries and their implications, there has always been odd importance assigned to secret knowledge and "damned facts." While the "first" science fiction author, H.G. Wells, displayed an interest primarily in the scientific, the precursors to the genre blended scientific innovation with the damned, secret knowledge often hidden or shoved aside as pseudoscience or folklore. Note the example of Frankenstein's monster: this creature could not have come into being solely based on the science taught to Victor Frankenstein—he must research into the "pseudoscience" of the occult scientist Agrippa. As Freud would note, the horror of the Hoffmann short story and SF precursor, "The Sandman," does not come from the technological innovation but rather the terrifying folklore of the Sandman mixed with the figure of Coppelius (himself a proponent of the "secret science" of alchemy). While highly sensationalized in the present, there is support for the idea that even ancient folklore was inspired by similar secret knowledge. Regarding a specific type of hidden knowledge, prominent ufologist Jacques Vallee asks: "If aerial phenomenon have been reported throughout human history, complete with interaction with luminous beings and floating apparitions behaving very much like contemporary ufonauts, then larger questions arise: what is the impact of these images on our culture, on our beliefs, on our religions?"[2] Vallee points to the fact that our literature, both oral and written, has been haunted by a secret knowledge which authors can only grasp at in vain. He also mentions "the works of the alchemists and hermetics" who were intensely intrigued by "beings who mysteriously appeared, dressed in shiny garments or covered with dark hair and with whom communication was hard to establish."[3] Secret knowledge and SF have always been connected. This influence does not go away, despite SF's initial "true" beginning with Wells. It has always existed and shows no signs of fading.

Despite hints of influence in proto-SF, it is more succinctly since the writing of Charles Hoy Fort, himself part of a movement directly against the ideology of Wells and his compatriots, that this secret knowledge (what Fort would call "the damned facts") has been an active influence in the SF genre. Fort's immediate influence can be tracked through SF writers from his appearance in pulp magazines, which developed a trend of posting similar pieces of "occult" research. Because of the existence of the Futurian phenomenon, explored by Damon Knight, it is generally accepted that the readers of these pulp SF magazines became SF authors and editors themselves and, as such, Fortean and occult influences remain in contemporary works. Fortean connections lurk in every corner of SF; even historians such as Knight were heavily interested in the subject. In some cases, the secret knowledge draws from places other than the pulps, but the influence from these magazines is too large to be ignored. Fort and similar writers' influences on the SF genre are often mentioned in passing with little exposition on the matter. This book aims to be an in-depth clarification and tracking of Fortean writing's impact on SF by using the work of religious studies scholar Jeffrey J. Kripal as a starting point and a sounding board. With this track in mind, the book will look at the works of numerous authors with Fortean leanings, ranging from interest and involvement in Fortean groups to casual reference to Fort in their works. The book examines four specific modern SF authors in depth (Arthur C. Clarke, Philip K. Dick, Robert A. Heinlein, and Robert Anton Wilson), to illustrate how influential the secret knowledge of occult texts weaves its way through every step of SF's development and into the modern SF era. The work intends to be an original analysis of Fort's influence on SF and the continuation of Fortean ideologies in the genre.

This work requires a clarification of terms and even an invention of terms. The genre of SF suffers from its consideration as largely lowbrow and with little literary merit. Writings of the unexplained and anomalous are often relegated to the "occult" genre, suffering the same lack of merit that SF has. While the moniker "occult" certainly implies the "secret knowledge" that these works dole out, it does not give enough credit to how these works function narratively. Many of the key figures involved with this genre postulated that reality as we know it is a narrative written by a higher intelligence. The simply plot-driven examples of 1900s occult writing (as opposed to those with verified data) often function just as an SF text would, except with an emphasis on the true nature of the tale. As one of the hollow earth stories from Richard

Introduction: The Damned Facts   7

Sharpe Shaver decries: "What I tell you is not fiction! It is tragic that the only way I can tell my story is in the guise of fiction."[4] This is a common plot device, but most would agree that it is at the very least uncertain whether the story was meant to be taken as fact or fiction. Often, a story's status as pretending to be true is abundantly clear to the reader as a narrative device. These other stories do not make this distinction; the stories are meant to be taken as truth. Sometimes the device is reversed, and true stories must be "in the guise of fiction" as Shaver's stories were. Because of their uncertain veracity, this book will deem these occult writings "maybe-fiction." To call them fiction would not be giving them enough credit—but calling them non-fiction would give them perhaps too much. They exist in the ambiguous and contentious divide between fiction and fact, covering a variety of topics: ancient astronauts, cryptids, mysterious disappearances, folklore, UFOs, teleportation, time distortions, and much more. Writings of this nature were not widely published or distributed—the works themselves have always had a limited audience, much like the cult appeal of Fort himself—until after the publication of Fort's work or the proliferation of SF in popular culture. Maybe-fiction's eventual rise in popularity can be attributed to both factors: Fort was among the first to cover every paranormal topic and SF utilized these topics in stories. A maybe-fiction work is a story presented as truth at the time of publication (even if later disputed or debunked) and ranges from data-backed entries and explorations to anomalous experiences to those likely to be hallucinogenic visions and pure fabrications. Their actual truth value holds little importance to this exploration, but the texts are nearly always about contentious subjects. What truly matters is maybe-fiction's influence on SF and its odd placement in the ether between fiction and non-fiction—a fascinating but often ignored area of literature. Furthermore, an examination of various maybe-fiction works may prove useful in understanding just why Fort's writings were influential to SF, a fact which does not always make sense given much of SF's predilection for a harder form of science.

The book uses this general formula: Chapter 1 serves as an introduction to Fort and his literary status within his time period. From the very beginning, Fort's work was related to SF even before the term was commonplace. Furthermore, Fort presents a complex character study of a man both adored and despised by other literary figures. Chapter 2 is a description and explanation of the aforementioned "maybe-fiction," tracing its existence as both a continuation and extension of Fort's work that has a similar appeal to SF and continually remains inspirational to SF texts. This chapter is crucial because there is consistent overlap between maybe-fiction and SF—which will be continually acknowledged in the chapters that follow Chapter 2—and Fort was pivotal in the establishment of both cultural forms. After examining this broad range of maybe-fiction texts, Chapter 3 focuses on

Fortean SF authors and works from the pulp fiction era—H.P. Lovecraft, Eric Frank Russell, Fritz Leiber, and Frank Herbert among others. These authors all reference Fort's work directly as an inspiration or elicit some form of ideological cohesion with Fort (e.g., reference otherworldly manipulators or Fortean phenomena). Chapter 4 goes deeper down the Fortean rabbit hole, examining the SF editors and historians who have Fortean ties. These include many of the major figures in both editorial and historian positions of the pulp era: John W. Campbell, Raymond Palmer, Damon Knight, and Sam Moskowitz all show some familiarity or appreciation for the works of Fort as it relates to their chosen genre of literature. Chapters 5 through 8 are in-depth Fortean analyses of four different SF authors: Arthur C. Clarke, Philip K. Dick, Robert Heinlein, and Robert Anton Wilson. This quartet serves as the most major SF figures to exhibit significant Fortean influence, but it is all presented in different ways. Some merely take inspiration from the strange reports Fort collated. Others find Fort's theories to be compelling or possibly credible evidence that human potential is greater than assumed or that our reality is not what it seems. Others still find Fort's work to be important texts in the establishment of a broader conspiracy theory of cosmic proportions. The difference in utilization and continuation of Fortean themes is one of the reasons the concept of maybe-fiction plays a key role: Sometimes the authors receive inspiration or possible thematic cohesion through Fort's texts, but at other times they come through maybe-fiction, which often contains or perpetuates these themes. The penultimate chapter is a collection of Fortean "footnotes," examples of authors referencing Fort or his work in more contemporary SF or other forms of contemporary popular culture. This section hopes to illustrate the longevity and broad reach of Fort's influence as it is not completely bound by genre or time period. This will further be extrapolated upon in Chapter 10, which explores the overarching takeaways of this investigation into Fort and SF, continuing to attempt an answer to the question of *why* Fort left such a footprint on SF literature. Furthermore, this book hopes to determine why Fort continues to matter to this day, more than a century after his first book of anomalous phenomena was published.

1

A Fortean Emergence
The Early SF/Forteana Relationship

> *Back in the 1920s, Charles Fort, the first writer to explore inexplicable events, observed you can measure a circle by beginning anywhere. Paranormal phenomena are so widespread, so diversified, and so sporadic yet so persistent that separating and studying a single element is not only a waste of time but also will automatically lead to the development of belief. Once you have established a belief, the phenomenon adjusts its manifestations to support that belief and thereby escalate it.*
> —*John A. Keel*[1]

The oeuvre of H.G. Wells is groundbreaking literature in the realm of SF. One of these works was his 1895 book *The Time Machine*, which is largely considered the first book to feature a time-traveling device. It also popularized the concept of time travel as a staple of numerous SF narratives. As is the case with most of H.G. Wells' writings, *The Time Machine* sees a narrative heavily interested in evolution and biological science. The Time Traveller in the book hypothesizes about the nature of the dismal future he finds himself in:

> The people might once have been the favoured aristocracy, and the Morlocks their mechanical servants: but that had long since passed away. The two species that had resulted from the evolution of man were sliding down towards, or had already arrived at, an altogether new relationship.[2]

The advancement of time in the novel is always focused on evolutionary changes. When The Time Traveller goes into the even further distant future, he encounters a devolution of sorts: As the world moves towards its end and the sun expires, he comes across crablike beings as if from the earliest stages of evolution, when creatures first started moving out of the ocean.[3] *The Time Machine* is not alone in its interest in evolutionary theory as it is explored in the works of H.G. Wells. With 1897's *The War of the Worlds*, readers see a race of Martians killed off by diseases which humans have become immune to:

> These germs of disease have taken toll of humanity since the beginning of things—taken toll of our prehuman ancestors since life began here. But by virtue of this natural selection of our kind we have developed resisting power; to no germs do we succumb without a struggle.[4]

As revolutionary as the works of Wells may be (and SF is greatly indebted to him), something is lacking in his fantastic visions. The scientific determinism which defined his era pervades his work, rendering the fantastic inevitable or somewhat cold and sterile. Perhaps this is because Wells, an intellectual opposite of Charles Fort, found himself defending science above all else, possibly motivated by his college biology teacher, the highly influential Thomas Henry Huxley. Despite his less than spectacular scientific qualifications, however, "Wells had acquired a clear vision both of the past and the future that would never leave him and which had a profound impact on his thought. That vision was founded by T.H. Huxley's teaching of the evolutionary process."[5] Huxley was known as Darwin's Bulldog, taught by the evolutionary science founder himself, and was a staunch advocate for evolution in a time when religion and science seemed to be at war. The Scopes Monkey Trial was a few decades away, but this head-to-head matchup of two juggernaut ideologies represents well the kind of war Huxley and Wells seemed to be fighting. Huxley promoted a sort of cosmic pessimism which is underlined in Peter J. Bowler's *Evolution: The History of an Idea*. The author, quoting Bertrand Russell, gives a salient picture of the cultural climate of the era:

> (T.H.) Huxley's scientific naturalism was repudiated by the new generation of analytical philosophers, but his cosmic pessimism seemed to resonate with the mood of the time. [...] Bertrand Russell summed up the image of humanity's place in the world thus: "[...] all the noonday brightness of human genius are destined to extinction in the vast death of the solar system, and the whole temple of Man's achievement must inevitably be buried beneath the debris of the universe in ruins."[6]

Wells mirrors this indifference and pessimism in *The Time Machine*: "(The Time Traveller) thought cheerlessly of the Advancement of Mankind, and saw in the growing pile of civilization only a foolish heaping that must inevitably fall back upon and destroy its markers in the end."[7] Wells' future is a dismal one and the Time Traveller observes it dutifully: "Looking at these stars suddenly dwarfed my own troubles and the gravities of terrestrial life. [...] All the traditions, the complex organizations, the nations, languages, literatures, aspirations, even the mere memory of Man as I knew him, had been swept out of existence."[8] Wells' work is nevertheless imaginative and groundbreaking, but SF needed further captivating influence to avoid going bland quickly. Much as was needed for Frankenstein to create his monster, revolutionary science needed to mediate with stranger, possibly pseudoscientific subject matters, in order to supplement creative thinking.

1. A Fortean Emergence

The religious backlash to the all-encompassing explanatory nature of the scientists of the time was intense. Paul Jerome Croce wrote of the beginnings of this culture war which first escalated in the middle of the 19th century: "This fraying of the culture over fundamental truths broke the edifice of consensus in nineteenth-century American culture and cracked the expectation of uniformities in thought and culture."[9] Jeffrey J. Kripal writes of the religious response, pointing to the resurrection of spiritualist beliefs: "The psychical rose into prominence at a particular moment in Western intellectual history, a moment when Darwinism, materialism, and agnosticism (a word newly coined by [...] Huxley, to capture and advance the spirit of the new era), were becoming dominant." The religious establishment and even those just wary of this cosmic pessimism felt that "the universe was looking more and more indifferent to human concerns with each new discovery and every passing year." Some "chose to reject the science, or at least those parts of it that could not be reconciled with their particular belief system."[10] Indeed, even Darwin's Bulldog, Huxley, promoted agnosticism. This philosophy will find itself adopted by many of the authors examined in this book, principally the "hero" of it. The era needed an oddball to mediate, or perhaps lambast, both ideologies. Enter Charles Hoy Fort.

Fort was in some ways a failed fiction writer, selling a few short stories to magazines with the help of Theodore Dreiser, who saw great value in his work. Eventually, he became obsessed with pieces of abnormal data that science refused to explain or investigate. He wrote two works based upon theories surrounding his collation of anomalous data, X and Y, but these were never released and burned after the publication of his first two books. Some ideas from these volumes made their way into Fort's non-fiction debut, *The Book of the Damned* (1919). The typical writing of Fort was an assortment of anomalous data which Fort came across in his meticulous reading through newspapers and scientific journals. The oddities were interspersed with Fort's comments on the possibilities behind such occurrences, flip-flopping between serious and tongue-in-cheek. Some of the first phenomena he examined would remain a staple in his works to follow: strange objects falling from the sky. Upon reading the entirety of Fort's works, one would be hard-pressed to name a material that had *not* fallen from the sky.

L'Année Scientifique, 1888–75: That, Dec. 13, 1887, there fell, in Cochin China, a substance like blood, somewhat coagulated.[11]

In *Notes and Queries*, 8-6-190, it is said that, early in August 1894, thousands of jellyfish, about the size of a shilling, had fallen at Bath, England.[12]

Annual Register, 1821–681: That, according to a report by M. Lainé, French Consul at Pernambuco, early in October 1821, there was a shower of a substance resembling silk. The quantity was as tremendous as might be a whole cargo, lost somewhere between Jupiter or Mars, having drifted around perhaps centuries, the original fabrics slowly disintegrating.[13]

The list could go on. The common fall attributed to Fort is that of frogs, a phenomenon which occurred more often than might be assumed, mentioned in each of the first three books. These quoted selections are but a small sample from his first book, *The Book of the Damned* (1919), which was published with the help of Fort's friend Theodore Dreiser. Dreiser is a key figure in Fort's life, helping his fiction become published in magazines and eventually threatening to drop a publisher unless they released Fort's first book. Sales were respectable enough to warrant the release of three more books, *New Lands* (1923), *Lo!* (1931), and *Wild Talents* (1932). These works continually expanded the type of anomalies Fort covered, eventually spanning practically the full gamut of paranormal events. In *Wild Talents*, for instance, he cited reports of poltergeists and spontaneous combustion, sometimes of the human variety.

> There is a story of "devilish manifestations," in the *Quebec Daily Mercury*, Oct. 6, 1880. For two weeks, in the Hudson Hotel, in the town of Hudson, on the Ottawa River, furniture had been given to disorderly conduct: the beds had been especially excitable. A fire had broken out in a stall in the stable. This fire was quenched, but another fire broke out. A priest was sent for, and he sprinkled the stable with holy water. The stable burned down.[14]

Fort was primarily interested in finding these reported anomalies and did not attempt to go and investigate himself. He simply offered his opinion on how scientists responded to these events with hyper-rational skepticism, no matter how improbable their answer may have been. He was interested in keeping science honest, endlessly wary of science not accepting anything that breached its specific rational data set.

Likewise, Fort pitted himself against the scientific culture of the time. While this aligned him with the goals of the religious establishment, he was equally skeptical of religion. But he mainly took issue with scientific dogmatism and the idea that humanity knew all that it could ever know. His work was almost entirely composed of secret knowledge: "The power that has said to all these things that they are damned, is Dogmatic Science."[15] To fight this battle, he took a bold but peculiar offensive. "I have gone into the outer darkness of scientific and philosophical transactions, ultra-respectable but covered with the dust of disregard," wrote Fort. "I have descended into journalism. I have come back with the quasi-souls of lost data. They will march."[16] Determined to collect and preserve the oddities which science could not explain, Fort became "America's unique literary phenomenon, the 'foe of science.'"[17] Biographer Jim Steinmeyer writes in his introduction to Fort's collected works: "Fort deliberately pushed his 'damned facts' on his readers," and negotiated with the fact that "science couldn't explain (them) and, even worse, it seemed determined not to try."[18] His negative view of science is all too evident in his more scathing passages: "Every science is a mutilated octopus. If its tentacles were not clipped to stumps, it would feel its way into disturbing contacts. To a believer, the effect of the contemplation of a science is of being in the presence of the good, the true, and the beautiful. But what he is awed by is Mutilation."[19] Fort is critical of Darwin in particular, making the claim that his theories could be proven just as well as Darwin's. "The fittest survive," he writes. "What is meant by the fittest? Not the strongest; not the cleverest—weakness and stupidity everywhere survive. There is no way of determining fitness except in that a thing does survive. 'Fitness' then, is only another name for 'survival.' Darwinism: That survivors survive."[20] While Fort's theories lack the scientific merit that could even marginally discredit evolutionary science, his beautifully prosaic style and combative tone are an eccentric breath of fresh air in a smog of dogmatism. For these reasons, he was able to gain a respectable number of disciples.

Others were not so accepting. H.G. Wells received a copy of *Lo!* gifted to him from Dreiser. He was not happy with the gift.

> Lo! has been sent to me but has gone into my wastepaper basket. And what do you mean by forcing "orthodox science" to do this or that? Science is a continuing exploration and how in the devil can it have an orthodoxy? The next you'll be writing is the "dogmas of science" like some blasted Roman Catholic priest on the defensive. When you tell a Christian you don't believe some yarn he can't prove, he always calls you "dogmatic." Scientific workers are first rate stuff and very ill paid and it isn't for the likes of you and me to heave Forts at them.

The unhappy Wells ended his letter bitterly: "God dissolve (and forgive) your Fortean Society."[21]

As badly received as Fort's works were by Wells, they remained influential to SF. Before he delved into research, Fort himself was a fiction writer and presented some of the first instances of numerous ideas present in SF, particularly the concept that we are but small pieces in a larger, vastly more intelligent system. "It is of some note that Fort was writing during a time in which the terms and rules of the science fiction genre had not yet been established," writes Kripal. Indeed, Fort's own fiction writing was pioneering despite its lack of success or recognition. An early short story, "A Radical Corpuscle," was markedly proto–SF, involving a group of cells who become aware that they are living within another organism, "a larger, cosmic body."[22] The concept of this short story sounds radically innovative for its publication date of 1906 but did not make enough waves to be considered influential. His non-fiction works, however, were more accessible and captivating to readers. They tread similar territory to "A Radical Corpuscle," postulating that humanity knows very little about how the world works and that we are perhaps mere playthings to a vastly superior force. "I think we're property," wrote Fort. "I should say we belong to something: That once upon a time, this earth was No-man's land, that other worlds explored and colonized here, and fought among themselves for possession, but that now it's owned by something: That something owns this earth—all others warned off."[23] It is here that Fort seems to predict the coming of what now is considered the flying saucer phenomenon, a key component to modern science fiction: "We shall have data as convincing as our data of oil or coal-burning (that of) aerial super-constructions."[24] The serious nature of Fort's hypothesizing sets him apart from Wells and his Martian spaceships. Wells' vision is pure fantasy, but Fort theorizes that the data shows the possibility that UFOs are more than mere whimsies of imagination. Fort compares humanity to cattle, ignorantly blissful of the fact that they are possessed by something greater and unseen. The only hint of this presence is in the glimpses of the anomalous phenomena which Fort meticulously catalogued. Fort was convinced that science ignored these "damned facts" because the conclusions to be drawn by them were uncomfortable: humanity does not actually know its place in the universe and is, in fact, a tiny corpuscle in a vast organism. Fort's system could expand endlessly—atoms within molecules within cells within organisms. These ideas are now commonplace generic traits of SF, but oftentimes Fort goes uncredited as one of the original minds behind this concept of being property, playthings of the gods. This is a disturbing hypothesis, echoed by both the SF community and the paranormal non-fiction community, perhaps speaking to a common human anxiety.

Opposed to the public image that Wells' staunchly anti–Fort view might imply, Fort had followers. His philosophy drew in a broad swath of New York writers, beginning with Dreiser and extending to others once Fort's works reached a larger audience. The Fortean Society was organized in 1931 by Fort's greatest supporter Dreiser and drew in a varied crowd of New York's literati. Amongst them were Tiffany Thayer (who would later lead the society into disarray), Booth Tarkington, and fascinatingly some members of the Algonquin Round Table such as Dorothy Parker and Alexander Woollcott. Even famed screenwriter Ben Hecht was a member, writing a favorable review of *The Book of the Damned* while still a newspaperman. "I am the first disciple of Charles Fort," he wrote. "He has made a terrible onslaught upon the accumulated lunacy of fifty centuries. […] Whatever the purpose of Charles Fort, he has delighted me beyond all men who have written books in this world."[25] The Society also drew in the beginnings of Fort's SF influence; characters like Edmond Hamilton began to correspond with Fort and from overseas, Eric Frank Russell contributed to the Society's journal.[26] The Fortean Society has continued to exist in some form or another into the present, eventually becoming the International Fortean Organization when the remainder of the original society's materials fell into the hands of the Willis brothers, Paul and Ron.

Fort's works were more than just theories that resembled SF. Fort also had a strange and often indeterminate philosophy weaved throughout his texts. The most intriguing sections from a literary standpoint are when he makes bold claims like "we belong to something." But, he would further claim of existence, "that ours is a pseudo-existence, and that all appearances in it partake of its essential fictitiousness."[27] This claim and similar philosophies weave their way into both prominent maybe-fiction and SF texts, notably Philip K. Dick's *VALIS* (examined thoroughly in Chapter 6). Kripal notes that Fort's 1925 work, *New Lands*, "is about *us as someone else's adventure and land*."[28] As later Fortean researcher John A. Keel would put it, "this planet has always been a Disneyland for the Gods."[29] These perspectives resemble the modern-day SF concept of living in a computer simulation, except for many Forteans this is a genuine possibility. There is also a hint of monism in Fort's works, as Steinmeyer points out, quoting an excerpt from one of Fort's short stories: "Martin Gardner and Ian Kidd have analyzed Charles Fort's monistic philosophy, a search to identify continuity through all things: 'That all things are one, that all phenomena are governed by the same laws; that whatever is true or what we call true, of planet, plants and magnets, is true of human beings.'"[30] Indeed, Fort believed that much of the phenomena he was investigating came from similar or the same sources. As for his view on the nature of reality, Fort's "A Radical Corpuscle" gives a good insight: we are akin to cells living within a body, but that body may very well be one of many cells inside of another body. "If our existence is a relationship between the Positive Absolute and the Negative Absolute, the quest for finality in it is hopeless," he writes. "Everything in it must be relative, if the 'whole' is not a whole, but is, itself, a relation."[31] However, a skeptical mind must shudder to think that Fort postulated the existence of a Super-Sargasso Sea called Genesistrine which would every now and then dump some sort of material onto the Earth, organic or inorganic, explaining the weird data which Fort logged obsessively. But Fort's work cannot be shoved aside as blatant pseudoscience; within its vast array of anomalous data, a complex and intriguing philosophy unfolds. Upon reading Fort, it is hard to treat him as a full-blown, fringe wingnut. He seems intelligent and completely aware of how improbable his theories were. Perhaps he reasoned that the only way to battle the absurd was to explain it away tongue-in-cheek with more absurdity. It makes Fort both endearing and readable in the face of what some would call eccentric anti-scientific chaff. Maybe it *is* anti-scientific chaff, but this conclusion seems to matter very little because of the interesting nature of the curiosities he investigated. The nature of his material is perhaps the reason why his influence has remained so firmly in place within both SF and maybe-fiction.

While Fort's work may give the impression of an eccentric man who could easily be a hermit, the nickname given to him, "the hermit of the Bronx," was not entirely accurate. Damon Knight writes that "people forget he was a newspaper reporter. He lived most of his life in tenements and he had a sociable wife. [...] He did not see its inhabitants quite as anyone else saw them, but he knew and loved them."[32] Fort is largely described as quiet and reserved, but he engaged in regular conversation with some of the most prestigious literary figures of New York. In London, he also took great joy in going to Hyde Park, "where he had found a congenial group of loungers to argue with."[33] While Fort enjoyed his solitude, his work was not that of an isolated mind; rather, it was a carefully established philosophy that he developed through dialogues with others, many who were notable minds of the era. This is perhaps part of the reason why Fort's ideas spread amongst the literary community; his philosophy was novel yet accessible enough for this spread to take place.

Fort's health began to fail while he was writing his final book, *Wild Talents*, in 1932. Knight writes of his sad final day:

> Fort would not see a doctor, but on the morning of May 3 he was so weak that Anna called an ambulance and had him taken to Royal Hospital. (Aaron) Sussman brought him advance copies of *Wild Talents*, but he could not lift his hand to take them. He died that day.[34]

His wife, Anna, died five years later. Before her death, she recalled to Dreiser an experience where the deceased Fort came back to comfort her after an argument with his aunt. "I was never so glad to see anyone in my whole life," she said.[35] It is difficult to deny the poetry of Fort making a posthumous appearance, adding his own personal addition to the myriad reports of strange phenomena. Yet this is not the only instance of the spirit of Fort living on; the spirit of his work wove its way into literature, SF and maybe-fiction specifically, for years to come.

Fort's influence on these genres truly began when his works were republished in pulp SF magazines. Kripal notes that SF had not yet become an established genre, the works of Wells and Verne still considered "voyages extraordinaires" and "scientific romances." "It was the American pulp magazines of the 1920s—so named after the thick, cheap, and quickly yellowing paper on which they were published—that science fiction came into its own and was first named as such."[36] Kripal further notes that the first pulp was published the same year as Fort's *The Book of the Damned*, in 1919. Perhaps this is some supernatural synchronicity; SF and Fort's relationship to one another has been tightly knit ever since. Fort's work appeared in *Astounding Stories* with sections of *Lo!* appearing two years after his death. It was promoted as "the greatest collation of factual data on superscience in existence."[37] To see it alongside SF stories is not altogether surprising because of the fantastic nature of Fort's research. The table of contents lists the *Lo!* excerpt as the "Fact Feature" of the issue, again not seeming to hierarchize either fact or fiction.[38] Besides, as Fort would postulate, maybe our reality is nothing but a higher intelligence's fiction. The editor, F. Orlin Tremaine, intended to "inject new life into a field which was rutted by habit-driven vehicles" via what he called "thought-variants," an idea whose precursor was Fort.[39] Dave Langford continues to postulate on this influence in an article about Eric Frank Russell:

> The SF hacks, while paying lip service to scientific dogma, were just as keen as Fort to locate science's contradictions and loopholes—preferably loopholes wide enough to drive faster-than-light spaceships through, in defiance of Einstein's tiresome speed limits. It made for better stories.[40]

Langford notes the key balance SF must strike between science and Forteana, but also says the oft-repeated notion that Fortean thought served as an excellent source for good SF stories. Pulp fiction's investment in Fortean subjects serves the dual purpose of highlighting works influential to the SF genre and including those works in order to sell magazines to SF fans who would have an interest in this type of material. (Writing as a fan of both SF and maybe-fiction, it must be said that the major draw to each are the narratives which both mirror and distort our own reality. These are not unlike genres.) "This is how Fort's career in science fiction began," writes Kripal. "As fiction and fact wrapped up in fantasy."[41] There is another a moment of indebtedness to Fort in the pulps when the editor of *Fantastic Story*, Samuel Mines, wrote: "No truly complete understanding of science fiction is possible without at least a nodding acquaintance with the works of Charles Fort."[42] Even before Fort's actual appearance in the pulps, some writers already exhibited his influence in their pulp SF short stories and novellas. Yet some writers, often from the same publishing circles as SF, continued Fort's research in earnest. These writers opted to not merely inject Fort's ideas into fiction, they continued researching the anomalous events that Fort saw plaguing the world. Fueled by an indeterminate mixture of human curiosity, anomalous experience, and perhaps the chance at monetary gain, maybe-fiction was born.

2

Defining Maybe-fiction

I've given up fiction, you see—or in a way I haven't. I am convinced that everything is fiction; so here I am in the same old line.

—Charles Fort[1]

These phenomena serve as a support for human ambition, a framework for human tragedy, a fabric of human dreams. We react to them in our movies, our poetry, our music, our science fiction. They are part of the control system for human evolution, like the nuclear process inside the Sun and the long-term changes in the Earth's weather. But their effects, instead of just being physical, are felt in our belief systems. They influence what we call our spiritual life. They affect our political institutions, our history, our culture.

—Jacques Vallee[2]

To Love a Strange Reality

When discussing Charles Fort, it is necessary to address his status as the premier writer of anomalistics, paranormal or occult non-fiction, or any similar type of literature. Others nearly immediately continued this work. These authors often had texts in conversation with one another, as illustrated by the case of the devil's footprints appearing in the works of Fort initially, then investigated by Rupert T. Gould, R. Dewitt Miller, and others. Fortean writers were also SF writers. Miller, for instance, exemplified the SF writer turned Fortean as he appeared in the same magazine as Fort, *Astounding Stories* (with his 1936 short story, "The Shapes") and later wrote works of "occult" non-fiction such as the sensational book *Impossible—Yet it Happened!* (sometimes known as *Forgotten Mysteries*) which involves snippets of paranormal research reprinted from the magazine *Coronet*. Miller illustrates immediate shared sympathies with Fort, decrying scientific dogmatism in his introduction: "Determinism is, and always will be, an empty concept."[3] Miller also praises and acknowledges both Fort and Gould in his introduction, noting that "evaluating Charles Fort is not a matter to be lightly undertaken." He further says that "(Fort's) great aim in life was to roust men out of complacent dogmatism. That in itself is a noble purpose."[4] Gould's 1928 volume of anomalous phenomenon titled *Oddities* appeared in Fort's lifetime and the two operated concurrently in America and Britain. It is then no surprise that Miller paid tribute to both the forefathers of anomalous phenomena who worked independently across the Atlantic. Their aims and hint of self-deprecating humor also seem to align:

> I fear that the book might more appropriately have been called Old Wives' Tales or [...] Tales of My Grandmother. Scientifically-minded persons can, with good reason, call it superficial; the general reader may, with no less justice, find it dull; and both will, I have no doubt, be tempted to echo the Irish bishop who remarked of Gulliver's Travels that seemed to him full of improbable statements, and that for his part he scarcely believed half of it. Still, I have done my best to show, by giving chapter and verse, that my facts are facts; for such opinions as I have offered I am, of course, solely responsible.[5]

Gould never mentions Fort directly (probably because he didn't consider Fort himself a factual source like newspapers or scientific journals), but he covers the same types of phenomena. For instance, they each had their own theories on what caused the Devil's Footprints phenomenon in South Devon, UK in 1855—mysterious footprints in the snow (which appeared to look more like hoof prints) and covered nearly 100 miles in length. Theories abound, although none were conclusive, and the mystery endures. Miller covers this convergence in interests by saying, of the Devil's Footprints: "Charles Fort suggested that they were not footprints at all, but rather imprints made by—as I understand him—rays shot at the earth from somewhere in space, possibly some sort of code dispatched in an effort to communicate with the earth, or with a lost expedition from another planet which met disaster here."[6] Gould's theory seems, by comparison, less outlandish but equally improbable: "Gould suspected an unknown creature which emerged from the sea, made the footprints, and departed whence it came." Miller himself is "unimpressed by any of the theories."[7]

Much of this early occult non-fiction includes SF-esque covers which are sensational and provocative, advertised in the same alluring manner as an SF paperback. A 1973 reprinting of Miller's book features a writhing mass of naked women falling through the center of an hourglass.[8] A 1969 reprint of Gould's book features a black cloaked figure on a psychedelic plain.[9] Indeed, Ace Books, later more strictly a publisher of SF and fantasy, published numerous paranormal non-fiction texts under their "occult" tag. Among these were Miller's aforementioned *Impossible—Yet it Happened!* along with books like parapsychologist Hans Holzer's first published work,

Ghost Hunter, in 1965, and even reprints of Fort's *The Book of the Damned* and *Lo!* Ace would also go on to reprint the Richard Shaver-esque schizophrenia memoir *Operators and Things* by Barbara O'Brien (explored more in Chapter 4) with the tagline "the real-life adventure that is stranger than science fiction!"[10] These works were all anomalies marketed as entertainment. No extraordinary experience or "out there" theory was discredited, because it was all in good fun. These works have been cropping up on the literary fringes ever since, either evading scholarly evaluation or invoking their disdain.

For the sake of this investigation, all literature of this nature will be placed in a broader genre called maybe-fiction. This type of literature is by and large Fortean, although Fort purists might decry some inclusions which stray from the basic Fortean structure of being reported in journals and newspapers. Included in this genre are, of course, the Fortean reports of anomalous phenomena, personal accounts of strange events, scientific and historical documents that go against the established grain, and even some urban legends. The key factor in each maybe-fiction text is that they describe the reality we live in as remarkably different and stranger than what most people consider it to be. It functions similarly to the SF plot device outlined by SF scholar Darko Suvin in which a *novum* or "strange newness" is introduced to a fictional story in order to create *cognitive estrangement*. The latter is described by reviewer Perry Nodelman as "the 'factual reporting of fictions,'" adding that, "for Suvin, this has the significant effect of separating or 'estranging' us from our usual assumptions about reality."[11] This is a key feature of all maybe-fiction, regardless of veracity. Each story or report colors the world as we know it as functioning differently than is usually accepted.

Fort proposed what he called "the hyphenated state of truth-fiction," which emphasized that "there is a fictional colorization to everybody's account of an 'actual occurrence,' and there is at least the lurk somewhere of what is called the 'actual' in everybody's yarn."[12] The term truth-fiction gestures toward a broader definition of this type of literature, illustrating that truth and fiction are much more malleable than most people assume. Fort seems to suggest that humanity inhabits neither truth nor fiction but the hyphen between the two. However, Fort's term does not illustrate a form of literature as much as it does a state of being—maybe-fiction is the literature based around this state of being, a highly varied gradient of fact and fiction that maybe-fiction intends to describe more concretely. In this realm of literature, fact and fiction are not clear-cut categories sprinkled with bits of their respective antitheses. Rather, the ratio of fact to fiction or fiction to fact can be ever-changing on a text-to-text basis—often on a reader to reader basis. The very concepts of fact and fiction get distorted with texts like these, perhaps because of the highly contentious subject matter.

2. Defining Maybe-fiction 21

Beyond this basic attribute of maybe-fiction texts existing on the fact-fiction gradient, this new term, maybe-fiction, will be expanded upon so that its qualities become clearer. This somewhat lengthy chapter is dedicated to this clarification, although its length is necessary in order to establish its importance to the SF genre. It is worth noting that maybe-fiction intends to describe a type of literature and the literature itself only. The verifiability may matter to scientists and others digging for the objective truth, but for this exploration, the literary or entertainment value of these texts matters more than whether they are true or false. The term maybe-fiction is meant to describe a mode of entertainment; it is not a dismissal or approval of any narrative or scientific study dealing with the paranormal. An objective truth seeker would shudder at the inclusion of someone like Jacques Vallee amongst urban legends and schizophrenics. Yet, it is not uncommon for maybe-fiction readers to give Vallee a home on the bookshelf with psychics, poltergeists, and Bigfoot. They are the misfits of the literary world, grouped together for being too weird, too uncomfortable, or too contentious to find their place in the non-fiction or fiction sections of libraries. Instead, they are often relegated to philosophy sections—metaphysics specifically—although they appear remarkably lowbrow next to their highbrow philosophical neighbors. Since maybe-fiction texts are often grouped together despite their wildly different subject matter and reputability, they must have some qualities in common. This is an attempt to establish those qualities and explore the culture behind the genre.

Exploring this definition of maybe-fiction will shed light on its numerous similarities to SF. These similarities are aesthetic, cultural, and even technical—the two genres and their subcultures have existed near one another since Fort's works were first published. They share common influences, communities, mythologies, and perhaps most importantly, page space. It is because of this communal relationship that an explanation of the broader genre of maybe-fiction is necessary to understand Fort's influence on SF more completely. Without Fort, there would be no maybe-fiction as it exists today. Without Fort, SF's development would have been radically different than it is currently understood. Without Fort, the strange would be remarkably less strange. We as readers love strangeness, and the true beauty of maybe-fiction is that it allows us to love our reality differently; it allows us to love the strangeness inherent in our reality. While Fort himself initially described his "damned facts" as "corpses, skeletons, mummies, twitching, tottering, animated by companions that have been damned alive," he had higher aspirations for them: "The damned won't stay damned; [...] salvation only precedes perdition. [...] Some day [sic] our accursed tatterdemalions will be sleek angels."[13] The damned facts might still seem quite damned based on their subject matter, but with their rise into the public consciousness, some sort of salvation may have been achieved. They have become as angelic as the bastard children of literature could ever hope to be.

The Qualities of Maybe-fiction

The term maybe-fiction can be distilled into four major qualities:

1. Maybe-fiction contains fantastic or SF-esque stories and events.
2. Maybe-fiction involves often contentious subject matter.
3. The authors claim the stories to be true and/or the resulting hypotheses to be entirely possible.
4. Maybe-fiction creates a vast web of intertextuality between the various texts.

While these are the basic tenets of this literary concept, other scholars have touched upon some key points of maybe-fiction literature in alternate terms. Texts of this nature have been studied infrequently by scholars. However, in the last decade they have been increasingly recognized by scholars of religious thought. At the forefront is Jeffrey J. Kripal, whose work has greatly influenced my own thinking about the topic. One such facet of Kripal's work that aided the conceptualization of maybe-fiction is his concept of the "Super-story," "a deep, often unconscious narrative that underlies and shapes much of contemporary popular culture."[14] This Super-story was largely initiated by Fort:

> There is a consistent narrative or Super-Story woven into the heart of his four books, a story without which these texts would have little power over their astonished readers. [...] This is where things cease to be abstract and philosophical and become eerie and numinous. This is the same fantastic narrative that would later take on visionary, even physical, forms within the UFO phenomenon, a stranger story still that Fort saw in almost every detail over thirty years before it finally appeared on the public stage in the late 1940s. Prophet indeed. What we have here, in the end, then, is much more than a philosophy. It is the beginnings of a new living mythology.[15]

While maybe-fiction refers to individual texts that supposedly take place in our reality, their key feature of intertextuality renders them akin to Kripal's Super-story. The Super-story is the suggestion of an underlying narrative woven throughout texts, both fact and fiction. Maybe-fiction is the suggestion of a broader set of texts, all stories that claim to be true, that suggest a similar underlying narrative. However, uncovering this underlying narrative is part of the enjoyment that readers can obtain from maybe-fiction. Maybe-fiction is also not necessarily limited to involving the mythemes suggested by Kripal, although many of them follow the trends Kripal sets forth (e.g., "Western culture has been influenced for millennia by forms of intelligence that have appeared under the divine and demonic masks of local mythologies and religions," or "an author, artist, or reader begins to realize that paranormal events are real, and, moreover, that they reveal a dimension of the world that works remarkably like a text or a story"[16]). Again, maybe-fiction broadens the boundary of these texts to include *any* work surrounding paranormal or anomalous events.

More recently, D.W. Pasulka wrote *American Cosmic*, a work about UFOs and religion that has some overlap with this broader concept of maybe-fiction. Particularly, Pasulka covers the cognitive effects of texts (and films) that fall in the maybe-fiction category. "I knew that screenwriters used a particular technique, made popular by the graduate student writers of the screenplay for the movie *The Blair Witch Project* (1997)," Pasulka writes. "They increased their sale by pretending that the movie was based on a real event. I was intrigued by this strategy."[17] Pasulka notes that films often rely on the "based on true events" card at the beginning of a movie (or in the case of *The Blair Witch Project*, outright saying that it is true found footage), and also through "realist montage" which "splices different scenes together to create a narrative and establish a cognitive connection between them."[18] Maybe-fiction has a similar cognitive effect, though I believe this effect is closer to the cognitive estrangement of SF suggested by Suvin. Maybe-fiction does not make the gentle suggestion of truth by claiming to be "based on true events" or by use of realist montage; rather, it claims to be a wholesale true tale. *The Blair Witch Project* during its initial release is an example of this effect, though not long after its release it was outed as a fictional tale with only a slight basis in reality. Before this revelation, the film was an almost perfect example of maybe-fiction, even using other texts (in this case promotional TV mockumentaries intentionally marketed as documentaries) to further solidify the reality of the project. Pasulka uses the work of neuroscientist Jeffrey Zacks to illustrate the cognitive results of works like this: "We *know* it is not real, but Zacks's research shows that our brains process the information and then categorize these productions as equally realistic."[19] Pasulka is referring to "fictionalized factual" productions here, fictional works that are presented as fact, usually for entertainment reasons. As Pasulka notes:

> I do not take these productions to be metaphors. They are real-life examples that reveal how fictional characters from *Star Wars*, as well as other intergalactic objects like UFOs and extraterrestrials, exist as realities that inhabit our childhood and adult memories and inform our future behaviors. They are cultural realities, infused with meaning and emotion.[20]

Speculatively, it is possible that maybe-fiction heightens the effects seen in "fictionalized factual" productions because the realities these texts inhabit are supposedly our own. The stories are no longer distant possibilities: real, often credible people claim that a strangeness has already made its home in our reality. How does a reader's mind grapple with this claim?

Erik Davis' 2019 book *High Weirdness* perhaps bears the most similarity to the concept of maybe-fiction, primarily aesthetic similarities. Davis's term "high weirdness" refers to "a mode of culture and consciousness that reached a definite peak in the early seventies, when the writers and psychonauts […] pushed hard on the boundaries of reality—and got pushed back in return."[21] It is a cultural form that encompasses all varieties of weirdness simultaneously: "the uncanny, the fantastic, the perverse, and the macabre side of the supernatural," the "anomalous" and the deviant.[22] More succinctly, Davis says: "As a genre of culture and a mode of enjoyment, […] high weirdness […] has elements of all these attitudes. But high weirdness is an infectious project; it breaks down the distinction between subject and object; it loops and stains."[23] Maybe-fiction is decidedly similar in nature, albeit much broader in scope. Davis focuses on a specific subset of "wordsmiths and garage philosophers who brought all their existential, intellectual, and […] spiritual resources to bear on awesome experiences that blazed beyond the pale," writers like Philip K. Dick, Robert Anton Wilson, and Terrence McKenna.[24] This book as well takes an interest in these writers; Davis' writings on PKD and RAW are particularly relevant when studying their Fortean leanings. My exploration will also focus on other writers who did not witness extraordinary psychonaut experiences but nevertheless established interest in related, Fortean subjects and draw inspiration from them. These non-experiencers are writers of both maybe-fiction and maybe-fiction-infused SF. Regardless, Davis's book is monumental in documenting both the literature and subculture of "high weirdness," which in turn aids in my postulation of a maybe-fiction genre. For instance, a shared facet of both Davis's definition of "high weirdness" and maybe-fiction is a connection to the "uncanny" as described by Freud, who "stressed the double character of uncanny objects or events: they are both familiar, even quotidian, and unexpectedly peculiar or macabre."[25] Maybe-fiction, too, is filled with instances of the uncanny; Freud himself described the uncanny as sometimes an "ominous recurrence," relatable to the Fortean subject of synchronicities or meaningful coincidences. Branching off from Davis' work, the concept of maybe-fiction aims to broaden what works qualify as this particular type of "weird" literature. This exploration also, while considering the experiences of the writers, has a focus on the reactions of readers to these strange texts, how they affect the reader and how the reader interacts with them. This work, while approaching the topic in a manner like Davis, will hope to expand the types of texts into which this "high weirdness" permeates.

Kripal, Pasulka, and Davis all take an interest in how curiosity toward or belief in paranormal events and topics can expand creativity. This idea of the paranormal as a source of inspiration is where the idea of maybe-fiction aligns with each of these critical texts, amongst other facets of their individual arguments. Where the maybe-fiction concept primarily differs from these other critical works is its broadness, covering the vast swath of literature that followed the thought of Fort. These texts vary greatly in topic, but each suggests a more fantastic reality. Each text shares a common community or fandom that actively engages with them, doing the critical work of drawing comparisons between them and further solidifying the notion of an overarching plotline developing in our reality. Belief in the stories can come into play, but it is not necessarily required; a suspension of disbelief when reading the tales is just as valid. Whether these works are taken seriously by readers or simply instill entertainment value, the result is the same: a bizarre, science-fictional story that can be enjoyed on its own merits. I would argue that there is inherent entertainment value in strange but true stories. SF writer Jack Womack collected a wide variety of UFO literature and eventually published musings on his enormous collection in 2016's *Flying Saucers Are Real! The UFO Library of Jack Womack.* In an interview about this book, Womack spoke about the appeal of UFO literature:

> "I can study TB without catching it, preferably, and I can be a student of the Bible without being a Christian," Womack says, explaining his intense interest in these claims without actually believing any of them. "I collected these books because they gave me the same kind of escapism kicks other people get from reading science fiction, or my friends get from writing it."[26]

Importantly, Womack notes that appreciating these texts does not require belief or religious devotion to the subject. It is akin to reading the bible for fun, although the "escapism kick" Womack mentions is noticeably less prevalent (but not nonexistent) in religious texts. This "escapism kick" is an important feature of maybe-fiction, and while UFO literature seems the most well primed subset to have an SF-esque appeal, it is not the only maybe-fiction subset that offers a form of SF escapism. Virtually any text within the realm of maybe-fiction can offer the same appeal as UFO literature, because they function under essentially the same guidelines. Womack himself writes about the inception of his varied interest in this type of literature in an internet post:

> (I) then found on the racks a new Ace book, a republication of an older book. On the back I found a listing within the blurb of what I would find therein, and midway down I saw something that immediately caught my attention: The Cow That Gave Birth to Two Lambs. I bought it. Fifty cents well spent, I thought.
>
> The book, of course, was Charles Fort's *Lo!* His best, I've always believed, certainly from the literary viewpoint. But if Frank Edwards was Kentucky field-grown marijuana from the pre-hybridization days, Charles Fort was (and is) pure Owsley blue.
>
> I've talked to David Hartwell and others about the sense of wonder so often inspired

by the reading of science fiction at a young age; but my sense of wonder was stirred by Charles Fort, who to this day I will happily admit to as an influence, a very real one.

Lo! terrified me, really. Fort pulled the rug out from underneath everything, or appeared to, and did it so extremely well. I hid it at the bottom of the drawer, as if it were pornography. Pulling it out occasionally, drawn time and time again to the lovely notion of steam-engine time, and such lines as "All of us are skating over thin existence," and "I shut the front door upon Christ and Einstein, and at the back door extend a welcoming hand to little frogs and periwinkles."

The latter line is the guiding motto of the Womack Collection.[27]

This "Womack Collection" he speaks of is the so-called "Womack Collection of the Human Mind at Work and Play," a collection with decidedly maybe-fictional qualities:

> What I get from the books I collect is a sense of the human mind in all its possible manifestations, good, bad, indifferent, and crazed (sometimes, delightfully, all four in the same book). This gives me ideas. It increases my appreciation of the workings (or lack thereof) of the brain. It enables me to see how extrapolation can not only go off on a tangent, it can slide off the edge of the world. The comic aspects, almost inevitably inadvertent, of course delight me.
>
> Making myself familiar with the way people think, confronted with what they *perceive* to be outré, arcane, or paranormal situations, allows me to allow my characters, and situations, to more believably take that all-important sudden left turn into WomackWorld (sic), as it were, when the time comes for them to do so.[28]

Womack is expressing his Fortean and maybe-fiction influences in this post, but he is also illustrating the maybe-fiction concept well. The description of his collection covers the broad range of subjects and its literary quality while also noting the varied reader reactions to the texts. These can range from genuine appreciation of the human mind's potential to comic relief. To these potential reactions, I would add the possibility of deep scorn of the text by skeptics or genuine entertainment—much like that which comes from reading SF. Womack's collection is expansive, fostering any and all bastard children of literature. Maybe-fiction also welcomes these throwaways with open arms, with an emphasis on the science-fictional and a few other caveats. The following sections will more firmly establish tenets of maybe-fiction, as well as examine its broad range of texts and its community or fandom. Throughout the sections, examples of maybe-fiction will be used to further solidify the variety of texts but also help to establish their encapsulating categorization. This explanation is necessary before exploring the works of SF authors influenced by Fort because their Fortean inclinations normally do not stop at Fort alone. Usually, the authors are interested in the broad range of maybe-fiction, often spurred on by an interest in Fort. The Fortean relationship to SF cannot be fully understood without an exploration into Fort's broader influence on the literature of the unexplained.

A Matter of Contention

Though virtually unlimited in terms of subject matter (from UFOs to ghosts to psychics), all maybe-fiction tends to be contentious in that most subjects are not acknowledged as valid by science. This follows a similar dichotomy of science versus religion as in Fort's time, although now it is a battle fought between different brands of skeptics and believers. Many subjects are outright ridiculed by skeptics. Author and notorious abductee, Whitley Strieber was met with such a reaction with Robert Sheaffer of The Bay Area Skeptics writing of *Communion*'s 1988 sequel *Transformation: The Breakthrough* that:

> In the final analysis, Strieber's visions of "the visitors" undoubtedly have more to do with religion and psychology than they do with anything extraterrestrial. Strieber is far from the first person in history to experience visions of bizarre beings, and then become transformed into a tireless evangelist seeking to convince the world that they are real.[29]

The publisher of *Transformation* seemed to concur, labeling the book fiction soon after its release. Strieber went back to writing what he understood as fiction because of "the pure opprobrium and public disinterest with which his accounts were routinely met."[30] Kripal writes: "In terms of reception history, both official religion (Fort's first Dominant) and official science (Fort's second Dominant) derided and demeaned the book."[31] The three "Dominants" Kripal refers to are "totalizing system(s) of thought that defines reality for a particular culture or period,"[32] the first two being the omnipresent foes of Forteana—the very reason these works are contentious. Strieber is no outlier when it comes to criticism against maybe-fiction; virtually every account of anomalous experience is immediately discredited as being a hallucination or falsehood. This is not to say that all experiences are to be believed or disbelieved—my goal in this new definition is to express that it is acceptable for fact and fiction to be ambiguously blurred. The obscuring of these labels is part of the charm of this type of literature. When discussing the works of Strieber, most of the emphasis is on discussing whether readers believe Strieber's accounts as genuine experiences. His abductions and various meetings with the entities he calls "The Visitors" are, to a skeptic, either a hoax or hallucination. To believers, they are accounts of abduction by extraterrestrials or some other manipulating entity. Yet others are simply impressed by Strieber's ability to weave a compelling narrative out of his experiences. Maybe-fiction is more inclined toward the latter, though pondering whether the text is genuine or not is part of the journey.

Fort himself was subject to immense criticism by the skeptical community. Regarding Fort, noted skeptic Joe Nickell wrote, "Fort was not an investigator—that is, one who seeks neither to foster nor dismiss mysteries but attempts to solve them. The power of science is its unmatched ability to provide explanations, and indeed the progress of civilization can be seen as a series of solved mysteries, a concept Charles Fort could scarcely comprehend."[33] But Nickell acknowledges that although "his brief mystifications about poltergeists, spontaneous human combustion, Bermuda-Triangle type vanishings, and similar reputed phenomena have largely been overshadowed by much more comprehensive, specialized efforts, [...] Fort was a major figure in establishing the genre of the 'unexplained.'"[34] However, this feat did not make up for many of Fort's failings, which Nickell alludes to, quoting 20th century skeptic Martin Gardner:

> When his more astute admirers insist that he was not the arch-enemy of science he was reputed to be, but only the enemy of scientists who forget the ephemeral character of all knowledge, they are emphasizing the sound and healthy aspect of Forteanism. It is true that no scientific theory is above doubt. It is true that all scientific "facts" are subject to endless revision as new "data" are uncovered. No scientist worthy of the name thinks otherwise. But it is also true that scientific theories can be given high or low degrees of confirmation. Fort was blind to this elementary fact—or pretended to be blind to it—and it is this blindness which is the spurious and unhealthy side of Forteanism.[35]

Much like Gardner's complicated feelings about Fort, maybe-fiction authors fall in both the healthy and unhealthy sides of Forteanism. Others seem clearly more invested in telling a good story, its "truth" immaterial to its enjoyment. Even when this is the case, the topic covered is still scoffed at by critics, while some readers believe the text wholesale.

While the battle between skeptics and believers is fought, a group of neutral readers in the middle tend to be less recognized by scholarship. Nevertheless, this middle ground represents a prominent subculture of readers simply fascinated by maybe-fiction as an entertaining escape from reality without worrying about the credence of the texts. Within this subculture are those who side closer to believers (without outright belief) who use the texts as exercises to think about reality differently. On the more skeptical side of the spectrum, some will casually poke fun at the texts as entertainment without outright debunking them. This middle ground, I would argue, is the underrepresented reader populace of maybe-fiction—and this is the subset of readers that many SF authors who use Forteana in their texts often fall into.

The Truth is Out There / In Here: A Survey of Maybe-fiction Types

The fact that these texts all claim to be true functions as a unique literary device, whether this is the intention of the author or not. In most maybe-fiction, the statements that the works are true come across as genuine statements from the author, either encouraging leniency from a possibly skeptic reader or pleading for their words to be taken at face value. In many cases, as seen with Strieber, reaction can be negative and even hostile to introducing fantastic elements into a work of non-fiction. In a few cases, the plea seems to be a plot device and nothing more, but these texts can still garner belief or suspended disbelief for the sake of entertainment.

This happens in the preface to Richard Shaver's first Lemuria story, as the author laments: "To me it is tragic that the only way I can tell my story is in the guise of fiction."[36] Though the author described a vast system of underground civilizations inhabited by malicious beings known as Deros and benevolent proto-humans known as Teros, he (and *Amazing Stories* editor Ray Palmer) insisted that these tales were true. A similar concession was made in 1992 with Preston B. Nichols' book *The Montauk Project*, detailing the author's experiences with a secret government research facility that supposedly achieved both teleportation and time travel. "This work is being presented as non-fiction as it contains no falsehoods to the best knowledge of the authors," he writes. "However, it can also be read as pure science fiction if that is more suitable to the reader."[37] This claim of truth has been a literary device for centuries: *Robinson Crusoe*, often considered the first novel, employed this literary device; Defoe "promoted the illusion" of the tale being true "by telling readers that *Robinson Crusoe* had been written by Crusoe himself, including a preface, supposedly written by the book's editor, asserting the story as 'a just History of Fact.'"[38] Literary scholar Michael Gavin says the book "is among the most prominent examples of a made-up story that could not quite call itself fiction."[39] *Robinson Crusoe* came so early in the development of literature as we know it today and fact and fiction already exhibit a heavy blurring. Gavin further argues that "made-up stories are part of the world and share it with us, that they are, in some important sense, real."[40] What are we to make of stories where this dichotomy of fact and fiction is blurred even further?

The following sections will list and briefly examine the vast range of literature that makes up the maybe-fiction subset—all stories that claim to be true and contain a science-fictional portrait of reality, full of bizarre events and seemingly fantastic conclusions. They cover inherently contentious subject matters. These texts come in a variety of forms because, as stated earlier, this range of literature is very broad. A survey of these texts will be explored throughout this section, covering the varying modes of narrative, topics, and the different levels of "believability" these texts can contain. While this section covers a relatively small number of maybe-fiction texts out of the medium's expansive catalogue, it is intended to give pertinent examples and indicate which texts not covered within this volume can be considered maybe-fiction. This line of investigation will be continued into the exploration of intertextuality between maybe-fiction examples. It is worth noting that maybe-fiction texts can often be a combination of the different modes presented here. For instance, journalists investigating Fortean phenomena often find themselves encountering paranormal experiences of their own, rendering the text a combination of Fortean journalism and personal experience narrative. In John Keel's *The Mothman Prophecies* (explored in the next section), Keel finds himself experiencing the same phenomena he came to investigate (e.g., strange phone calls with metallic voices). Most case studies of paranormal phenomena (owing to the very nature of the paranormal) rely on personal testimonies of anomalous experience, bridging together anomalous experience literature and "forbidden science" literature. While complicating the categorization of maybe-fiction, this hybridization also plays into the omnipresent intertextuality at play in maybe-fiction. These examples are the basic formulas of a maybe-fiction text, but these formulas intermix often. A more complete survey of maybe-fiction could fill multiple books, so this section aims to narrow the literature to that which most resembles SF and/or bears the clearest relationship to Charles Fort. Many of these examples come from my personal Fortean library as an attempt to convey how writers have continually expanded Fort's catalogue of oddities and anomalies. As a result, SF has seen an expansion of possible fodder for explicitly fictional stories.

Detectives of the Damned: Fortean Journalism

Just as Fort "descended into journalism," countless maybe-fiction authors have made the same journalistic dive into anomalous events. Fort himself rarely went to investigate unexplained phenomena (although there are a few examples of others investigating on his behalf), but others following his lead put themselves in the midst of the events. John Keel is perhaps the best example of this investigative journalism style of maybe-fiction, writing numerous books on paranormal phenomena in which Keel throws himself right into the action. His 1957 non-fiction debut was *Jadoo*, a book describing his experiences with miracles and paranormal activity during his travels throughout Asia, but his real success came with 1975's *The Mothman Prophecies*. The book involves Keel's investigations into sightings of a giant grey creature in Point Pleasant, West Virginia. The town became plagued by reports of various other paranormal events, such as the appearances of Men in Black, a man who was abducted by an alien named Indrid Cold and taken to his planet, and ample UFO sightings by the locals. After Keel himself gets bombarded by strange telephone calls consisting of veiled threats and odd noises, the book eventually culminates in the collapse of the local Silver Bridge. Keel ruminates on whether this tragedy is somehow connected to the strange events plaguing the town.[41]

2. Defining Maybe-fiction

A more recent maybe-fiction journalist is George Knapp, most famous for his 1989 interview with supposed Area 51 whistleblower, Bob Lazar. Lazar claimed that "he saw documents and photographs of UFOs and alien autopsies while working at Area 51; Lazar also said that he saw nine extraterrestrial craft and witnessed some of them in flight."[42] The supposed goal was to reverse-engineer the crafts for the military. Knapp's work took an even stranger turn with 2005's *Hunt for the Skinwalker*, coauthored with biotech research scientist, Colm A. Kelleher. The book was a terrifying tale of a Utah rancher's family besieged by a wide variety of paranormal events, ranging from strange lights in the sky to poltergeist activity to the appearances of large wolf-like creatures, seemingly physical manifestations of the Native American Skinwalker myth. The book follows a team of National Institute for Discovery Science (NIDS) members who observe strange occurrences but struggle to get any concrete proof, as if the supposed force behind the phenomena knows when it is being recorded.[43]

Our science-fictional reality is not limited to book-length journalistic investigations—various Fortean publications have long been a source for journalism of the strange. The *Fortean Times* is the longest-running and most prominent of these publications. Single issues run the full gamut of Fortean journalism—a 2013 issue included a re-evaluation of Helena Blavatsky, spontaneous combustions plaguing a Turkish family, rumors of Princess Diana's dresses being haunted by her spirit, a supposed Iranian time machine, and more.[44] While the magazine is perhaps the most representative of Fort's style of journalism, cataloguing any and all oddities to grace our planet, more field-specific publications with a narrower focus on a narrower range of phenomena are still Fortean journalism. *The Flying Saucer Review* is a UFO-specific journal that has been published nearly continuously for 70 years, starting in 1955. *Animals & Men*, published by the Centre for Fortean Zoology, collects reports of anomalous animals—those supposedly extinct or previously undiscovered. A variety of other small newsletters, many short-lived, have attempted to continue Fort's research throughout the decades. These newsletters and the subsequent community engagement that results are not unlike SF fandom, though this thread will be explored further in this chapter. A few choice titles are the *Journal of Abnormal Abduction Research* (2014–2015), *Magonia* (1979–2009), *Caveat Emptor* (1971–1990), and the *Journal of the Fortean Research Center* (1986–1989). An issue of the latter included a report from 1969 Nebraska of "an amoeba-shaped blob, about six feet across, and about 18 inches thick, moving along the ground [...] by extending a gelatinous pseudopod, and then pulling itself along in that direction, or rather flowing into itself."[45] Perhaps the world has become more science-fictional since Fort's time. As with all maybe-fiction, the reputability of these works varies greatly; the truth of the stories is never certain, but some works certainly have more physical and anecdotal confirmation than others. Typically, journalistic maybe-fiction maintains an unbiased stance, and simply reports on these oddities and gives credence where credence is due. However, some publications, such as the *Weekly World News*, continuously mix their journalism with true strange tales and journalistic parody. The publication's most famous character, Bat Boy, was introduced in 1992 and the initial story reads like a direct sendup of earlier, earnestly reported tales of inner earth civilizations or cryptozoology. It is only with subsequent publications featuring Bat Boy that the tale gets too ludicrous to pass as anything but pure fiction (e.g., a cover story entitled "Bat Boy Led Our Troops to Saddam's Hole!").[46] Yet other stories reported by *Weekly World News* actually draw from true reports or interviews, such as a 1993 story featuring an actual ufologist, Stanton Friedman. Of course, some journalistic integrity was forgotten when the story was sensationally titled "UFO Expert Warns Earthlings: Space aliens will invade if we lay one finger on 'em!"[47]

At the Cosmic Confessional: Anomalous Experience Literature

The type of maybe-fiction that most resembles SF is perhaps that of anomalous experience literature. These texts consist of writers conveying their Fortean experiences from a first-person perspective. Some of the SF authors examined in this work (particularly Richard Shaver, Philip K. Dick, and Robert Anton Wilson) wrote texts that could be considered maybe-fiction in this sense, because while some their works are published as SF, the authors are clear to say that the experiences were real or based on real events. These texts are numerous, but perhaps the most well-known of anomalous experience narratives is Whitley Strieber's *Communion*. First published in 1987, the book was subject to much criticism and debate, largely stemming from the fact that Strieber was originally a fiction writer specializing in horror novels. But his experience, while certainly remarkable, is one seen quite regularly in anomalous experience literature. It seems Strieber's background as a writer helped him to convey the terror, confusion, and awe of this experience far better than those before him. The plot of *Communion* unfolds like an excellent soft–SF work. Even sections that are word-for-word transcripts of his and his wife's hypnosis sessions leave the reader on the edge of their seat, wondering if some tidbit of information can unshroud the mystery behind Strieber's experiences. *Communion* especially resembles an SF novel when Strieber offers suggestions as to what the "visitors" could be. This is in the last section of the book where he examines the history and meaning of the abduction experience more broadly. One such hypothesis Strieber outlines is akin to Arthur C. Clarke's works (explored thoroughly in Chapter 4): "Maybe you and I are larvae, and the 'visitors' are human beings in the mature form."[48] This possibility is tied to the idea of an afterlife, a post-mortem human evolution that turns humans into these visitors who are concerned with their lesser forms: us. Strieber mentions that "we are consuming our planet's resources with at least the avidity of caterpillars on a shrub."[49] Abductees often report the humanoids bringing messages of warning against nuclear power and resource abuse; perhaps Strieber is not wrong in assuming these entities are some kind of cosmic babysitter.

However, Strieber is a bit of an outlier when it comes to abductee literature. He was an accomplished writer with ample ability to convey his experience well. Before *Communion*, there were myriad other first-person accounts of alien abduction, often written by inexperienced writers. This results in two juxtaposing features of most abductee literature: First, it is unlikely that this broad swath of normal, unassuming people would risk their credibility by releasing an account of a fantastic story which tends to *add* credibility to the story. But secondly, because they are not experienced writers, the books are sometimes quite dry, despite the science-fictional story being told. Other abductee tales are more flowery and peaceful, such as that of Howard Menger, who was taken by brotherly Venusians to the far reaches of our solar system. Later he tried to recreate the music he heard on Saturn with a 1957 record entitled *Authentic Music from Another Planet*.[50] As usual, UFOs tend to dominate the realm of maybe-fiction, likely because UFO-related experiences are among the most common paranormal experiences. Anomalous experience literature, however, is not limited to UFO-centric literature. For instance, there is the bizarre narrative of a psychic treasure hunt in *The Green Stone*, a maybe-fiction text published in 1983. In this text, a ragtag group of people all around Britain receive psychic messages imploring them to locate medieval relics, like the titular Green Stone of Meonia, in order to ward off an evil force who would use the stone's powers for ill. It reads like a fantasy novel, but there are physical artifacts with supposed connections to the Knights Templar. It is a complex story and a blurb from *Psychic News* on the cover assures the reader: "If you only read one book in your life, read this one. If you only read two books in your life, read it twice!"[51] Other anomalous experience texts deal with people who have found themselves haunted and preyed upon by another presence, as is the case with Steven LaChance's *The Uninvited*. The book follows the author's horrific plight with demonic attackers who possess and injure his family and, eventually, the next homeowner.[52] Yet others are not haunted by otherworldly intelligences, but rather, their own government. Such is the case in David Morehouse's *Psychic Warrior*, a book in which the author reveals his role in the CIA's Stargate Program, where he was trained as a remote viewer and forced to live through countless tragedies on the psychic plane.[53]

If journalistic maybe-fiction is SF with third-person narration, anomalous experience literature is SF from a first-person perspective—a fact that renders many of the experience texts deeply personal, more emotionally inclined, but nevertheless fantastic and Fortean. Often, this personal narrative makes the fantastic nature of the story easier to swallow—though the motivations of these authors can often be questioned. Despite seeming honesty, most skeptics will wonder if the author of an anomalous experience piece stands to gain notoriety or money from telling their story. Anomalous experience narratives are among the most common maybe-fiction texts to appear in pulp SF and will play a major part in the chapters to come: many SF writers had anomalous experiences and utilized them to inspire their fiction.

Where Scientists Fear to Tread: "Forbidden Science"

Anomalies have become a subject carefully studied by researchers of varied credibility. These studies are still considered maybe-fiction under the current definition because the hypotheses are nearly as fantastic as any SF novel, journalistic maybe-fiction, or narrative of anomalous experience, and these hypotheses are presented as a real possibility. Among the most reputable sources of maybe-fictional science is Jacques Vallee, the astronomer-turned-ufologist who brought a higher degree of credibility to the fringe subject of UFOs. Kripal writes of Vallee:

> When I first read Jacques Vallee, I knew immediately that I had found a writer who had something important to teach us about the history of Western esotericism, about the truths of traditional folklore, about the mysterious attractions of modern science fiction, and about the reality of paranormal phenomena.[54]

Striking an impressive balance between the physical and psychological characteristics of the UFO phenomena, Vallee's work itself possesses the "mysterious attractions of modern science fiction." Much like the character based upon him in *Close Encounters of the Third Kind*, Vallee traverses the globe interviewing UFO experiencers, examining physical evidence, and searching the archives of the human record for analogous experiences in our early history. This results in numerous examinations of the UFO phenomena from a scientific standpoint, but Vallee, as a proponent of this scientific study, understands that boots-on-the-ground Keel-esque research is also necessary to study the elusive phenomena in its entirety. Kripal again: "(Vallee) makes the impossible possible through the sophistication of his suspicions and the complex ways that his comparative imagination puts together the pieces and parts of his historical data in order to form a radically different picture-puzzle of things."[55] However, Vallee has always butted heads with the academic establishment and UFO enthusiasts with his consistent refusal to align by their standard views of the phenomena. Kripal notes how Vallee has been "exiled [...] from both the rationalist debunkers of the scientific world and the true believers of the UFO community."[56] Only recently has Vallee been reevaluated by religious scholars like Kripal and Pasulka, who see the value of Vallee's work in bridging the gap between religion and science.

Other, less academically accepted researchers make up the "forbidden science" segment of maybe-fiction. Prominent examples are the proponents of alternative history research that have cropped up since before the days of Fort, often called pseudoarcheologists. Fort contemporary James Churchward claimed to have translated secret tablets that "unearthed secrets of great importance in the elucidation of that eternal problem, Man."[57] These translations culminated in his 1926 work *The Lost Continent of Mu*, published in the period between Fort's *New Lands* and *Lo!* Mu, like the mythical Atlantis, had been submerged and contained "a civilization far superior to our own."[58] Churchward claims that many ancient civilizations sprung forth from Mu and thus several artifacts of Lemurian culture survive in the succeeding ones. Noted skeptic Martin Gardner wrote of these works:

> The Mu books are uniformly crude in writing, and such a mishmash of geological and archeological errors that they are widely regarded, even by other Atlantean and Mu scholars, as a deliberate hoax. It is significant that no one ever saw the tablets which were the chief source of the Colonel's knowledge, nor did he anywhere identify the monastery where he found them.[59]

This crude archeology continued later in the century when Erich Von Däniken's 1968 book *The Chariots of the Gods* made waves in popular culture. Von Däniken's oft-disputed research follows a similar method to that of Fort: collecting various anomalies and outliers, this time within the field of archeology, and forming a science-fictional hypothesis via this evidence. Furthermore, Von Däniken questioned the accepted theories of respected archeologists and remolded them to mesh with his conception. *Chariots of the Gods* was not the first work of its kind and it was certainly not the last. Following Von Däniken, in later decades, Zecharia Sitchin postulated that the creation of the ancient Sumerian civilization was orchestrated by a race of beings from the planet Nibiru called the Annunaki. Again, respected scholars found these to be gross mistranslations of Sumerian texts. In the present day, writer Graham Hancock is perhaps the most prominent proponent of alternative history research, receiving similar skepticism. Pseudoscience expert Brian Regal wrote of Hancock, calling him "the most successful modern purveyor of the hidden history concept":

> As with all hidden history aficionados, Hancock holds the line that experts and other academics (he has no training in science or archeology) are engaging in a major

cover-up of humanity's golden past. He sees himself as part of a noble coterie of amateur investigators who are all that stands between humanity and the forces of darkness.[60]

Despite the criticisms leveled against them, these alternative historical texts have proven to be a cultural force and wellspring of creativity.[61] The television show *Ancient Aliens* has aired for (at time of writing) fourteen seasons, and is a project widely criticized for promoting the pseudoscience of several of these alternative history proponents (Von Däniken and Hancock appear as talking heads semi-regularly). However, the show functions along the basis of maybe-fiction, explaining its popularity via its entertainment value as opposed to true believers in their viewership. The science-fictional hypotheses are presented as truth, along with over-the-top computer-animated recreations of events and supposed artifacts, reminiscent of the faux-documentaries explored in the following section on urban legends and ambiguous fiction. *Independence Day* director Roland Emmerich has noted his inspiration from the works of Sitchin and Hancock in his movies, finding that such works "let your creativity run wild because there is no historical record."[62] Run wild it has—alternative history theories have appeared in fictional works as dissimilar as *Prometheus* (2012) and a recent incarnation of the Scooby-Doo cartoons, *Scooby-Doo! Mystery Incorporated* (2010–2013).[63]

Maybe-fictional hypotheses are varied but never fail to suggest a fascinating reality. Pilot-turned–amateur researcher Carl W. Feindt collected and examined hundreds of unidentified submersible object (USO) cases in his 2010 book *UFOs and Water*, his stated purpose being, given that human technology is incapable of making a device that can function completely in both air and water, studying these cases might hold the key to solving the UFO enigma. Feindt writes: "By examining what a UFO does *to* that medium (water), which is not as evident in the atmosphere, we can pick up clues as to its operation."[64] D. Scott Rogo and Raymond Bayless attempted a serious study of phantom phone calls in 1979's *Phone Calls from the Dead*, crafting the most thorough survey of cases available to discern the trends and outliers of the subject. Within this text, another science-fictional theory: "If nothing more, [...] the phantom phone call mystery indicates that perhaps one day, direct-voice or other forms of electronic communication with the dead will be a common occurrence."[65] The hypotheses proposed by these maybe-fictional investigations could function as a sourcebook for SF stories, just as Fort's work did during the pulp era. But the "forbidden science" texts also remind us that SF can provide a sourcebook for scientific explorations, if the science is permitted to be speculative enough. Andrew May notes how this pseudoscience has a similar end goal to SF:

2. Defining Maybe-fiction

Pseudoscience is a creative undertaking—effectively a branch of the entertainment industry. Its end users read books ... and for a book to be successful, it needs to say something large swathes of the public want to read. Pseudoscience is much better than real science at giving the audience what it wants.[66]

What the audience usually craves is a picture of our reality that resembles SF.

Legends and Ambiguous Fiction

Some urban legends fall within the maybe-fiction genre. Folklorist Jan Harold Brunvand, who specializes in urban legends (ULs), describes these stories as "too good to be true":

These popular fables describe presumably real (though odd) events that happened to a friend of a friend. And they are usually told by credible persons narrating them in a believable style because they *do* believe them. The settings and actions in ULs are realistic and familiar [...] and the human characters [...] are quite ordinary people. However, the bizarre, comic, or horrifying incidents that occur to these people go one step too far to be believable.[67]

While many urban legends are not maybe-fiction, functioning rather as humorous or strange anecdotes, Brunvand's definition of UL bears an uncanny resemblance to the description of maybe-fiction as established through Suvin's concept of cognitive estrangement. ULs rely on a realism disrupted by "the bizarre, comic, or horrifying," inducing estrangement in the reader just as SF and maybe-fiction works do. Fort regarded ULs as a form of his truth-fiction, noting that even the stories that are "too good to be true" are not devoid of truth. He referenced the common ULs of "the fellow who found the pearl in his oyster stew—the old fiddle that turned out to be a Stradivarius—the ring that was lost in a lake, and was found when a fish was caught. [...] But these often repeated [*sic*] yarns are conventional yarns. And almost all liars are conventionalists."[68] Yet Fort concedes that "even in the matter of the talking dog, I think that the writer probably had something to base upon. Perhaps he had heard of talking dogs."[69] In this sense, even the most "fictional" fiction available has some modicum of truth to it. Urban legends are no exception.

In recent decades, common forms of maybe-fictional entertainment have been creepypastas and augmented reality games (ARGs). Both of these mediums rely on the basic mechanics of urban legends (i.e., word-of-mouth, narrated in a believable manner, etc.), but are more science-fictional, Fortean, or supernatural in nature than most urban legends. Among the first ARGs were pamphlets circulated about a commune of estranged scientists who created a dimensional gateway at a secret laboratory in Ong's Hat, New Jersey. This story circulated through early internet boards throughout the eighties and nineties, perpetrated by the "gamemaster" Joseph Matheny, who went so far as to give an interview on *Coast to Coast AM* with Art Bell, expressing the truth of the stories about Ong's Hat.[70] While it has since been revealed to be an ARG, the narrative struck a chord with its followers. Religious studies scholar Michael Kinsella wrote that Ong's Hat was "a far-reaching, open-ended narrative [...] that chronicles the efforts of several groups and organizations conspiring to either liberate or enslave man through the distribution or repression of technologies enabling travel to parallel worlds."[71] The relations to Fort and SF are both relatively clear. The phenomena, including mysterious disappearances and parallel dimensions, are among the tropes of the Fortean SF explored later. The very idea of a hunt for some hidden truth that this ARG left open to a community of readers (as well as a dark force hoping to keep this truth hidden) is reminiscent of Fort's own catalogue of anomalies. He left these collections open for future readers to puzzle over. Even his disdain for "dogmatic science" which strived to keep its own narrative the only acceptable one is a theme within the Ong's Hat ARG. These are not uncommon themes in ARGs, or maybe-fiction in general. While maybe-fiction has proven to be a collection of largely splintered camps, the act of connecting them together to try to gesture towards an overall solution to the unexplained is one worth taking seriously in the cultural sense. This act relates to the thrill of the hunt and transmedia nature of ARG and creepypasta storytelling. While some of these examples are confirmed fictional, they still illustrate the consistent functions of the maybe-fiction genre. Kinsella's conception of the purpose of legends relates specifically to maybe-fictional texts: "We use legends as manifestations of a collective imaginary in order to create, substantiate, and contest what we believe to be reality."[72]

However, even explicitly fictional tales can keep up this veneer of absolute truth. As mentioned earlier, if *The Blair Witch Project* had maintained its early-on "authenticity," it would still be an example of maybe-fiction. When no one could confirm that actors had *not* died during the making of it, it functioned just as any maybe-fiction text would, despite being markedly spookier. Indeed, despite the fictional nature of *The Blair Witch Project*, it clearly has Fortean leanings. English scholar Stephanie Moss compared the film to the gothic novel *Dracula*, as both works are presented as documented proof that "becomes a scientifically flawed collection of strange anecdotes, a conclusion that implies the difficult, often contentious relationship between the objective research paradigms recognized by the scientific community and the goals of those who seek validation of the subjectively determined data of the paranormal."[73] Intriguingly, Moss suggests that "when the willing suspension of disbelief engages audiences of (*The Blair Witch Project*), they, like Seward witnessing Lucy arisen from her grave, participate in the observation of unexplained events."[74] Part of maybe-fiction's appeal is certainly the secondhand experience of seeing a stranger world. I corresponded with filmmaker Ben Rock, the production designer on the film and creator of the famous "stick men," the pagan stick constructions that are placed throughout the makeshift outdoor sets. Rock also directed two mockumentary promotional videos for the film and its sequel, *The Burkittsville 7* (2000) and *Shadow of the Blair Witch* (2000). Both features imitate a real documentary and give no indication that they are fiction. Without the revelation that *The Blair Witch Project* was entirely fictional, these two pieces of media are very convincing. The second feature, *Shadow of the Blair Witch*, takes a "meta" route and claims to be an investigative report on the murders that inspired the second *Blair Witch* film. Again, we see the fact/fiction gradient become further distorted, and intertextuality continues to play a key role, even in the realm of the most clearly fictional maybe-fiction. Rock also happens to be a subscriber to the *Fortean Times*. He says that these Fortean interests began with *In Search Of...* (1976–1982): "I loved the idea of monsters and aliens and whatnot. In my school library there was a book about the Loch Ness Monster that really sparked my imagination."[75] But Rock is not a total believer by any means and reading these texts made him more skeptical: "There was also this book about a guy who proved that the ancient Inca had the technology to make hot-air balloons to look down on the Nazca lines, which maybe was the beginning of a foundation for my current skepticism."[76] Despite this skepticism, Rock still sees value in texts that are more rumor, speculation, or urban legend. "Storytelling-wise I find it all fascinating," he says. "I never miss an episode of *Ancient Aliens*. [...] They (*FT*) always have a new angle on some of these older ideas and if I suspend my disbelief, the stories are a lot of fun." With regard to how these types of stories have influenced his filmmaking, Rock says that his mockumentaries were "100% [...] fueled not just by my fascination with mystery and folklore, but even more [...] trying to emulate the way those ideas are presented in documentary form." Rock clarifies that "the fun of it [...] is not about saying anything is true—it's more about how a piece of folklore gets filtered through the telling by so many people. In all the stuff I've had a hand in writing, we gave each person an intentionally different version of the story so they wouldn't all line up perfectly."[77] Again, we see the omnipresent shades of grey on the fact-fiction spectrum become further ambiguous. This blurring appears to be a continual part of the entertainment appeal of maybe-fiction.

Intertextuality

The work that truly inspired this book was not Fort himself, but a little-known maybe-fiction text published in 1989, *The Vertical Plane* by Ken

Webster. I first heard about this text through the maybe-fiction-centric podcast *Mysterious Universe*.[78] After hearing the tale, I was inclined to revisit the vast catalog of Forteana. The author is a schoolteacher from Dodleston, UK, who found himself involved in one of the strangest paranormal events I have ever heard about. Via a 1980s Macintosh computer (with a word processor but no internet) he claimed to receive messages from a certain Tomas Harden, a man living in the same location but in the 1500s. The story is fantastic, and hardly believable in most regards, but there is always some note of believability in the author's presentation of the events that supposedly occurred. Allegedly, the type of English used was accurate to the 1500s and a knowledgeable friend of Webster says that the writings would take a long time to emulate accurately. In historical records, Webster found evidence confirming the claims of the man that left him messages on his computer. Poltergeist activity occurred; a picture of a Jaguar Coupe disappeared and reappeared reputedly looking hundreds of years old; and the messages continued for around two years. The most baffling development was when another person claiming to be from the year 2109 contacted Webster and his wife, leaving cryptic messages that seem to imply that the communication with Tomas Harden was part of some strange test. Again, we see an instance of the phenomenon being some type of manipulation, which is especially cruel when many experiencers think they are having a joke played on them. The story is bizarre, but its author never falters in how truthful he claims he's being. Webster conveys an intense emotionality in the book, expressing his deep bond with Harden (sometimes spelled Hawarden) and the power of an unlikely friendship in disparate temporal realities. The book is a fascinating example of maybe-fiction, and one that was recently republished after years of languishing in obscurity.[79] Many will doubt its claims and, perhaps, they are correct in doing so, but the narrative is fascinatingly accessible, as much as a work of SF is accessible. While much SF stirs the question in the reader, "could our world become like that?" a maybe-fiction text like *The Vertical Plane* instead stirs the question, "is our world already like this, so irrational and strange? Are we being manipulated?"

    Little did I know, *The Vertical Plane* was a perfect example of the intertextuality between maybe-fiction texts. I was astounded to learn that the story did not end with Webster's book, but that the same forces behind the communication seemed to return to yet another experiencer. Surprisingly, a German physicist named Ernst Senkowski published a 1995 book entitled *Instrumental Transcommunication*, which examines cases of alleged contact with entities through "magnetic tapes, sounding out of loudspeakers and telephones, computer texts, images on video tapes, TV screens, and monitors."[80] I cannot vouch for the veracity of the work as a whole (maybe-fiction can rarely be totally vouched for), but I was shocked to discover that

2. Defining Maybe-fiction

Senkowski not only mentions Ken Webster's experiences in the 1980s, but also that of an Adolf Homes who managed to contact the 2109 entity in the year 1995. However, I hold great doubts to whether this was genuine contact as opposed to an attempt to replicate the phenomena from Webster's book, and the wording is sometimes so confusing that I fear something may be lost in translation. One of 2109's messages to Homes reads as follows:

> Identification of 2109 consists of innumerable time- and space-less mind structures of the formation/becoming of psychic species.—Thousands of billions (am.: quadrillions) of systems exist, in all (these) we exist.—Your existence/being consists of complex facets of earlier, present, as well as partly of future information and forms.—We can also say all life on your object is a continuous experiment of other intelligences. You consequently act by distant hypnosis.—From our viewpoint all your researches [*sic*] are useless because you have drawn away. Vulgata MATTH. 22,37/40.—All biological processes are manipulations.—AARON do understand, remain true to yourself.—We have contact with all that was, is, and will be.—2109 greets AARON and MOSE as well as every mind/spirit.—What has been created is (will be) preserved. A metamorphosis is needed.[81]

As can be seen, the message is at once vague and terrifying, recalling specifically the language used in many of the UFO cults Jacques Vallee investigated in his 1979 book *Messengers of Deception*.[82] For instance, the entity says that a metamorphosis is needed—a facet of the phenomena that Vallee notes as constant in contactee literature: the concept of guided evolution by a force much greater than humanity itself. This message is a shift for the 2109 persona from Webster's work, which painted the entity as much less threatening although still in total control of the communications. The 2109 messages are a prime example of the intertextuality inherent in maybe-fiction. Because of the vast quantity of anomalous reports and personal experiences, there is nearly always a story that corresponds with another, forming a Fortean trend. Maybe-fiction is a vast tapestry of strangeness that forms a blurry and often indecipherable picture of our reality, yet it leaves the notion that a clearer picture can be determined if one goes far enough down the rabbit hole. Maybe-fiction is not unlike fan fiction, using our own reality as the canvas. Fan fiction, or fanfic, finds a basis in fictional texts and expands the mythology and worlds of those texts. Maybe-fiction seems intent on expanding the boundaries of our own world, past what most people consider conceivable, and attempts to form a cohesive rendering of our reality out of thousands of maybe-fiction texts.

Intertextuality can be seen in several works already mentioned. Keel's *The Mothman Prophecies*, for instance, features Keel's investigation into Woodrow Derenberger's contactee experience with a grinning being from "Lanulos" named Indrid Cold. Derenberger wrote his own narrative of the events in the 1971 book *Visitors from Lanulos* and Derenberger's daughter

Taunia added even more to the tale with the 2016 book *Beyond Lanulos: Our Fifty Years with Indrid Cold*. Certainly, there is a narrative intertextuality to these works, but this intertextuality can become more complex.

To give a further example of how maybe-fiction forms its network of intertextuality, consider the following example and the numerous other texts to which it can be connected: A clerk at a St. Louis hotel had a bizarre night in 1970. Writing a message to the local UFO newsletter, *The UFO Enigma*, Dorothy Simpson relayed an incident involving a suspiciously out-of-place family that appeared at the front desk following a "whistling sigh" noise. All were diminutive despite two of them supposedly being children. Simpson recalls that they all had on expensive looking clothing and that their hair did not appear real. The man spoke up, but in a surprisingly high-pitched voice and broken English: "Do you have a room to stay?" He asked the question twice. Simpson gave the man details about the accommodations, but the man did not seem to understand. Seemingly unmotivated by Simpson's questioning, the man still pulled out a giant wad of cash; "the bills were so crisp and new that Simpson wondered if they were counterfeit." The man checked in under the name A. Bell. Befuddled by their appearance and behavior, Simpson questioned them further:

> "Where are you from?"
> The little man's answer was odd. He shot an arm upward, pointing at the sky, and said: "We come from up there. Up there."[83]

The female companion immediately tried to correct the man's answer by saying that they were from Hammond, Indiana. Even after checking in, the odyssey of this strange family did not stop. In a nearby restaurant, "the little man read the menu aloud and kept asking odd questions about where milk, vegetables, and other common food come from." Though past the struggle of ordering, eating seemed an entirely new challenge: "Each picked up a single pea with a knife, brought it to his or her tiny mouth, and inhaled it with a sucking sound." The man could not consume any of the steak he ordered because this method did not allow for such a large chunk of food. Simpson awaited the departure of the family but never saw them leave, "though the front door was the only door they could pass through without setting off a security alarm." All employees interviewed by the *UFO Enigma* staff seemed "sincerely bewildered" by these surreal experiences.

The story is tantalizingly bizarre on its own, but it also can be connected to other maybe-fiction texts. The odd behavior that suggests a fundamental misunderstanding of how humans behave is reminiscent of some Men in Black reports where similar behavior takes place. John Keel wrote of Men in Black sightings in Point Pleasant, West Virginia, where the figures also acted suspiciously "off":

> He was slightly built, about five feet seven inches tall, with black, piercing eyes and unruly black hair, as if he had had a brush cut and it was just growing back in. [...] His hands were especially unusual, [...] with unduly long, tapering fingers. He wore a cheap-looking, ill-fitting suit, slightly out of fashion and his tie was knotted in an odd old-fashioned way. Strangely, he was not wearing an overcoat despite the fierce cold outside.[84]

Keel also notes that the MIB could hardly speak. Instead, he notes a particular encounter where an MIB stammered semi-incoherently while threatening a reporter, advising against her printing UFO stories. When Jerome Clark published the St. Louis motel account in *Extraordinary Encounters*, he related it to a section entitled "Extraterrestrials Among Us" that explore various stories of possible extraterrestrials living amongst humans, often getting some facet of human behavior incorrect.[85] One such story follows a similarly behaving short-statured couple and Bruce Lee, the editor of Whitley Strieber's first foray into his personal experiences, *Communion*. As Lee tells it:

> I noticed a couple come into the store and head directly for *Communion*. [...] You could just see them come in—they didn't know where the book was, you couldn't see it from the street—and they came in and headed right back for where the rack was. [...] They were very short. [...] And they were wrapped up. Long scarves, wool hats that you pull down, and they picked up a copy of the book and they started thumbing through it—the man was doing this. And it was obvious that they were speed-reading, too. And they would say, "Oh, he's got this wrong, he's got that wrong." And they were sort of giggling. [...] So I went over and introduced myself and said I'm from the publisher, and could you tell me what you think is wrong with the book. I think it was the woman that looked up. She was wearing those big sort of sunglasses that girls keep up in their hair. And they really sort of hide the face. But by God behind those dark glasses was a goddamn big pair of eyes. [...] And they were shaped like almonds.[86]

Lee only saw the eyes of the short woman, but the look she gave him filled him with an intense dread, differing from the strange family in the St. Louis hotel. Another strange detail: The pair spoke in normal human voices that "sounded like Upper East Side Jewish" accents, more unsettling than the garbled speech of the hotel encounter as it implies an ability to fit in remarkably well. Yet this brief anecdote has the effect of connecting Whitley Strieber's work to the St. Louis story, extending the web even further.

Beyond this similarity to reports of people behaving strangely, the diminutive figure at the St. Louis hotel gave his name as A. Bell, presumably referring to Art Bell, the host of longtime host of paranormal radio show *Coast to Coast AM*. With this inclusion, the web of intertextuality transcends even the textual medium, possibly relating to any number of Bell's radio shows or even Bell's personal life which "has also been the source of speculation and conspiracy theory."[87] The story can be connected to others based on location and date. Were there other bizarre instances in St. Louis or on May 15, 1970? This is the thrill of reading maybe-fiction. Patterns emerge and plots develop, not unlike fiction unfolding in our world. The conspiracy theorist with the corkboard and connecting strings is not too far off from the activities of maybe-fiction readers, and often conspiracies play into even the most otherworldly stories.

Continuing the thread of Art Bell, maybe-fiction over the airwaves has also led to more intertextual works, connecting the mediums of radio, literature, and art. In various episodes of *Coast to Coast AM* between 1997 and 2002, a caller going by the name Mel Waters spoke to Bell and told him a fantastic story of a seemingly bottomless hole located on his property:

> He said he lowered a weighted fish line down the hole, and he ran out of several reels of heavy line at more than 80,000 feet without it touching bottom. [...] The hole had paranormal properties, despite the fact locals dumped their garbage there for years. He said a rural resident tossed his dead dog into the hole only to see it later alive outdoors with a hunter. The dog wouldn't come to him. [...] Others had seen a black beam coming from the hole and still others claimed portable radios held close the hole's entrance would play programs and music from the past. Metal held close to the hole's 9-foot diameter opening would change into other metals or substances.[88]

A considerable number of Fortean events seemed to be concentrated on this particular spot of Kittitas County, Washington, along with a dash of conspiracy: Waters claimed that federal agents forced him to lease the land to the government, citing a downed aircraft as the reason (though Waters never saw this aircraft), and Waters fled to Australia.[89] This story, while certainly one of the most intriguing to appear on the show, was not out of the ordinary for *Coast to Coast AM*. A wide range of guests with a variety of fantastic stories and claims have appeared on the show, but Mel's Hole inspired some of the most visible intertextuality in maybe-fiction. I say "visible," because while other works are inspired by or in conversation with maybe-fiction texts, those relationships are not necessarily perceptible without research and analysis. A seasoned reader of maybe-fiction may notice immediate similarities or even motifs between stories, but Mel's Hole is interesting in that much creative and critical work has been written in response to it. This is collected in *Aspects of Mel's Hole: Artists Respond to a Paranormal Land Event Occurring in Radiospace*, originally an art installation organized by art critic Doug Harvey at Cal State Fullerton's Grand Central Art Center. Harvey notes in his introduction to this collection that Mel's hole has "engendered" a "vast range of interpretations" which he believes "is well represented by the work" of the various artists and writers who contributed to the exhibition.[90] As Harvey writes:

> Underlying the richly detailed folk yarn is a mythological progression from a predictable hierarchical materialism to anarcho-feminist, humanist-mystic indeterminacy, and this I think, is what excites so many artists about the story of Mel's Hole, regard-

less of their respective individually nuanced interpretations and enthusiasms—the aspects they respond to. The radio broadcast itself conflates a remarkable set of contemporary art theory concerns—the legacy of Land Art, paranormal phenomena, vernacular narrative and more—into an eruption of profound possibilities, and may be the most remarkable single artwork related to this exhibition.[91]

Harvey hints at the creative wellspring that is maybe-fiction. It is a mode which has profound implications on our art and culture through the simultaneous ambiguity of its messages and intimacy between the reader and the text. Put simply, maybe-fictions are left open to interpretation, making them an easy target for creative personalities to either craft art or propose an alternative to the currently accepted standard of reality. It is a medium that seems to tell us as much about ourselves as it tells us about the world we inhabit. It is connected to fiction nearly as often as it is connected to other maybe-fiction texts. For instance, psychoanalyst Judy E. Vida-Spence was immediately reminded of the L. Frank Baum novel, *Tik-Tok of Oz*: "There was an uncanny similarity of Mel's Hole to The Hollow Tube, a passageway from one side of the earth to the other, right through the center, presided over by the terribly just Tititi Hoochoo."[92]

Brian Tucker, a curator of art exhibits dedicated to the work of Richard Shaver (explored thoroughly in Chapter 4), finds obvious connections to the story of Mel's Hole:

> To some extent Shaver's concerns remain alive today. Red Elk, a Native American shaman who claims to have been introduced to Mel's Hole by his father decades ago, offers a theory about the hole that is largely consistent with Shaver's Deros: "There are people down there. Alien people to us that were here even before man. They cannot stand our weather. They can't stand the sunlight, or the cold. The planet they come from is a desert planet, so they live underground. [...] And they want to control us: as slaves, as food, as sex items."[93]

As said before, this collection of works inspired by Mel's Hole is a visible example of intertextuality, but it is also one of the clearest instances of maybe-fiction as creative inspiration—even the subsequent research is a unique creative outlet. The various contributors make their appreciation for Mel's Hole clear in this regard, as said by the editor, Harvey, the hole serves as "an eruption of profound possibilities." The results of this eruption range greatly, from writers seeing relationships between other fiction and other maybe-fiction, to being inspired to create art. Doug Harvey notes that the Center for Land Use Interpretation even went so far as "organizing an investigative excursion to the relevant regions in hopes of documenting tangible evidence of the alleged geological formations."[94] Mel's Hole is unique in regard to the visibility of its intertextuality and creative influence, but it is certainly not the only maybe-fiction story to have these qualities. This intertextuality plays into the texts examined earlier in this exploration, and it will certainly continue to come into play as connections to SF authors are investigated later in the text.

Of course, critics and skeptics are quick to say that coincidences happen—most maybe-fiction has a conventional explanation. But, in the spirit of Fort, a conventional explanation is anathema to a maybe-fiction reader. Why not, instead, embrace the strangeness of our world? Maybe-fiction readers and writers can mold paranormal happenings into SF plots with fantastic and horrifying implications on our world. Even if the connective tissue between maybe-fiction texts are assumptive leaps, they nevertheless remain a valid form of entertainment and community engagement. Such a reliance on intertextuality to research stories in lieu of scientific study seems to inevitably result in a "fandom" of sorts, not unlike SF fandom. While some paranormal researchers and writers would be offended by the title "fan," the gist is largely the same: a group of people with similar interests come together, write and research these topics extensively, and try to come up with some coherent answer. More so than most groups, these maybe-fiction communities have been plagued by fragmentation from the beginning, an inevitability given the number of available hypotheses regarding the various phenomena. Yet, these groups continue to exist on the fringes and persist in trying to piece together a story of our reality that is strange—perhaps stranger than fiction.

Maybe-fiction: A Fortean Affair

Fort previously covered virtually every topic in the realm of maybe-fiction. The strange aerial phenomena reported by Fort became popular maybe-fiction fodder; stories of UFOs and their occupants are perhaps the most numerous of any type of maybe-fiction, now investigated by private individuals and governments alike. Fort's most direct successor was William R. Corliss, who continued to collect anomalies from print sources. Arthur C. Clarke regards Corliss as "much more scientific" due to the fact that "unlike Fort, Corliss selects his material almost exclusively from scientific journals like *Science* and *Nature*, not newspapers."[95] Corliss's Sourcebook series was a logical continuation of Fort's work, focusing only on the verifiable bizarre cases through "a filtering process which [...] remove(d) most hoaxes and reports from obvious cranks" from consideration.[96] But Fort's research was continued by a gaggle of indirect successors, writers of more specific maybe-fictional works. Former police officer David Paulides continued the Fortean research of strange disappearances, authoring a series of books on the topic entitled *Missing 411*. The reports of strange creatures in Fort's work have evolved into the ever-compartmentalized study of cryptozoology, with certain researchers choosing to focus their efforts on their personal favorite cryptids, Bigfoot being the most obvious cryptid craze. Fort's out-of-place artifacts are still seriously considered by numerous proponents of alternative history and ancient aliens. Even the oddities among the oddities found a home in the studies of "high strangeness," with authors like John Keel leading the parade. Books about ghosts and poltergeists are perhaps as abundant as books on UFOs. It cannot be overstated just how influential Fort was in validating the practice of writing about anomalistics. Each writer of strange phenomena is indebted to Fort in numerous ways, whether it is because he made the practice more acceptable or because the writer alludes to his previous research.

Donald Keyhoe's *The Flying Saucers Are Real*, largely considered the first widely read book on the UFO matter, caused quite a stir when it was first published. While the subject of UFOs died down shortly after the 1947 Kenneth Arnold sighting of a flock of crescent-shaped crafts and the subsequent flying saucer craze, Keyhoe revived it. Modern ufologist, Richard Dolan, expressed the importance of Keyhoe's contribution to the burgeoning field of ufology: "Thanks largely to Keyhoe, and despite all efforts by the Air Force and even the White House, UFOs became an important media issue for the first time in three years."[97] Yet, it was Fort who had some influence on Keyhoe's final opinions on the matter. John Keel wrote of Keyhoe's research:

> Major Donald E. Keyhoe digested Fort, talked with witnesses, and produced "Flying Saucers are Real" for *True* magazine. His conclusion was one Fort disagreed with: UFOs were extraterrestrial. H.G. Wells' 1898 novel, *The War of the Worlds*, had suddenly crossed the borderline that separates fiction from reality. To Keyhoe, and thousands of others, flying saucers were very real. Their reported maneuvers seemed to prove their superiority to any known earthly aircraft, therefore they had to come from some other planet.[98]

While their final conclusions differed, Fort's work was valued by Keyhoe. This is likely because Fort's was the only book with comprehensive reports on strange aerial phenomena at the time. Again, Fort proves a valuable resource to further study on anomalies. Even his broader philosophy weaves its way into the thinking of maybe-fiction authors. Keel's theories of a universal connection between unexplained phenomena are markedly like Fort's approach. Praising Fort, Keel writes that he "put bread on the table of generations of science fiction writers when, in his 1931 book *Lo!*, he assembled the many reports of objects and people strangely transposed in time and place."[99] In 1975, Keel wrote his best-selling work, *The Mothman Prophecies*, an exploration into sightings of an apparent hulking, winged creature in Point Pleasant, West Virginia, interspersed with various other paranormal events. He ended the book with the Damon Knight phrase that is often attributed to Fort; Keel credits the latter: "If there is a universal mind, must it be sane?"[100] Whitley Strieber also reflected on Fort's work in his book *The*

Super Natural, coauthored with Kripal, taking a particular interest in Fort's "we are property" line: "We are little, curious animals, as it were, peering through the slats of the fence that surrounds our barnyard, and seeing beyond the edge not another world, but a more real vision of ourselves reflected as noumena and wondering, 'What is *that*?'"[101]

Prominent ufologist Jacques Vallee is yet another author of the unexplained that found Fort's work useful. In *Passport to Magonia*, Vallee lists Fort as one source of information for his collection of "A Century of Landings," quoting directly from the 1941 Holt edition of Fort's collected works to give information on specific sightings.[102] Fort is especially valuable for some of the earliest UFO reports. For instance, Vallee includes incidents from *Lo!*, one of which features as the earliest report in the *Magonia*'s appendix:

> Zoologist, July, 1868—something that was seen in the sky, near Copiapo, Chile—a construction that carried lights, and was propelled by a noisy motor—or "a gigantic bird; eyes wide open and shining like burning coals; covered with immense scales, which clashed together with a metallic sound."[103]

Vallee utilizing this report is a fantastic example of maybe-fiction's interconnectedness—how one maybe-fiction can explain, contradict, or be compared to another. It is also indicative of the importance of Fort's work: His collection of data retains meaning and usefulness long after his death. The Chilean sighting is, after all, one of the strangest and earliest reports of UFO-like activity—nearly a century before Kenneth Arnold's sighting at Mount Rainier. Vallee again pays tribute to Fort in *Messengers of Deception* when he says of Fort's *Book of the Damned*: "Many of the typical tricks of what we now call UFOs have been described in the journals of bygone days, collected by this man...."[104] Vallee shares a similar Fortean disdain for so-called scientific "rationalism" that teeters into scientific dogmatism. Fascinatingly, Vallee feels that this disdain of rationalism is warranted even if the UFO phenomenon is human trickery:

> To prevent such a scientific study from being organized, all that is needed is to maintain a certain threshold of ridicule around the phenomenon. This can be done easily enough by a few influential science writers, under the guise of "humanism" or "rationalism." UFO research would be equated with "false science," thus creating an atmosphere of guilt by association which would be deadly to any independent scientist.[105]

Regardless of whether UFOs are an alien or human creation, to Vallee, such a separation from science would be beneficial for those who use UFOs to manipulate people, as is explored in *Messengers of Deception*. Vallee again broaches the topic of Charles Fort with fellow highly respected ufologist J. Allen Hynek in their 1975 co-authored book, *The Edge of Reality*. In a transcribed discussion between the two authors and psychologist Arthur Hastings, the latter brings up Fort, to which the two ufology icons respond:

HASTINGS: What about Charles Fort? Of course, it's not scientific documentation, so how would you see those books as being interesting?

HYNEK: I wouldn't put them in myself, except for the sake of historical perspective.

HASTINGS: Just for their historical value...?

HYNEK: Well, the point is that Fort has three chips on his shoulder. He was out to absolutely vilify anyone who looked like a scientist. Scientists were stupid, in his view. The man has completely disregarded the stupendous and positive things that scientists have done. Good Lord, look what's been done in astronomy and celestial mechanics and bacteriology! He made a specialty of picking cockeyed things, not particularly documented, completely uncritically, he just wanted to show up these damn fool scientists.

VALLEE: Well, I think scientists need people like that to keep them humble! *The Book of the Damned* is a remarkable document, you know.

HYNEK: He'd have been much more effective if he hadn't been quite so blatant, if he'd been a little more scholarly in his presentation. A guy on a soapbox waving his arms at sixteen rpms doesn't inspire confidence.

HASTINGS: That could be said.

HYNEK: But he's got a valuable collection of things there from the standpoint of popular accounts.

VALLEE: Even from the standpoint of scientific journals. And I like the way he writes.

HYNEK: This recent book on "Strange Phenomena," did you ever get a copy of that? That's another good one...

VALLEE: Yeah, but it doesn't say anything about UFOs.

HYNEK: Neither does Charles Fort, a great deal. All sorts of fishes that fall from the sky. I hope I'm not being unfair and have not overlooked something, but most of the books just get you nauseated....[106]

Between Vallee and Hynek, the former was clearly the bigger fan of Fort, repeating the "remarkableness" of *The Book of the Damned*. Yet, Hynek is not without light praise; despite being "nauseated" to a certain extent, he admits that Fort's work has some historical value, assumedly to the field of ufology.

Even more obscure maybe-fiction texts show an indebtedness to Fort, such as Adi-Kent Thomas Jeffrey's pulpy-covered *Parallel Universe*, released by Warner Books in 1977. The front cover includes the subtitle "UFOs! Mysterious disappearances! Eternal spirits! Are they all evidence of a world of anti-matter—the mirror-image of our own?"[107] Fort retains his title as a sourcebook for later works of both fiction and non-fiction; Jeffrey makes note of Fort's additions to the field of unexplained phenomena. Calling Fort "the master writer and researcher of all things strange and mysterious," Jeffrey goes on to use numerous cases that Fort catalogued, primarily disappearances, to put together her hypothesis of parallel universes infringing on our own. Among these is the case of Issac Martin covered in *Lo!* where the young farmer had disappeared during his field work.[108] Further explored is the disappearance of Judge Joseph Force Crater, which Fort also catalogued amongst a slew of strange happenings in the New York City area in *Wild Talents*.[109] The 1980s book *The Dark Gods* shows Anthony Roberts and Geoff Gilbertson's attempt to expand upon John Keel's work into the realm of the occult; the authors note, rather ominously, that Fort "was yet another breaker of the cosmic code and a valuable addition to the ranks of real human beings."[110] The authors see Keel as an extension of Fort and believe that "Fortean data contain much that is of interest to students of the ultraterrestrial (interdimensional) phenomenon and all manifestations of what is loosely termed 'magic.'"[111]

Beyond these authors referencing Fort as an important researcher or thinker in their fields, all maybe-fiction bears this influence from Fort—even if it is sometimes an unspoken influence. He was, after all, the "Prophet of the Unexplained" and maybe-fiction is a genre of attempting to explain or report on the unexplainable. If Fort prophesized anything, it was the emergence of this broad field of literature that relies on the unexplained as a subject matter. But Fort did more than incite the emergence of this literary medium; he also incited a culture of the unexplained—groups and communities of people who are drawn to anomalies, oddness, and the inherent weirdness of reality.

Hardcore UFOs / Letters to INFO: Scattered Maybe-fiction Communities

When speaking with a former member of the now-defunct International Fortean Organization (INFO) about the group, the member immediately pointed me to Robert Putnam's *Bowling Alone* to grasp INFO's current state. Putnam's 2000 work outlines the decline of participation in groups and "clubs" in American society over the last half-century. Putnam writes:

> For the first two-thirds of the twentieth century a powerful tide bore Americans into ever deeper engagement in the life of their communities, but a few decades ago—silently, without warning—that tide reversed, and we were overtaken by a treacherous rip current. Without at first noticing, we have been pulled apart from one another and from our communities over the last third of the century.[112]

Fortean communities were victim to this community death in a manner more pronounced than the neighboring SF fandom. Paranormal researcher George P. Hansen notes that "Fortean 'organizations' are some of the most anti-structural of any in the paranormal subculture."[113] This lack of structure is in no way unexpected, given the fact that Fort himself was non-committal to any of his hypotheses—any individual hypothesis regarding Fortean phenomenon would inevitably collide with another. Forteana is perhaps too broad and requires an agnosticism too staunch for a cohesive group to form. Yet, Fortean groups still exist, much more quietly than they

2. Defining Maybe-fiction

did in the past, residing deeper in the fringes of culture. They are often met with scorn or are not studied efficiently. As Rafael Antunes Almeida notes:

> The social sciences have been resistant to study the collectives formed through the relation with [...] UFOs and [...] ETs because, as Pierre Lagrange argues, the claims of these groups have been frequently reduced to a "psychological phenomena ignored by reason," and this justified the refusal to treat them as more than a community of believers.[114]

Again, while ufological groups are the example used, the same point could be made of Fortean groups in general: they are not taken seriously by most scientists, researchers, and laymen.

Though much less fractured and compartmentalized than groups of maybe-fiction fans, SF fandom resembles and overlaps with much of the maybe-fiction community. Darko Suvin wrote of SF as "exiled since the beginning of the 20th century into a reservation or ghetto which was protective and is now constrictive, cutting off new developments from healthy competition and the highest critical standards."[115] Maybe-fiction never had the protective exile that benefited SF, rather being isolated to the fringes of literature where texts were unchallenged by competition and critical standards. Virtually any fantastic tale or hypothesis is fair game in this niche, leading to a community made up of eccentrics, brilliant minds, crackpots, and storytellers. The group functions as a sort of dysfunctional family where the dinner table talks are about UFOs, conspiracy theories, ghosts, and cryptids. It is a raucous existence. The maybe-fiction community consists of wildly different people who approach the phenomena at a variety of different angles: To some, it's a spiritual matter, to others it's one of science. To others still, maybe-fiction is entirely a mode of entertainment. While this exploration is focused on the latter, to say that maybe-fiction is *purely* entertainment would be selling it short. Examining it as a literary medium requires the entertainment aspects of maybe-fiction to come to the forefront. However, in examining the communities behind maybe-fiction, it is clear that while maybe-fiction is an exercise in creativity and entertainment for some, it is a matter that deserves serious study to others. These two camps have been warring factions since the beginning of Fortean communities—as if the skeptics did not give them enough grief.

Precise histories of these groups are hard to come by because there are so many specialized varieties. UFO buffs hang around ufology circles, cryptid enthusiasts are part of cryptozoology groups, ghost hunters socialize with other ghost hunters, etc. The groups that most resemble a broad maybe-fiction community are the various Fortean groups. Even within Fortean groups, however, members specialize in their own subset of Forteana, such as those explored throughout this chapter. Cohesion has never been Forteans' strongest suit. Even the original Fortean Society devolved into dysfunction shortly after Fort's death. While an ethnography in the vein of Janice Radway's *Reading the Romance* would prove helpful to the study of maybe-fiction groups and cultures, some extant work on specialized groups can give us an idea of how maybe-fiction culture functions in general. The various groups dedicated to the work of Fort himself are particularly helpful. These include the Fortean Society, the Fortean Research Center, the International Fortean Organization, and, most recently, the Charles Fort Institute. One of the most important Fortean groups to form after the initial Fortean Society was INFO, a group that sprung up out of the ashes of the dying Society. Talking with former INFO members provided valuable insight into the overlap between SF fandom and Fortean communities.

While the authors examined in this book, both briefly and at length, can be denoted as Fortean on the merit of their fiction alone, some of them are rumored to have engaged with Forteans more personally. According to the Wikipedia entry on INFO, the authors Philip K. Dick, Fritz Leiber, and Robert Anton Wilson all corresponded with the group and its editors. This entry is intriguing because it is one of the only places such correspondences are mentioned. The entry also mentions rather impressive anecdotes about Heinlein's involvement with the organization. The limits of this engagement are hard to pin down because of INFO being, at present, largely inactive. However, upon talking to numerous former members and looking at INFO's history, I believe there is a possible precedence to believe the Fortean connection beyond an uncited Wikipedia entry. In my own search for these letters, I wound up emailing a former member of INFO who goes by Mr. X. Of course, I thought immediately of Fox Mulder's own informant in *The X-Files* of the same name, giving my search a hint of intrigue. Whether these letters still exist somewhere is perhaps questionable, but there is reason to believe they once existed. Mr. X provided numerous leads, several of which this work has greatly benefited from. I was put in contact with several former members of INFO in my search for these letters, each one adding some insight into how they could have been lost. The connection between SF and Forteana became further solidified through the information given to me by these former members. SF author and prominent INFO member during its heyday, David Drake gave the following insight into the magazine and the possibility of finding the correspondences:

> INFO was a follow-on to the fanzine *Anubis* which brought out four issues in the '60s. Paul (Willis) was the enthusiast behind both magazines; he was also a drunk. Ron (Willis) was a solid citizen, with a wife, child, and home in Arlington. (I think he was an EPA statistician.) He funded things. Both were very smart. The *INFO Journal* was run off on an offset press in Ron's garage. Paul visited the PO Box occasionally and carried the mail to his apartment in Alexandria. There was a huge stack of *Anubis* contributions in his hallway when I visited, still in their envelopes.

Ron died of a brain tumor in 1975. Paul kept INFO going and expanded the Fortfests from cookouts in Ron's back yard into fairly major events. Booze kept wearing him away.

I have no idea of what could have happened to INFO correspondence; I was never involved in that end. I suspect it went into a dumpster when the Alexandria apartment was emptied.[116]

It is worth noting that *Anubis* was an SF fanzine, which would explain why the Willis brothers would have had SF correspondences. The organization struggled even in its brightest days, resulting in files being consistently mismanaged or lost through flooded basements and unexpected moves of the offices. I found, and former member Richard Leshuk concurs, that whoever wrote the Wikipedia entry for INFO seems to have held great knowledge of the organization and was likely a member. Even through countless emails to former members, however, this mystery author remains unidentified. The source of this information is presumably the "Notes and Letters from Robert Heinlein from the Collection of the International Fortean Organization," listed in the sources at the bottom of the page. However, I am told that the collection of INFO documents is in storage, unsorted, inaccessible, and likely incomplete. Another dead end. By gauging each of these authors' knowledge and interest of Fort via other channels, the likelihood of letters like these being written is within the realm of possibility. Nevertheless, if evidence of these correspondences could be found, it would prove excellent documentation of the engagement between the fields of SF and Forteana.

The Wikipedia entry also notes that Heinlein subscribed to *The INFO Journal* and became upset to learn that his checks were never cashed because they were hung up on the office walls.[117] Stephen Webb says that Heinlein was a member, but this anecdote is not documented elsewhere.[118] The last editor of *The INFO Journal* and avid SF fan, Michael Shoemaker, says he thinks "it unlikely that Heinlein was an INFO member, because he was a no-nonsense engineer and liked order and authority, generally not a trait of the Fortean community."[119] Shoemaker says that he heard the Heinlein story from a former INFO member "who was not above drawing the long bow" and that the author was on INFO's mailing list, but never saw any evidence of the story.[120] Perhaps these correspondences between the Willis brothers and SF greats was in no way connected to INFO, instead being related to the brothers' other venture, the SF fanzine *Anubis*. This would make more sense while still being simple to misconstrue as the authors having Fortean correspondences with the major journal in the field. *Fortean Times* founder Bob Rickard stated regarding the check: "I have no recollection of seeing such a thing on the walls of his old flat. That is not to say it wasn't there. But it wouldn't surprise me. The Willises were SF fans of the old school and knew Heinlein, James Blish and a galaxy of other stars."[121] Again, while not being an answer to the existence or nonexistence of the correspondences, it is clear that this Fortean group was enmeshed with SF authors and fans.

Though concrete proof of these letters remains to be found, I believe that the following examination of the authors involved gives credence to the idea that the correspondences *might* have occurred, given their Fortean tendencies. Their connections to Fort can be found through other means, yet these letters, if they do indeed exist, would provide important documentation of both SF and Forteana. Yet this search led to my contact with various members of INFO during its heyday which, in turn, led me to see clearly how intertwined SF and Forteana are. Many past members were active in both fields, two of whom were some of the most prominent SF historians. Other members were SF writers and hardcore SF fans. On writing the first comprehensive biography of Fort, Knight commented: "No one who has tried to write a biography of a man thirty years dead can realize how impossible it is to find out the whole truth. The past is a black hole. Records have vanished, correspondence and photographs have been destroyed, friends and relatives are long dead. The miracle is that it is possible to write of such lives at all."[122] The same could be said of succeeding organizations of Fort's followers. Like the Fortean Society and Fort himself before it, INFO only exists through a few remaining members and documents in non-accessible storage. Though I feel confident that I have found alternative ways to highlight these authors' Fortean inclinations, I cannot help but feel as though a vital part of SF history may be lost, known only by a nameless Wikipedia editor who is no longer active.

The Overlap: Maybe-fiction Authors and SF

Despite some opposition between them, maybe-fiction authors and Fortean communities tend to overlap with SF and its fandom. This overlap will be explored further in succeeding chapters, but this section will present a brief survey of maybe-fiction authors who display an interest in SF. The overlap can be seen not only in the SF authors examined in the following chapters having Fortean interests, but conversely, in maybe-fiction authors having an interest in SF. Even the first stirrings of maybe-fiction publications seemed to directly follow SF publications. Raymond Palmer, who will be explored in Chapter 4, eventually felt constricted by the push for a more scientific *Amazing Stories* towards the end of the Shaver debacle and shifted his priorities to publishing magazines dedicated to fringe topics like *FATE*, *Mystic*, and *Search*. But the SF texts do not always precede the maybe-fiction texts, or vice versa; rather, there is a constant dialectical relationship between the two. As Kripal has stated, "It's the paranormal that produces the science fiction and then the science fiction loops

2. Defining Maybe-fiction 55

back and influences the paranormal."[123] This section is a brief journey into this phenomenon, to reiterate just how intertwined these two literary cultures are before delving into SF explicitly. It examines three representatives from three different types of maybe-fiction (Fortean journalism, forbidden science, and anomalous experience narrative, respectively) and tracks their interest in SF and how it relates to their maybe-fiction writing. The maybe-fiction/SF overlap is certainly not limited to these authors, but these three prominent personalities in contemporary Forteana illustrate well how maybe-fiction and SF intersect, even for authors whose interest in SF seems secondary to their Fortean interests.

The most prominent figure who continued the Fortean cause is John A. Keel, whose investigations into the unexplained throughout the sixties and seventies remain popular amongst fans of paranormal non-fiction. Kripal calls Keel "a kind of *X-Files* Agent Mulder of the real world,"[124] which is not an exaggeration. Trekking the globe looking for Fortean phenomena, and sometimes the phenomena finding him, Keel became perhaps the most noted paranormal journalist. As with most, if not all maybe-fiction, Keel's work "reads like the sci-fi, monster, and horror tales that Stan Lee was telling the 1950s and early '60s," writes Kripal. While speaking of his third book, *Strange Creatures of Time and Space*, this can be applied to most of Keel's work. Kripal notes: "Keel was suggesting that such monsters had a kind of intermediate or subtle reality of their own. This was not quite hard fact. But it was certainly not fiction either. We are back, once again, to Fort's truth-fiction."[125]

Somewhat unsurprisingly, given the trends explored in this book, Keel is yet another writer whose interest in Forteana was spawned by reading pulp SF magazines. Keel immediately connects his initial interest in Forteana to Fort himself and SF publications:

> I read Charles Fort when I was very young, when I was about 14 or 15 years old. I was reading *Amazing Stories* in those days too, and they were getting letters to *Amazing Stories* about things people had seen in the sky—this is before 1947—and I was writing a newspaper column at that time for my home town newspaper and I did a couple of columns on that kind of thing, lights in the sky and people who saw contrails high overhead and thought that that was some kind of spaceship or something.[126]

He published an SF fanzine called *The Lunarite* in the 1940s, copies printed on postcards with very limited circulation (the second issue says at the top: "CIRCULATION THIS ISSUE. 200 COPIES"). Keel was still a teenager when publishing this fanzine. Interestingly, in the first issue of *The Lunarite*, Keel is quite critical of the Shaver Mysteries in *Amazing Stories*, saying that Shaver "ought to give up writing. He's lousy." He even sends a jab at the publication itself saying that "*Amazing Stories* is still trying to convince everyone that the BEMs (Bug Eyed Monsters) in the caves run the world. And I was blaming it on the democrats."[127] Keel's early interest in Forteana yet disapproval of the Shaver stories indicates a seriousness in his research early on, not accepting every anomalous story that claims to be true. As his career went on, this must have grown quite difficult. Later, like many intrigued by the paranormal, Keel became an investigator like Fort himself, gathering reports from around the world of anomalous phenomena and attempting to make sense of it all. *The Lunarite* was not his only foray into SF criticism. In 1987, a piece by Keel about Philip K. Dick's experience and fiction appeared in the Philip K. Dick Society newsletter. Entitled "Was PKD a Flake?," the piece examines PKD's paranormal experiences through the lens of Keel's own experiences and research. He concludes that "like all writers, PKD was a neurotic. Like all those who allow their minds to probe into the misty corners of man's spiritual existence, he suffered." Keel connects Dick's experiences to the UFO phenomena, occult phenomena, and psychic phenomena. "We were all being manipulated," Keel writes. "Many of us were on a great voyage of self-discovery. PKD was learning of powers he had never been fully aware of."[128] Given PKD's possible involvement with INFO and his conversation with Brad Steiger (outlined in Chapter 6), it seems as if Keel considered Dick a Fortean brother-in-arms. The cover of *The Mothman Prophecies* (as well as another non-fiction book with an SF title, *Strange Creatures from Time and Space*) was done by famed pulp artist Frank Frazetta. The cover is highly sensational, featuring a large red-eyed Mothman with colorful wings gesturing towards a scantily clad woman and, less prominently, a terrified man. Two classic flying saucers with portholes hover behind Mothman. As astounding as the artwork is, Mothman was described as not looking so much like a moth, but the depiction fits the SF aesthetic. Keel was not perturbed by the sensationalism and even "attributed the success of that book to the cover."[129]

The more scientifically inclined Fortean author Jacques Vallee has also delved into the world of SF, writing several SF novels throughout his career as a ufologist. Kripal writes:

> Vallee rejects such speculations as scientifically groundless, but one suspects—I do anyway—that he is more drawn to this kind of impossible science-fiction thinking than he will allow himself to admit in print here. Vallee, after all, had already won the prestigious Jules Verne Prize in 1961, at the age of twenty-one, no less, for his first science-fiction novel, *Sub-Space*, and he would go on to publish four more science-fiction novels, the last in English, *Fastwalker*. The Jules Verne medal is now proudly displayed among his books, significantly in the section on parapsychology and paranormal studies.[130]

Despite his scientific background, Vallee's attitude to SF is perhaps more reflective of his belief in the power of human consciousness, SF being a vessel through which this power can be shown fully. As Vallee says in the conclusion to his 1975 work, *The Invisible College*: "The solution lies where it has always been: *within us*. We can reach it any time we want."[131] But Vallee's non-fiction work is not averse to connecting Forteana and UFOs to SF stories. In *Messengers of Deception*, he compares one hypothesis on the UFO phenomenon, the idea that human governments are behind the matter, to two SF novels. Yet again, we see our reality needing to be equated to SF to make sense of it. The books Vallee uses as examples are Bernard Newman's novel *The Flying Saucer* (1950) and Leonard Lewin's *Report from Iron Mountain* (1967), the latter of which is a spoof of a government document still considered a truthful account by conspiracy theorists to this day. Both works feature the concept of governments utilizing a faked imminent invasion by extraterrestrials to achieve world peace.[132]

In terms of anomalous experience literature, Strieber poses an interesting case in this brief chapter. While he began as a fiction writer, he soon became embroiled in a non-fiction saga of contact with the Visitors, then he went back to writing fiction that was clearly inspired by his seemingly reluctant foray into the strange. As the events of *Communion* unfold, Strieber is quick to say that his mind was not preoccupied with any fiction that would resemble his experience: "At this time in my life, I wasn't even working on horror stories, and at no time had I ever been in danger of being deluded by them."[133] He describes a short story he wrote in the immediate aftermath of the encounter, entitled "Pain":

> It is about a man who encounters an enigmatic woman named Janet, who proves to be some sort of superhuman being, perhaps an angel or a demon. She draws this man into a strange experience of capture and incarceration in a tiny, magical cabinet. From the agony that ensues, he gains immense insight and new spiritual strength.[134]

He finds that these themes have appeared in his past horror novels:

> The visitors could be seen as the Wolfen, as Miriam Blaylock in *The Hunger*, and as the fairy queen Leannan and her soldiers in *Catmagic*. The theme is always the same: Mankind must face a harsh but enigmatically beautiful force that, as Miriam Blaylock describes herself, is "part of the justice of the world." This force is always hidden between the folds of experience.[135]

As stated, Strieber presents an interesting case where critics are quick to use this thematic consistency as proof that *Communion* is also fiction. Strieber notes how the themes present in our fiction—particularly our SF and horror novels—are also present in both our experiences with and writings about the unexplained. Nevertheless, Strieber is illustrative of the consistent overlap between SF and maybe-fiction. Perhaps his occupation as a fiction writer rendered him predisposed to experiences that resemble such fiction, or maybe some anomalous experience trapped deep within his subconscious predisposed him to write fiction that resembled his experience. Which came first is undoubtedly a chicken-or-egg scenario, and some of the SF writers examined, Dick especially, will acknowledge such a relationship. However, in the case of SF, many of these ideas were drawn directly from Fort and, later, by works related to Fort. This continuation of Fortean themes is explored in the chapters that follow, but maybe-fiction will always lurk in the bigger picture.

3

Lo! Forteana!
Early Fortean SF Authors

> Unquestionably, Fort's collected facts are important. Only—no one has been able to find out just how or why, or what they mean. They are, in other words, a perfectly magnificent source-book and challenge to writers and readers of science-fiction. [...] It probably averages one science-fiction or fantasy plot idea to the page. And—if only we could find the pattern hidden there among the vast jumble of facts—it probably contains the root truths of about four new sciences. It's not all light reading, but it's a vast mine of fascinating material for either science-fiction or fantasy.
> —John W. Campbell[1]

Prelude

Fortean SF falls into two categories, with texts sometimes falling into both simultaneously. The first category is SF which is inspired by Fortean philosophy or experience. This means that the SF could be said to thematically follow from Fort's writings or an unexplainable experience. The second category is SF that could be said to explain Fortean phenomena. This is to say that the SF seems to answer the question of what's behind the phenomena, sometimes including examples that would not be out of place in Fort's books. Some Fortean SF does both, such as Eric Frank Russell's *Sinister Barrier*, which both utilizes Fortean phenomena as a plot element and attempts to explain it via its narrative. Other works do not directly acknowledge Fort or Fortean thought but contain plots that explain Fortean phenomena. This book attempts to collate a variety of this Fortean SF into an original analysis of various SF texts that have some connection to Charles Fort. Some authors will be undoubtedly omitted—it is oft repeated by editors, biographers, and writers that creating a complete database of Fort's SF influence is a herculean task. However, collected here are some of the most key examples of such a phenomenon, hopefully forming a coherent picture of continual influence through subsequent eras and movements of SF.

Lovecraft's Fortean Writings and Experiences

One of the most famous pulp SF writers to exhibit Fortean influence is H.P. Lovecraft, an author whose stories often dealt with an unseen world filled with freaky phenomena. Apart from similar thematic areas, Lovecraft apparently read at least some Fort, mentioning him by name in a story fragment titled "The Descendant": "Books like Ignatius Donnelly's chimerical account of Atlantis he absorbed with zest, and a dozen obscure precursors of Charles Fort enthralled him with their vagaries."[2] Here he acknowledges Fort's importance to research of the unexplained and it comes as no surprise that Lovecraft was aware of Fort. Lovecraft's philosophy of cosmicism bears similarities to Fort's own; both emphasize that humanity is largely insignificant in a cosmic sense, but not in the same way that T.H. Huxley might believe. Lovecraft's views on this subject were nightmarish, not merely pessimistic. He also seemed to believe, like Fort, that there are other entities which are superior and vastly more intelligent than humans. Lovecraft's philosophy is marked with occult influences, further alienating him from writers like Wells. It is with Lovecraft that Fort's work and similar philosophies appeal to a cosmic dread, as opposed to Huxley's cosmic pessimism. Not only are we insignificant in the grand scheme of the universe, but the universe is out to get us. We should be afraid. Like the work of Eric Frank Russell (explored in the following section), Lovecraft also wrote stories regarding "secret knowledge" and how the discovery of this knowledge would be lethal to humans. The trend is common in Lovecraft's works. For example, the titular character of Lovecraft's "Herbert West—Reanimator" (written 1921–1922) discovers the secret knowledge of reanimating life and pays dearly for it. This tale contains hidden knowledge reminiscent of that within *Frankenstein*, but in this case the reanimated corpses are much more monstrous and with an animalistic drive not inherent in Frankenstein's monster. In Lovecraft's "From Beyond" (written in 1920) characters discover a parallel reality (reminiscent of some of Fort's theories) coexisting and overlapping with our own while unseen. This is where the terror becomes cosmic in nature. Once these boundaries are crossed—once the hidden knowledge is discovered and utilized—literal hell breaks loose. Alien creatures from the other dimension attack and kill the scientists' servants. Lovecraft scholar George T. Wetzel also notes Fort's probable influence on Lovecraft: "The influence of Fort is obvious in HPL's story 'Call of Cthulhu' (1926) in which Fort is named. The plot of the story (just as in Fort's

3. Lo! Forteana! 61

controversial collations) depends on dissimilar but simultaneous phenomena being explained as the results of a common cause."[3] Wetzel also notes how Lovecraft's "Whisperer in the Dark" contains "an idea right out of Fort's *Book of the Damned*, chapter 10, that extraterrestrial creatures have walked this earth disguised in human masks."[4] Yet, Lovecraft rarely seems to blame scientific dogmatism like Fort. Despite the deterministic nature of most of his plots, he rather focuses on human curiosity and the destructive consequences of secret knowledge. He manifests a tendency towards interest in hidden knowledge and cosmic dread as opposed to Wellsian SF and Huxley's cosmic pessimism. This cosmic dread wound up infecting the pulps that exhibited Fortean influence. As Steinmeyer writes, "it wasn't the myriad of Fort's phenomena that stunned readers, but one underlying suggestion that human beings have always found to be hair-raising: The world is actually irrational."[5] SF writers seemed to find the provocative entertainment value in this suggestion.

Beyond simply a direct influence from Fort, Lovecraft was influenced by Fortean phenomena in general. In his book *Gef! The Strange Tale of an Extra-Special Talking Mongoose*, Christopher Josiffe notes the parallels between Lovecraft's work "The Dreams in the Witch-House" and the supposedly true tale of Gef. The Gef debacle involved the appearance of a strange rodent-type creature on an isolated farmhouse in the Isle of Man which could speak and manifest poltergeist-like activity. The activity went on for several years as the homeowners, the Irvings, dealt with its constant talking, rapping, and even pranking. Josiffe notes that like Gef, the witch's familiar in the Lovecraft story is "rat-like in size, sharp teeth, human hands, and a high-pitched voice with which it can speak other languages."[6] Josiffe admits that there is no direct confirmation that Lovecraft was influenced by the talking mongoose tales in the worldwide press, but "the time of writing is most suggestive." This purported connection has intriguing implications—Lovecraft was not only influenced by the darker side of anomalous phenomena that instills the omnipresent cosmic dread in his stories, he was also influenced by more obscure reports of Fortean events. Putting aside the possible hoax at play, the Gef saga is at times frightening. The little creature proclaimed that he was the devil and tried to intimidate the Irving family early on in his stay at their farmhouse. There were hints of a dark omnipotence in Gef's appearance, supposedly reading thoughts and knowing details about locations outside the cottage. This elevates the otherwise hokey encounter to a more Fortean dread of an intelligent paranormal force, perfect fodder for a writer like Lovecraft.

Lovecraft was not only possibly influenced by outside paranormal stories, but his writings stemmed from his own encounters. Paranormal researcher Nick Redfern explores fictional creatures that have seemingly maneuvered their way into our reality in his book *The Slenderman Mysteries*.

Redfern notes how Lovecraft is an early example of this phenomenon.[7] Using the work of Lovecraft scholar Donald Tyson, Redfern writes of startling events in Lovecraft's life. Shortly after coming across an engraving in a deluxe edition of Milton's *Paradise Lost*, Lovecraft found himself haunted by night-gaunts, figures that would eventually make their way into his fiction. The experience, however, was very real: "Lovecraft described these night-gaunts as lean, black, and rubbery to the touch, with barbed tails, horns, and bat-like wings. Their most horrifying feature was their complete lack of faces. In effect, they were living shadows."[8] While these figures appeared in Lovecraft's nightmares, the causality of encountering them after seeing "a bat-winged Lucifer" in the engraving makes the experience seem more paranormal in nature. A common theme of Lovecraft's work is the cosmic horror that develops from archeology and research. James Holloway in the *Fortean Times* notes: "In story after story, Lovecraft posits that archeological, historical or scientific investigation could well destroy mankind."[9] The fact that Lovecraft experienced a personal microcosm of this phenomenon implies that he may very well be an early instance of a pulp SF author placing true paranormal experiences in his fiction. Regardless, the very theme of history and archeology holding some horrible secret that can instill cosmic dread is a somewhat Fortean notion. Fort himself considered his research to be unearthing a hidden truth that humanity had been denied, with perhaps less horrific consequences than Lovecraft's writings. It should be noted that other readers have proposed that this theme may have arisen from Lovecraft's racist world view being revealed as an illusion; his personal reality was shattered and the universe seemed out to get him.[10] Regardless, Lovecraft proves a fascinating figure in Fortean SF, sometimes predating it. He was at once influenced by personal paranormal experience, Fort himself, and a worldview that at times seems a dark reflection of Fort's. There is no positivity to unearthing hidden knowledge; it can only lead humanity to its ruin.

Lovecraft stated in a letter to SF writer Fritz Leiber that he was wary of believing in anything supernatural:

> I have told my critics that in all probability, the reason I *want* to write about circumventions of time, space, and natural law is that I *don't* believe in such! If I believed in the supernatural, I would not need to create the aesthetic illusion of belief. Indeed, the supernatural would not seem strange and fascinating to me. I am preoccupied with the invention of a desired thing which I can get *only* through invention.[11]

In another letter to Leiber, he furthers this explanation:

> My own temperament, I should say, is one of *scientific indifferentism* (the solar system is a meaningless drop in an unknown and purposeless cosmos, but what the hell of it?) rather than melancholy—though I suppose my constant interest in fantasy expresses a subconscious dissatisfaction with objective reality which is not far from certain phases of the genuine article.[12]

Here, Lovecraft illustrates an important facet of Fortean SF as this exploration continues. An author need not believe in Fortean philosophy for it to permeate their fiction. Lovecraft states that his fiction is written as a sort of dissatisfaction with reality as it exists, but the cosmic pessimism he expresses still creates Fortean overtones in his stories. Lovecraft's work was also seemingly influenced by what some consider paranormal forces, others consider nightmares. Lovecraft himself clearly did not find the sources supernatural, unless he was for some unknown reason hiding this from Leiber. Regardless, he sees the value in Fortean philosophy for fiction, whether it be SF or the weird gothic tales. SF author and paranormal researcher, Colin Wilson, wrote: "What is so interesting about Lovecraft is the extraordinary consistency of his attempt to undermine materialism. His aim was 'to make the flesh creep': more than that, to implant doubts and horrors in the minds of readers."[13] Whether or not he believed in the supernatural or Forteana, Lovecraft's chief interest was in how these subjects can truly unnerve and terrify us. Later writers, however, would wholeheartedly claim and utilize a chiefly Fortean philosophy in their stories, perhaps for similar reasons. This type of philosophy just happens to create more intriguing stories.

The Premier Fortean SF Writer: Eric Frank Russell

Though he later became the foremost proponent of Fort in the SF community, when Russell first read *Lo!* in its *Astounding Stories* serialization, "it had made no impression on him." After finding a secondhand copy of the British edition, however, the author "went quietly mad, [...] his lifelong ambition became the resolve to obtain the three other books."[14] Mad he went, going on to write perhaps the most overtly Fortean novel in the pulps. Russell dedicates his 1939 book *Sinister Barrier* to Fort in the foreword and when published in an issue of *Unknown*, the work included this note amongst the introductory text: "I wrote the story—but, it isn't mine. It is a posthumous collaboration. [...] To Charles Fort, who was a sort of Peter Pan of science and went about picking up whimsies of fact, mostly from the rubbish heaps of astronomy."[15] Russell was a card-carrying member of the Fortean Society and not shy about it:

> But perhaps my greatest debt is to two friends, one of whom asked me, "Since everybody wants peace, why don't we get it?" while the other posed me this one, "If there are extra-terrestrial races further advanced than ourselves, why haven't they visited us already?" Charles Fort gave me what may well be the answer. He said, "I think we're property." And that is the plot of *Sinister Barrier*.[16]

It is astounding how often that one assertion of Fort's makes its reappearance in SF throughout the decades. *I think we're property.* Russell's work indeed treads this Fortean territory: After scientists discover a previously unseen force that feeds on humans called Vitons, chaos ensues in the Vitons' hostile reaction to being discovered. Not only does the novel address the concept of humankind as being a property of some unseen higher force, but the Vitons kill Fort-like scientists who search for evidence of their existence. "Quick death awaits the first cow that leads a revolt against milking," writes Russell.[17] The novel is full of Fortean research by these scientists, oftentimes using the same formatting that Fort used in his works. The scientist Beach is a prominent example. From the Paperback Library edition of the book:

> We've carried the devil on our backs perhaps a million years and only now are aware that he's there. [...] Only this morning I was studying a case to which no solution had been found in ten years. The details are given in the London *Evening Standard* of May, 16, 1938 and the British Daily Telegraph of several dates thereafter. The 5,456-ton vessel *Anglo-Australian* vanished at short notice, without a trace. She was a modern, seaworthy boat plowing through smooth, tranquil waters when she and her crew of thirty-eight abruptly became as if they had never been.[18]

This case occurred after Fort's death so did not appear in his works, but the case of the *Anglo-Australian* was indeed a real ship that disappeared—some suggest that the ship was a victim of the Bermuda Triangle. Clearly Russell must have been doing his own Fortean research, finding incidents that Fort might find interest in. There are further examples of Fortean events in the novel. The scientist Graham even keeps Fortean newspaper clippings on hand:

> *World-Telegram*, April 17: case of a fireball that bounced through an open window into a house, scorched a rug where it burst. Same day, another hopped erratically two hundred yards down a street and popped into nothingness with a blast of heat. *Chicago Daily News*, April 22: case of a fireball that floated slowly across a meadow, entered a house, tried to rise up a chimney, then exploded, wrecking the chimney.[19]

It is uncertain if these two cases came from actual reports, but again they do not appear in Fort's works. Russell's intro to the novel, when published in *Unknown*, indicates that all the "clippings" that appear in the story are real accounts that he collected. The characters of the novel hypothesize that the fireballs collected in the works of Fort could be dying Vitons. Graham reveals more connection between Beach and Fort:

> He has a huge collection of clippings dating back one hundred fifty years. Nearly two thousand of them deal with fireballs and similar phenomena. When you look through them, knowing what at long last is known, they look different. They're no longer a mere collection of off-trail data. They're a singular collection of cogent, highly significant facts which makes you wonder why we've never suspected what has now been discovered.[20]

Again, the parallels between Fort are practically plainly stated. One cannot help but read into Russell's novel that this was how he saw Fort's work, "cogent, highly significant facts" that piece together a puzzle of reality. Continuing to go quietly mad, perhaps, Russell formulated an SF story out of anomalous data, some of which are actual reported anomalies. This is not too different from some of Fort's hypotheses, though he did not take the full foray into fiction with his anomalous data research.

Russell is but another example of pulp SF exhibiting a Fortean sense of cosmic dread while also displaying an interest in the power and danger in hidden knowledge. He coined the phrase "sinister barrier" which has since reappeared as a title of an issue of the comic book character, *The Spectre*, with a cover that highly resembles the cover of *Unknown* that Russell's story appears in. In both, a demonic figure cradles the Earth in its arms, displaying ownership.[21] Russell completed other Fortean novels including 1948's *Dreadful Sanctuary* which was serialized in *Astounding*. Like *Sinister Barrier*, Earth was being utilized by an outer force, this time not as a cattle farm but as an insane asylum. As seems to be common in the pulps, it is primarily Russell's early work that bears the most Fortean markings. In addition to his Fortean SF, Russell released his own Fortean non-fiction, oftentimes treading the same ground as Fort and other anomaly researchers. The year 1957's *Great World Mysteries* covered several different instances of unexplained phenomena, including "The Creeping Coffins of Barbados" which had previously been explored by Rupert T. Gould in 1928's *Oddities*. Russell was familiar with Gould, being a British SF writer and Gould being Fort's British equivalent. He thanks Gould in the introduction to *Sinister Barrier*, crediting Gould as writing works that inspired the novel.[22] Like Fort before him, Russell's "Creeping Coffins" was also published in the pulps, appearing in *Fantastic* a year after *Great World Mysteries'* publication.[23]

Furthermore, Russell was the president of the British chapter of the Fortean Society, his name listed as the main contact for readers of *Doubt* in England.[24] Russell remained in the Fortean Society despite Tiffany Thayer's reign as leader, which many described as an egotistical venture. Russell insisted even after Thayer's death that the Fortean Society "never dissolved and thus still exists." His claim that the group was *un*organized, not *dis*organized seems to ring true to the present as illustrated by the previous section regarding INFO.[25] In an essay about Russell's Fortean leanings, Dave Langford notes that many SF authors had what he calls "Fortean Awareness."[26] Russell was at the forefront of this trend, becoming the first SF writer well known as a Fortean. But Langford's term, "Fortean Awareness," will come into play later in this exploration. While few authors were as blatantly and proudly Fortean as Russell, many SF authors hold this awareness of Fort's work regardless of whether it appeared in their fiction.

The True Beginning: Edmond Hamilton

Usage of Fortean themes and references was not a trend that Lovecraft or Russell initiated. Rather, as SF historian Sam Moskowitz notes, "Eric Frank Russell was to popularize the bizarrely logical intimations of Charles Fort in *Sinister Barrier*."[27] However, Russell never had direct contact with Charles Fort, discovering *Lo!* after its posthumous serialization in *Astounding Stories*. One SF writer penned stories with Fortean themes in Fort's lifetime *and* communicated directly with Fort:

> It was Edmond Hamilton who had actually introduced Fortean themes to the science-fiction field [...]. After reading *The Book of the Damned* (1919) and *New Lands* (1923), he had sent a batch of newspaper clippings about strange phenomena to the Bronx belittler of science, Charles Fort, and they struck up a correspondence. In one letter he asked Fort what he would do if the Fortean system were taught in schools as right and proper. Fort wrote back, "Why, in that case I would propound the damnably heterodox theory that the world is round!"[28]

Such a correspondence is remarkable as most of Fort's followers up to this point were highly regarded writers such as Theodore Dreiser, Booth Tarkington, and members of the Algonquin Round Table like Dorothy Parker and Alexander Woollcott. Pulp SF at this point had a minuscule audience, but as usual, Fort's work seemed to draw together a rather varied crowd. Hamilton "remained the high spot" of Eric Frank Russell's visit to America. The two bonded over a shared SF occupation and Fortean Society membership and "Hamilton gave (Russell) his own copy of *New Lands*, completing Russell's Fort collection, as well as a letter from and a photo of Charles Fort."[29]

One of the instances of anomalous phenomena that Hamilton sent Fort was "a newspaper account of a Princeton geology professor who had inexplicably found small living frogs in a puddle of water in the hot Arizona desert." Hamilton wrote to this professor putting forth his own Fortean hypothesis that the frogs fell from the sky but received a staunchly negative response. Fort himself found the professor's response nothing out of the ordinary: "Like you, I noticed the learned gentleman's use of the word 'absolutely.' If he could apply that word to anything, say a frog, that Frog would be God."[30] The interactions between Hamilton and Fort seem largely cordial. Fort even confided in Hamilton "the difficulty of criticizing science," a point of weakness in his research:

> Poor old Theology hammered all around, but Science the great Immune. And as far as I know, mine are about the only books of impoliteness to scientific dogmas written by one who has not the theological bias. [...] I think I made it plain in the books that I am not out to restore Moses.[31]

These interactions are rare albeit interesting moments where the man who influenced an entire genre of fiction corresponded with a writer of said fiction. Hamilton's SF stories were the first to directly be influenced by Fortean themes.

As Moskowitz points out, Hamilton's *The Space Visitors* "was taken right out of *The Book of the Damned* and tells of a gigantic scoop that periodically descends from the upper atmosphere, scraping up samples for some unimaginable group of intelligences to examine. It was a strongly Fortean symbolic effort."[32] Like, Russell's *Sinister Barrier*, the foreword to *The Space Visitors* includes direct reference to Fort: "That such beings may have actually come near the earth, is asserted forcibly by Charles Fort in his amazing book, 'The Book of the Damned,' in which he brings forward evidence to show that over a period of the past 150 years there has been evidence of strange extra-terrestrial activity, presumably from sentient beings."[33]

A later story, *The Earth-Owners* is largely considered a precursor to *Sinister Barrier*, featuring "one group of radiant globes (similar to the Vitons) as protectors of the earth against raiding black clouds who feed on humans." SF reviewer Thomas S. Gardner was the first to write about the similarities:

> The same plot was developed with an unusual twist that Russell's *Sinister Barrier* does not contain in a short story by Edmond Hamilton in *Weird Tales*. [...] Even the same quotation from one of Fort's books is used in both stories. In order to appreciate *Sinister Barrier*, one should also read Hamilton's story and notice the difference in the endings.[34]

Whereas the humans can overcome the Vitons in *Sinister Barrier*, Hamilton's ending has noticeably different implications with the light-globes protecting the earth from the black clouds. "We know now that we and our earth are owned and we're glad they are," a character remarks at the conclusion. "As our knowledge and power increase, we'll come at our last point where we can live without the need of this guardianship of light-globes, able to fight our own battles against any beings."[35] While the ending is partially hopeful in humanity's ability to adapt to malign cosmic forces, Hamilton illustrates that earthlings cannot overcome their keepers at their present advancement. Russell's humans were able to take on earth's harvesters without the help of highly advanced keepers. Moskowitz accounts for "The Earth-Owners" lack of recognition stemming from the fact that it appeared in the same issue as a popular Lovecraft novelette (*The Whisperer in Darkness*) which grasped reader attention more strongly. Hamilton firmly established Fortean topics in SF long before anyone else, but it is Russell who is considered the one to have popularized it.

Fort's SF Friendship: Miriam Allen deFord

In addition to Hamilton, the other SF writer who contacted Fort was Miriam Allen deFord, who was fascinatingly namechecked in both *New Lands* and *Wild Talents*. deFord returned the favor in the short story "Slips Take Over."[36] She sent Fort two of her own Fortean experiences, the first from March 1922:

> She was in Chico and investigated. Went to the scene of falling rocks; discussed the subject with a person in the crowd. "While I was discussing it with some bystanders, I looked up at the cloudless sky, and suddenly saw a rock falling straight down, as if becoming visible when it came near enough. This rock struck the roof with a thud, and bounced off on the track beside the warehouse, and I could not find it. I learned that the rocks had been falling since July 1921, though no publicity arose until November."[37]

She again alerted him to Fortean happenings via a newspaper clipping from 1929:

> Newton, NJ—The county prosecutor's office here is baffled by the greatest mystery in its history. For days a rain of buckshot, at intervals, has been falling in the office of the Newton garage, a small room, with one door and one window. There are no marks on the walls or ceiling, and there are no holes in the room, through which the shot could enter.[38]

Whereas Fort mildly scoffed at Hamilton's submission, he went so far as to include deFord's reports in his books. More fascinating still is the fact that deFord went to the site of a previous instance of falling rocks, making her an early example of a person doing Fortean fieldwork.

DeFord went on to reference Fort in "Slips Take Over," a short story that appeared in the September 1964 issue of *The Magazine of Fantasy and Science Fiction*, with Isaac Asimov as the editor at the time. The story concerns a barroom conversation that takes an interesting turn into the subject of slipping from one dimension to the other. The story is full of references to Fortean happenings in history. This is started by the main character Davenant asking a stranger at the bar, "You don't believe, then, that beings from other planets are watching the earth?" The question itself is Fortean, but leads to another hypothesis by the stranger, that dimension slips are the cause of strange happenings. It is in this explanation that deFord mentions Fort:

> Ever hear about the farmer who went to his barn to milk his cows, and the cows were found un-milked and the farmer never seen again? Or the private plane that crashed with only the owner in it, and the plane was found, but never the pilot? Or the diplomat who walked around the horses of his carriage—and vanished? Hell, Charles Fort's books are full of cases—supposing you ever heard of Charles Fort. Take Dorothy

3. Lo! Forteana!

Arnold, and Judge Crater, and, away back in the early 19th century, Chief Justice Lansing. Where did they all go?

And how about the people who suddenly turn up on a park bench or on some busy street, years and miles from the life they used to know? Usually they say they can't remember. But where had they been?[39]

Further referenced is the case of Kaspar Hauser, whose mysterious life was explored in Fort's *Wild Talents*. Hauser is also mentioned in Eric Frank Russell's *Sinister Barrier* as a "man from nowhere" who was probably created in a Viton laboratory.[40] Even Heinlein, who is explored later, utilizes the figure of Hauser in a similar manner. deFord uses Hauser as an example of a "slipover," people who have inadvertently changed dimensions. Davenant finds himself questioning this notion throughout much of the story, until he becomes a slipover himself, falling into a panic when he finds himself in a different dimension in the conclusion. While the manipulators that appear in much of Fortean SF are not present in deFord's story aside from two slipovers who seem to try to teach Devanant a lesson, much of the story is reliant on Fortean phenomena for its premise.

When deFord passed away in 1975, *The INFO Journal* included an obituary, noting that both she and her husband, Maynard Shipley, were "outstanding Fortean(s)."[41] Shipley was primarily a science writer, having numerous works appear as Little Blue Books in the 1920s. He reviewed Fort's *Lo!* in the *New York Times*:

> Fort, it is true, writes thrillers—non-fictional thrillers, but more melodramatic than any mystery novel yet published. [...] Reading Fort is a ride on a comet. If the traveler returns to earth after the journey, he will find, after his first dizziness has worn off, a new and exhilarating emotion that will color and correct his future reading of less heady scientific literature.[42]

In the issue following her obituary, editor Paul Willis revealed that she had bequeathed the International Fortean Society's first editions of Fort's work that Fort himself had given her, two of them signed. She also passed on a "fairy cross" to INFO that Fort had gifted her and her husband years prior.[43] The stone is now in the possession of the final editor of *The INFO Journal*, Michael Shoemaker, who says that "unfortunately, it is one of the fakes that are sold to tourists, not an actual twinned crystal."[44] As the saying goes, it is the thought that counts. Clearly deFord and Shipley were notable acquaintances of Fort—such gift-giving from the researcher typically only happened to a few people who had corresponded with him, and the gift of the fairy cross seems especially unique. The passing on of these items to INFO also indicates that deFord was a Fortean to the very end and a remarkable one at that, holding the honor of being the only firmly established SF author to be quoted in Fort's books.

Letters to Lovecraft: Fritz Leiber's You're All Alone

Like Lovecraft, Fritz Leiber never corresponded with Fort directly. He barely was able to contact Lovecraft before his death, but these correspondences with Lovecraft reveal fascinating information about both authors, especially Leiber's enjoyment of the works of Charles Fort. They started their correspondence less than six months before Lovecraft died. The then 25-year-old Leiber was still unpublished at the time this exchange started, but Lovecraft was receptive to the young writer's questions and observations. In the letter to which Lovecraft responded with his nonbelief in the supernatural, Leiber mentioned to Lovecraft his high opinion of Charles Fort. Leiber was part of a group of panelists discussing Lovecraft at a Los Angeles Science Fantasy Society in 1963 where he mentioned this letter:

> In my short correspondence with (Lovecraft) one of the first that came up, I remember, was that I made some rather complimentary remarks about Charles Fort's books, saying something to the effect that these books showed that scientists didn't know everything and that there was lots of information that scientists were deliberately disregarding because they couldn't figure out any good explanation. He came back with a rather hot defense of the scientist; he pointed out that he was a materialist himself and that the scientist had to demand that recorded events be confirmed in the most detailed way, that if a thing be seen that you describe how an experiment could be set up to produce the same effect again. He assured me that although Fort's books, his collections of newspaper and magazine clippings, were very interesting and great background material for the writer, they weren't to be taken seriously in the way of a refutation of scientific theory. I just cite that as an example of his thoroughgoing scientific approach to life outside of his stories.[45]

Leiber's admiration of Fort is evident here, and Lovecraft's response, while somewhat wary of Fort's conclusions, speaks to a notion that is repeated in SF again and again. Fort's books are great background material for the writer, an SF source-book, as John W. Campbell claims. Fellow panelist and *Riverside Quarterly* editor, Leland Sapiro, replied to Leiber by quoting Sam Moskowitz: "Lovecraft was so knowledgeable and interested in the sciences, it became increasingly difficult for him to write a weird tale that was not plausibly explained and in most cases scientifically explained."[46] Perhaps this difficulty in finding the weird is why Lovecraft still considered Fort's work valuable as background material; they gave Lovecraft examples of puzzling phenomena that were left unexplained by science. This too would explain Lovecraft's possible interest in Gef the talking mongoose, a phenomenon which was never thoroughly explained. In a November 1936 letter to Leiber, he wrote that "so far as weird fiction is concerned, I always insist that the emphasis be kept on *the wonder of the central abnormality itself.*"[47]

In addition to revealing more about Lovecraft's Fortean tendencies,

Leiber had some of his own. Like many of the authors examined, this influence is not immediately apparent. Leiber was primarily known for his series of sword and sorcery novels, Fafhrd and the Gray Mouser, a subgenre he is often credited with helping to create. However, Leiber was allegedly amongst the numerous other writers who took part in lengthy correspondence with the International Fortean Organization. Leiber's own work illustrates his Fortean interests: Stephen Webb makes note of Leiber's *You're All Alone* and its Fortean leanings, comparing it to the more overtly Fortean stories "The Earth-Owners" by Hamilton and "They" by Robert Heinlein.[48] Webb says that the story "is one of the best examples of how science fiction authors have examined the big questions," referring to its existential nature. The story appeared in the July 1950 issue of *Fantastic Adventures* and follows the tale of Mackay, one of many automatons who somehow breaks free of the system. "The world seems to be running to its own script, a script from which the protagonist has vanished," writes Webb.[49] This is a Fortean notion—that our reality is being written, but we do not know for whom.

Early on, the novel opens the possibility of a Fortean reading. Jane Gregg, the young girl who "awakens" protagonist Carr Mackay from his pseudo-reality slumber expresses her disdain for patterns: "I hate patterns. Patterns are traps. If you live according to a pattern, other people know how to get control of you."[50] Recalling Fort's interest in the outliers of data, Jane seems to imply that accepting a foolproof system of reality is an easy way to find yourself trapped within it. Only via those events and decisions outside the norm does true reality seem to spring forth. This system is continually implied to be manipulated by an outside intelligence, again not unlike Fort's theories and the other SF stories that perpetuate such ideas. Mackay repeatedly ponders on the nature of the universe placing humans as cogs in a machine: "What was the real significance of the dark rhythm that was rushing him through life at an ever-hastening pace toward a grave somewhere? Did it have any significance—especially when any break in the rhythm could make it seem so dead and purposeless, an endless marching and counter-marching of marionettes?"[51] Leiber implies that the accepted view of reality is sedating, and any factors which seems to poke holes in it are to be dreaded as they make the world seem irrational. The same could be said of the incidents reported in Fort's work which made him question whether the nature of reality and human existence was as simple as the majority would make it seem. Perhaps the breaks in rhythm interrupting Leiber's marionette march were Fort's damned facts marching out of time, glaringly in opposition to the accepted rhythm. Certain passages have metaphorical Fortean implications, such as when Leiber's protagonist hides with Jane in a library past closing time, unbeknownst to the rest of humanity which is "asleep." The narrator says that "all around them was the pressure of the hundreds of thousands of books. But always the tunneling gaps, the peepholes, the gaps between the books."[52] Beyond such possible metaphorical relationships to Forteana, Leiber's story also posits a possible cause for Fortean phenomena. The people who are "awake" among the legions of the "asleep" include many who utilize their power like childish gods, "slipping plates of food out from under people's forks and watching them eat air, [...] half undressing the prettier girls [...] and sticking pins in them." The more devious "men in black hats" take particular joy in waking up the "asleep" enough so that they can feel pain at their hands. Their appearance and ominous nature are reminiscent of the Men in Black of UFO literature, although Albert Bender's work on the matter would not come out until six years later. Regardless, these mischievous god-people who take advantage of the sleeping masses qualifies the work as SF which explains some Fortean happenings, in this case, teleportation of objects and disappearances. Those who are still locked into the system are not able to comprehend what has happened to these objects or people.

You're All Alone's Fortean inclinations hint at the staying power of Fortean philosophy in current popular culture. Leiber's story is a precursor to numerous works of dystopia that relegate humanity to the role of unknowing cogs in a machine. As with most dystopian stories, and even most Fortean stories, the work could be read politically: a "good little citizen" wakes up from the mirage of utopia and sees the true way the world works, benefiting the chosen few and relegating others to live as zombies. Even Fort's "we are property" line seems ripe with political implications. Yet without these intentions being made explicit, and keeping Leiber's interest in Forteana in mind, one can see how the story also functions with a basis in some of Fort's theories. The "they" in the novel that utilizes humanity as some kind of machine is never clarified, but such a system seems to have some intelligence behind it. It is also akin to Fort's "A Radical Corpuscle" wherein certain cells of a larger system become self-aware. Whatever the case, Leiber serves as an excellent example as to how even stories that are not explicitly Fortean can be read through a Fortean lens. With knowledge of his interest in Forteana, it is also possible that some ideas made a quiet transfer to his fiction, maybe unintentionally.

Frank Herbert's "Rat Race" and Cryptozoology

Like the cosmic detective that Fort sometimes fancied himself as, Frank Herbert's 1955 short story "Rat Race" treads surprisingly familiar territory in Fortean pulp SF. Herbert's name most often goes hand-in-hand with his *Dune* series which falls farther into the fantasy SF territory than most Fortean SF would ever venture. However, with "Rat Race," Herbert proves himself a quite versatile author. From the opening paragraph, Herbert displays a knowledge of Fort. His detective protagonist, Welby Lewis, decries "his cynical police-peopled world transformed into a situation out of H.G. Wells or Charles Fort."[53] Strangely, like many other early Fortean pulp stories, like Heinlein's "They" or Russell's *Dreadful Sanctuary*, Herbert's also doubles as detective fiction. Perhaps this trend is a product of the paranoia that Fortean philosophy can instill in readers and writers alike. Welby investigates a mortuary after encountering the odd behavior of a mortician while investigating a separate case. He gets the distinct feeling that the mortician is "some kind of creepy freak."[54] Cold War anxieties make an appearance, Welby at one point thinks that the strange events in the mortuary are part of a "Communist set-up" to utilize corpse blood. Not unlike Heinlein's *The Puppet Masters*, also the product of Cold War anxiety, Welby uncovers an alien plot to manipulate humanity, but events take a decidedly Fortean turn. What results from Welby's investigations is truly frightening, a conclusion that echoes Fort's notion that humanity is the property of something else. Humans are but guinea pigs to some higher intelligence, they "fractionate the blood" of humanity in the same way that "we recover vaccine from chick embryos, how we use all of our test animals."[55] Welby, with the help of Dr. Bellarmine, makes a desperate effort to stop the harvesting of humans by this higher force, attempting to illustrate to them that humans are intelligent creatures. As Bellarmine says, if he found one of his lab rats to be intelligent and conscious of what was being done to it, "I think I'd have to put it through some tests to find out just how smart it was." The doctor disappears and Czernak hopes that he can pass the battery of psychological exams that the manipulators are putting him through, for the sake of mankind. Like the Fortean notion that we are property, Herbert's story makes this notion even more horrifying by having the captors harvest humans for the sake of medicine, not registering that they are intelligent. Welby is horrified at the possible scope of the manipulators' intelligence, noting that rats are vegetables compared to humans. He trails off thinking about humans being vegetables to this other force. Herbert is not a noticeably Fortean writer, with the popularity of *Dune* dwarfing short stories like "Rat Race." But "Rat Race" is an impressive piece of Fortean SF, very much in the vein of earlier works by Hamilton or Russell. The short story illustrates that Herbert is keenly aware of Fort's philosophy, not simply namechecking Fort in the opening.

Even in *Dune*, Herbert shows some possible Fortean inspiration, more specifically the cryptozoological side of Fortean interest. This possible point of interest is indicated by the presence of the sandworms throughout the story who pose a grand threat to all who try to harvest spice from Arrakis. These worms surprisingly have some basis in our reality. Roy Chapman Andrews says of the *allergorhai-horhai* (the mythical creature commonly referred to as the Mongolian Death Worm):

> It is shaped like a sausage about two feet long, has no head nor legs and is so poisonous that merely to touch it means instant death. It lives in the most desolate parts of the Gobi Desert, whither we were going. To the Mongols it seems to be what the dragon is to the Chinese.[56]

Andrews was an American explorer who came across the legend of the Mongolian Death Worm during an expedition to turbulent Mongolia and China. He does not seem convinced of its existence, but the worm has since become a widely recognized cryptid, a staple of Fortean zoology. Although Herbert does not connect the sandworms' creation to the legend of the Mongolian Death Worm, its presence still is explained in mildly Fortean terms. He speaks of the mythological nature of the sandworms' creation, saying that "the elements of any mythology must grow from something profoundly moving, something which threatens to overwhelm any consciousness which tries to confront the primal mystery. Yet, after the primal confrontation, the roots of this threat must appear as familiar and necessary as your own flesh."[57] What Herbert hits upon here is the fact that mythologies do not just spring up out of thin air; there is a primordial origin to them. Just as Vallee insists that our mythologies of ancient times could be based upon the same unexplained phenomenon in the skies we see today. The inspirations for our mythologies predate us and sometimes it seems as though something sinister and omnipresent was behind their creation. Less speculatively, the Mongolian Death Worm is a form of modern myth, like UFOs and Bigfoot. It follows Herbert's own conditions for the creation of a mythology. Even if Herbert did not draw at least some inspiration from the giant worms of Mongolia, both breeds of worms seem to stem from some primal fear. Even though no one that Andrews spoke with had personally seen the worm, no one doubted its existence. There is also the mythological connection Andrews draws between the dragon and the worm. Andrews is being speculative, of course, and yet he may not be entirely off base. Herbert also relates his sandworms to Chinese dragons "who carr(y) the 'pearl of great price' in its mouth."[58] It is, of course, coincidental that both worms are related to dragons in their respective texts, but it is in some sense telling of the primal fear of the unknown and more powerful. In Fortean terms, the reason science often relegates myth to pure fantasy is because *if* they were indeed real, our myths would destroy us. But as Vallee indicates, perhaps there is more to our myths than meets the eye.

Harold M. Sherman, "The Green Man," and Telepathy

Ray Palmer (the subject of the succeeding chapter) published Harold M. Sherman's full novel *The Green Man* in the October 1946 issue of

Amazing Stories, declaring it to be an excellent answer to the "question that has become a very real one: 'What would happen if a being came to Earth from another planet?'"[59] Palmer admits that, unlike the Shaver stories, this story is pure fantasy. "It is all in the spirit of fun, and in the delicate satire that characterizes a true and worthwhile fantasy," he writes.[60] The tale *is* largely satirical, featuring Numar the extraterrestrial giving his speech of peace to the spectators of a football game, perhaps because of Sherman's previous experience as a sports fiction writer. As if to further distance the story from the supposed realness of the concurrent Shaver Mystery, the entire ordeal ends up being the dream of its protagonist.[61] But as has been the case with much of pulp SF, this story somehow made it into reality. When the tale and its 1947 sequel *The Green Man Returns* were packaged together in the same book, the works were subtitled as "an amazing UFO pre-vision of the coming of the space people," implying that Sherman had predicted or intuited the later contactee reports. Perhaps the books were a product of some unintentional ESP, a subject with which the author also became fascinated.

Whether or not it was a "prediction," Sherman's story seems to have directly influenced the contactee experience of George Adamski. Fortean researcher Loren Gross examines this claim, citing the nearly identical messages of peace in Adamski's own story submitted to *Amazing* the same year. The tale was markedly similar to Sherman's "but in (Adamski's) version, instead of an alien it is Jesus Christ that lands in a spaceship."[62] Gross suggests that this narrative extended further into Adamski's purportedly true tale of alien contact with a Nordic alien from Venus named Orthon and others. Though this was to occur later in the 1950s, Adamski's earliest claim of a UFO sighting occurred the same month that Sherman's tale was published. Amongst other similarities between the supposedly true sightings and the SF tale are the fact that both occurred in Southern California, Adamski's first few sightings involved "cigar" shaped objects as did "The Green Man," and even his description of Orthon resembles Numar without the green skin. As Gross eventually puts it:

> Adamski's yarn sounds too similar to Harold Sherman's tale "The Green Man" to ignore the strong possibility that the unusual California occult leader had been inspired by the story in *Amazing* magazine. Unfortunately, Adamski's "Numar" didn't stick around to plea for peace among the nations of earth, but Adamski was only too glad to spread the word himself.[63]

Gross quotes an excerpt from Charles Fort's *Lo!* to illustrate how the researcher would probably differ from Sherman in the hypothetical reactions of humans to extraterrestrials visiting Earth:

> I accept that, if explorers from somewhere else should visit this earth, and if their vessels, or the lights of their vessels, should be seen by millions of the inhabitants of this

earth, the data would soon be conventionalized. If beings, like human beings, from somewhere else, should land upon this earth, near new York, and parade up Broadway, and then sail away, somebody, a year or so later, would "confess" that it had been a hoax by him and some companions, who had dressed up for their parts, and had jabbered, as they thought extra-mundanians should jabber. New Yorkers would say that from the first they had suspected something wrong.[64]

Fort, always the cynic, does not see visitors from other places promoting peace or starting an invasion, he only sees the people of earth quickly explaining away their visitations. Jacques Vallee would likewise see the narrative in "The Green Man" as a continuation of aliens saving humans from themselves, a dangerous form of *intellectual abdication* which renders humanity no longer responsible for its own problems. Perhaps "The Green Man" was a progenitor of the philosophies of various UFO cults and contactees that Vallee explores in *Messengers of Deception*. Seeing as Adamski was one of the first to promote such a message through contactee experience, perhaps "The Green Man" actually helped to create such philosophies of peaceful alien intervention.

His possible influence on Adamski was not the only Fortean connection that Sherman had. The author, not unlike Robert Heinlein (explored in Chapter 7), became interested in telepathy, but his interest was written about much more plainly and not relegated to more personal letters like Heinlein's. Amongst numerous works such as *How to Make ESP Work for You* (1964), *Wonder Healers of the Philippines* (1967), and *You Can Communicate with the Unseen World* (1974), his most famous work on Fortean subjects was released before *The Green Man* appeared in *Amazing*. In 1942, he released a supposed landmark study into telepathy between him and Sir Herbert Wilkins but it was received with much scrutiny. Entitled *Thoughts through Space*, the study involved Sherman exchanging telepathic messages with Herbert Wilkins while Wilkins was on an arctic rescue mission to save downed Russian pilots. While his other books appear more like psychic self-help books, *Thoughts through Space* is intended to be a more serious study of telepathy. The notion was that while Wilkins was in the Arctic to search for a downed Russian plane, he would periodically attempt to send telepathic messages to the receiver, Sherman, back in New York. The entire transcript of the messages is reprinted in the book, along with sections by each author entitled "My Experience as Sender" and "My Experience as Receiver." In the transcript of the communication, there are vague moments where it seems as though Sherman was picking up on what Wilkins was telepathically sending him. On Test 59, for instance, Sherman correctly gauges a shift to good weather. He also wrongfully "receives" that mail arrived that day and that a flight was initiated. There are a few partial "hits" that seem like a stretch. For instance, Sherman sees red and Wilkins suggests that it could be the red gas cans that airplanes fly from town to town.[65] This study had no scientific value, but it still marks Sherman as an oddity of an SF writer. He believed wholeheartedly in the "wild talents" that Fort wrote of and possibly inspired the experience of one of the earliest UFO contactees. Wherever SF goes, inherent strangeness follows.

4

Fort's Further Pulpy History

The Editors and the Historians

> *The night it all started I was sitting alone in the darkness of my living room, the rest of the family having long since gone to bed. I was thinking deeply of* Manfred, *the narrative poem by Byron. I was mentally stimulated by the strange evidence my thoughtful analysis had given me that Byron was not, strictly speaking, writing fiction. I sensed he was trying desperately to say that his subject was more factual than fictional; but that he could not say it outright because of some restriction, either prejudice or actual danger.*
>
> —Richard S. Shaver[1]

Prelude

The previous chapter's examples illustrate Fort's influence on SF as visible but critically understated. Robert Barbour Johnson includes Fort in a series of "Personalities in Science Fiction":

> Fort surely needs no introduction to devotees of science fiction and fantasy. Indeed, he may well be termed the spiritual father of both these literary fields. It was recently proposed to form a club that would be called, "Writers Who Have Stolen Plots from Charles Fort." The idea was dropped, however, when it was realized that such a group would include virtually every modern writer in the imaginative field, including many now deceased.[2]

Others have echoed this early account of Fortean influence. "In many cases, later science fiction reads like a series of imaginative riffs, with techno-realistic pictures now, on Charles Fort," writes Kripal.[3] But Fort's name now gets lost in the shuffle while his ideas and themes remain prominent in SF. My aim in this chapter is to track the continuous thread of Fortean influence on SF from the early pulps into more contemporary SF. This goal is achieved through an analysis of the editors of pulp magazines and the SF historians who saw value in Fort's work.

Raymond A. Palmer

The next step in the development of Fortean SF is succinctly stated by Kripal: "It was not Fort who would finally fuse science and fiction into a potent Fortean potion of truth-fiction that would confirm the paranormal experiences of many a reader and confuse the hell out of the rest of them. That man was Ray Palmer."[4] It is no secret that narratives gain effectiveness on their readers through a healthy suspension of disbelief. When the truth and fiction of a piece is blurred, this suspension of disbelief becomes heightened as the reader questions what is fact and fiction; what would otherwise be a straightforward SF story becomes more enticing as the reader asks themselves, "well, could this be true?" This enticement is how the essential examples of maybe-fiction retain their ability to affect their audiences deeply. Raymond A. Palmer clearly understood this phenomenon. Palmer was born in 1910 and Kripal notes the fantasticality of his "origin story": a freak accident with a butcher shop truck left his body stunted to the short height of four feet, eight inches. His height and SF interests inspired the secret identity of the miniature-sized superhero The Atom, although Palmer's true life was no less fantastic. Because of his early childhood injuries, he was resigned to reading pulp SF magazines which quickly grew to an obsession. He experienced a meteoric rise in the business of SF pulps and by 1938, he was editor of *Amazing Stories*. Seemingly analogous to his superhero namesake, Palmer claimed supernormal abilities, including being a casual psychic. His interests were eccentric, often within the Fortean realm of thinking. Kripal quotes a section of Palmer's *The Secret World*:

> Palmer claims that a book like this one "just 'happens' by some mysterious on-going process that sometimes seems to be the whim of chance Fate, but in an awesome number of instances, seems manipulated by a Deliberate Manipulator—some super Intelligence beyond normal comprehension." The conclusion dawns on one that "there is a Plan," which, alas, sometimes feels more like a "Plot."[5]

Palmer's musings of reality being a "plot" of some cosmic novel is unconventional. However, the injection of his beliefs into the magazines he edited proves highly influential in keeping Fortean elements alive in SF even after Fort's impact might have otherwise faded over time. Palmer was perhaps the most Fortean figure that could have risen to prominence within the pulp world. As stated earlier, Palmer thought himself a psychic, witnessed a flying saucer outside of the *Amazing Stories* office building (nine years before the flying saucer phenomenon reached the national vernacular with

Kenneth Arnold), and even believed that "somewhere, somehow, the total sum of all knowledge exists."[6] Kripal also sees parallels between Palmer's personal beliefs and Fort's work. Regarding his UFO encounter: "We are back to Fort's truth-fiction: an office publishing pulp fiction on alien invasions stops its work to watch a flying saucer hover over the city."[7]

This conflation of truth and fiction is how Palmer left his mark on *Amazing Stories* and the SF genre in general. In 1943, he received his first letter from Richard Shaver, a figure both infamous and thought-provoking. Shaver wrote of his experiences within the hollow earth where he was witness to an astounding civilization hidden to the surface world. His "elaborate, deeply paranoid cosmology" featured an ancient alphabet (a not too thinly veiled bastardization of the English alphabet; it still contained 26 letters) and a plot pulp SF fans would flock to: two distinct races (a la *The Time Machine*) at war with one another using the technology of the Titans and the Atlanteans.[8] From a scientific perspective, these are the ramblings of a madman. Palmer had to rewrite the story because of its many typographical errors and while "Shaver claimed he was suffering in the hollow earth, he was actually, according to Palmer himself, suffering in a mental hospital."[9] One cannot discount the fact that Shaver was schizophrenic; he spent nearly a decade in mental institutions, including the famous Ypsilanti State Hospital where Milton Rokeach researched *The Three Christs of Ypsilanti*, a brash attempt at curing schizophrenia by having three patients with the same delusion interact. Even Fort might balk at Shaver's assertions. Fort was only interested in the facts on record and developing theories based on them. Shaver said he received these stories quite literally from a voice inside his head, shot into his mind from a ray gun in the inner earth. If Shaver was schizophrenic (which he likely was), does this mean there is not some sort of substance to be gained from these writings? Palmer seemed to think that they had value. Kripal says that "this is a difficult but key point to our secret life: psychopathology and the paranormal go just fine together."[10] Palmer published these stories with a mysterious preface which blurred the truth value of them indefinitely. Whether this section was written by Palmer or Shaver himself is indeterminable but the message remains the same, the truth is in the fiction: "(The Author) claim(s) both that 'What I tell you is not fiction!' and that 'it is tragic that the only way I can tell my story is in the guise of fiction.'"[11] While Fort would be doubtful of Shaver's claims, one could see him admiring the author's amalgamation of fact and fiction, revealing the fictional nature of our reality. It is with the Shaver stories that SF and maybe-fiction seem indistinguishable from one another, a trend that has affected both genres permanently. SF gained paranormal influences and maybe-fiction was beset with narratives that seemed too good to be true.

One of the most fascinating facets of this new development in SF was how many copies it sold. Sales skyrocketed after the introduction of the Shaver Mystery, with Shaver's initial published letter to *Amazing* garnering what Palmer reckoned to be 50,000 letters in response. The publication was a phenomenon. Whether Palmer truly believed the stories or simply used them as a vehicle to increase circulation is ultimately ambiguous, and the truth probably falls somewhere in the middle. But he did tell fellow editor Howard Browne: "Any editor worth his salt has one goal: to increase circulation figures. When an opportunity to do that comes along, he has to know how to recognize it, make it work for profit."[12] Palmer saw the entertainment value that maybe-fiction has, the very reason that Fort's works had been such a draw to the SF community. The Shaver Mystery ultimately became an exploration into the unknown and unexplainable, areas that leave readers wondering and asking for more even if the mystery is never solved. This was intentional on Palmer's part; he heavily molded Shaver's stories to keep the mystery going. Shaver expert Richard Toronto notes that Palmer had a similar view to the UFO phenomenon: "If we knew exactly what the flying saucers were [...] we would have solved the mystery, returned to boredom, and stopped thinking again. I hope we never really solve the mystery of the saucers...."[13] Despite not wanting to solve the mysteries, Palmer nevertheless had Fortean motivations for publishing the Shaver stories. He viewed this type of writing as an educational tool, feeling that "science fiction and provocative ideas inspire people to think for themselves and become useful citizens, and this was far better than a classroom education."[14] Palmer emphasizes a questioning of science and indisputable facts is necessary to keep society thinking, not growing complacent in their role in the universe: "There is only the mysterious horizon beyond which lay unborn facts, and unresearched and unproved knowledge. If you don't see that, you are hopeless."[15]

Regardless, the minority of readers who made up the SF "fandom" were relentlessly against Palmer's decision to keep the Shaver Mystery going. One of the most popular writers of SF fandom, Thomas S. Gardner, wrote particularly scathing reviews of the stories. Gardner, quoted in Toronto's book, wrote that "the reader group catered to by Palmer consists of the average person with a sixth grade education level" and worried that these misinformed readers were "living their daily lives under delusions of grandeur, believing in lost races, 'ancient wisdom,' astrology, pyramidology, and the like."[16] Gardner implied that this mass of "lunatic" readers had truly dangerous implications, going so far as influencing the public school system. Repeatedly pummeled by the SF fandom for the anti-scientific Shaver stories, Palmer eventually exploded in repudiation, writing to one angry fan:

> Science says nothing exists that can't be proved. With five meager senses, if you please. What about the invisible? You can't SEE that? So, ergo, there is no invisible. You can't prove God in a laboratory, ergo there isn't one, and so, because a lot of people are reli-

gious "fanatics" science will just shrug its shoulders and say sanctimoniously "we don't know." They DON'T KNOW! What poor, blind, dumb bastards. [...] Science—a cult. Scientists—priests. Fen—kneeling, trembling, adoring, befuddled, unthinking, stupid worshippers.[17]

Palmer sounds like Fort, albeit with a bit more venom, decrying the state of SF fandom for treating scientists like gods and allowing scientific dogmatism to reign supreme. It is in this letter where, although he has clearly been incensed to the point of textual yelling, Palmer seems to defend the Shaver stories for purely Fortean reasons. The criticism which expresses the danger inherent in publishing the Shaver Stories would perhaps be warranted if they appeared in a science magazine as opposed to an SF pulp. Certainly, there was a lunatic fringe who suffered auditory hallucinations and wrote into the magazine (as explored in the following section). However, the average reader probably just saw a fascinating story, so long as the story is granted a small amount of suspension of disbelief. The Shaver stories are one of the earliest examples of a maybe-fiction that was clearly intended for reader pleasure.

It was also amid the Shaver Mystery that Palmer became interested in flying saucers. It is in this interest that Palmer reveals his knowledge of Fort, extending the influence beyond just similarities in their respective philosophies. Palmer writes in his July 1946 editorial: "If you don't think space ships visit the Earth regularly, [...] then the files of Charles Fort [...] are something you should see."[18] Palmer further mentions that he has done his own Fortean research, cataloguing different reports of objects in the sky. According to Palmer, these "could be nothing but space ships."[19] This claim, that Palmer believes there is no other answer to sky phenomena, truly forms the distinction between Palmer's personal beliefs and Fortean philosophy. Fort would never declare such a thesis as fact, only as his opinion, and then often, Fort would poke fun at his own statements. Throughout the course of the Shaver stories, Palmer seemed to grow slightly unhinged, more conspiratorial and more open to any wild claim of science to keep the mystery alive. Because of this, the Shaver Stories and *Amazing* in general began to devolve into a slight mess of what, at times, seems like semi-serious role-playing or pseudoscientific rubbish (depending on the reader). But circulation numbers were high, and the Mystery continued until Palmer decided to start his own publishing company, a place where his spiritualist beliefs would not be so vulnerable to criticism by the SF fandom. The strange SF experiment teetered out at *Amazing*.

Despite the short length of the experiment, the Shaver Mystery in turn reveals a great deal about Forteana in SF. Not only does Forteana provide entertaining SF inspiration, the maybe-fiction texts can be entertaining on the same level that SF is. Palmer considered these two genres largely equivalent in their goal to keep society from becoming complacent. Despite the entertainment value and the popularity these stories can stir, maybe-fiction is still derided as a literary medium. Most SF diehards were angered at the inclusion of these supposedly true stories, considering John W. Campbell of *Astounding* to be "the guru of highbrow science fiction" as opposed to Palmer's peddling of sensational chaff. Regardless, these stories sparked "an eclectic outpouring of enthusiasm, disbelief, and curiosity," according to Toronto. The controversial decision for Palmer to run the stories was a "cure (for) readers' war-weary gloom."[20] At the very least, despite any criticism Palmer and Shaver received from SF fandom, these stories *were* seen as entertaining, first and foremost. This is the true draw of the maybe-fiction work, despite lacking proof and requiring a healthy suspension of disbelief, these stories are enjoyable. It is largely unfair that Palmer was continually pitted against the juggernaut John W. Campbell as an SF editor in the 1940s. Despite radically different approaches, the magazines they ran were both ultimately enjoyable affairs carrying a consistent rivalry much like the endless competition between DC and Marvel comics. Besides, Campbell would not come away unscathed by the SF fandom, having his own closet full of maybe-fiction skeletons.

Interlude: Seeing Things and Hearing Voices

While many SF diehards looked upon the Shaver stories, and Ray Palmer's desire to print them, with scorn, the stories still had surprisingly far-reaching effects on readers. In turn, this reader response reveals a certain segment of psychological non-fiction that resembles SF. Richard Toronto has written the definitive survey of Shaver's life and work, *War over Lemuria*, which was started in collaboration between Toronto and Shaver before the latter's death in 1974. In this book, Toronto examines how the Shaver stories "tapped into a vast, marginalized group of citizens that did in fact hear voices." Toronto further explains that "in Shaver they saw a fellow traveler, for he was hearing the same voices that influenced their day-to-day lives, for better or worse."[21] Numerous letters were written to Palmer expressing this sentiment, supporting Shaver's stories and Palmer's decision to publish them, but one letter-writer eventually wrote a story of their own—a story which appeared alongside Shaver's "The Mind Rovers" in the January 1947 issue of *Amazing Stories*. The writer was a denizen of the "unintentional support group for sufferers of auditory hallucinations" that had developed through the Shaver stories, although she also seems to have suffered from visual hallucinations perhaps driven by drug withdrawal. She was Margaret Rogers, a woman who wrote letters to Ray Palmer expressing that while she also had experiences like Shaver, Shaver actually got many details of his underground society wrong. As Rogers writes in her first letter to *Amazing Stories*, which appeared in the September 1946 issue: "It seems incredible that any human alive today could remember so many things and still make so many mistakes or tell so many lies in his very frightening description of the underworld, the caves."[22]

The magazine was largely dedicated to the Shaver Mystery at the time of Margaret Roger's letters and eventual short story, and Rogers was not alone in writing Shaver-esque maybe-fiction. However, her letters to Ray Palmer preceding the publication of the story give comparatively more insight into the mind of the author and the motivations of Palmer to publish it. Even in her first letter, Rogers gives prominent plot points of her later story that seem just as fantastic and science-fictional as Shaver's:

> This much I can tell you. They are in face and form like earth peoples, but much larger and more beautiful. I have never seen an old, ugly or deformed person among them, and I spent three years there. I traveled many thousands of miles. Now understand me, I do not know and cannot speak of those who live in Europe's underworld. I only speak of those beneath the surface of these United States, Mexico, and the Latin American countries. I am grateful to them for they took me, a broken, sick, sinful, dope-ridden and hopeless woman and placed me under rays and brought me back to health.[23]

The eccentric Palmer was clearly enticed by this letter as indicated by the title he gave it ("Wow! Don't Stop Here!") and Rogers truly does leave the reader wanting more. She expresses that she is afraid of ridicule and therefore does not want to write the whole story. The story that begins to unfold is very much in opposition to the binary underground races in the Shaver stories, Rogers experienced gracious underground hosts who rescued her from the brink of ruin. She challenges Shaver even further in the letter:

> Ask him (Shaver) if his memory stretches back to the arrival of man on this planet. If he knows that all mankind sprang from the 100 who landed on this planet. I know all this, how and where we came from. I haven't the memory he claims to have, but it has been shown to me on their eternal records. Records that were made when the first spaceship was being built. Through these magic pictures I lived and journeyed through space.[24]

In a follow-up letter, Rogers seems noticeably relieved at the response to her first letter, particularly Ray Palmer's response. She writes to Palmer: "I feel as though you were not a skeptic, that I can talk to you as I would to a friend."[25] The next month, her story appeared as the first piece in the issue.

"I Have Been in the Caves" begins with Rogers in a sorry state, drug-addled and destitute in a Mexican hotel. "An outcast," she writes. "Thirty-nine years old, a slave of the drug, pitted by smallpox, ugly, ratted, and an object of pity and scorn to my countrymen."[26] Given some sort of divine intervention, Rogers is rescued from trouble with the law and detoxed by an electro-therapy doctor who leads her to the entrance to the caves. Underground, she is treated for her addiction by giant humanoids and given the opportunity to see the many wonders of this advanced civilization. Similar to Shaver's subterranean races, Rogers' Nephli are an ancient race vastly more technologically advanced than humanity. Amongst the numerous anecdotes that Rogers writes of, an intriguing section connects the Nephli's activities to Jesus Christ. A "great scientist" named Jas Whal grows tired of humanity's false gods and "was sent to the surface to teach of the true god and to give Man of the science he knew (sic)."[27] He shrunk himself down to human size and used the advanced science to perform "miracles." Of course, humanity turns on Jas Whal:

> They tortured him, and he who could have merely vanished from their sight, allowed even that in order to prove to them that he would die for them. He apparently died and was placed in a cave that was an entrance to the underworld. [...] Does not that sound like the miracles and crucifixion of Christ? The similarity is remarkable.[28]

Margaret Rogers' story and letters exemplify the maybe-fiction of 1940s pulp SF, sincere despite their outlandishness and SF appeal. Especially in her letters to Palmer, Rogers seems sincere in what she was saying and feared ridicule. Lucky for her, under Palmer's editorship, *Amazing Stories* was a great place to discuss Fortean conspiracy theories of underground civilizations messing with the humans above ground. According to Palmer, many people visited Rogers after her first letter and stressed that they felt her experience was real.[29] Regardless of the trueness of this tale, Rogers is an excellent example of how maybe-fiction ran rampant in the pulps after Fort's publication in *Astounding* in 1934, many perhaps unknowingly utilizing Fortean thought along the way. As opposed to the inhabitants of an unseen realm in the sky, we see a return to the idea of manipulation by hidden forces coming from below us once again. Margaret Rogers' story is but one of many stories which seemed to corroborate or be in discussion with Shaver in late 1940s *Amazing Stories*, indicating an extreme shift to maybe-fiction in a journal that was originally conceived as an SF publication.

Writers like Rogers who fed into the Shaver mythos were not the only hallucination-sufferers who were welcomed by SF publishers, and Palmer was not their only champion. As mentioned earlier, Ace Books, a publisher of primarily SF and fantasy, released the memoir of schizophrenia, *Operators and Things* by author Barbara O'Brien. O'Brien experienced schizophrenic symptoms suddenly after quitting her job, followed the instructions of the hallucinatory visions that hounded her, and traveled across the country on a Greyhound bus at their suggestion. After six months, the schizophrenic episode ceased on a third visit to a psychoanalyst. The account is remarkable not only for its briefness but its incredible intensity and the impeccable recall of the experiencer. Given its somewhat sensationalistic release by a publisher of fiction, these factors seem too good to be true. But a Boston

University psychology professor writes in the preface: "In this book, an intelligent, observant, and talented woman returns from a world of hallucinatory characters to join therapists and researchers in their pursuit of the causes of schizophrenia. [...] The author presents a startlingly clear account of our present state of knowledge and ignorance about schizophrenia."[30] O'Brien describes what she calls Operators, "a human being with a type of head formation which permits him to explore and influence the mentality of others,"[31] which closely follows the abilities of Shaver's Deros, who shot manipulating beams directly into his head. Both highly resemble the "influencing machines" of schizophrenia sufferers, outlined by psychoanalyst Victor Tausk, which "serves to persecute the patient and is operated by enemies."[32] Whether via the "hooks" of O'Brien's Operators or the rays of Shaver's Deros, both manipulate an individual's thoughts and bodily functions. The very term "operating machine" is science-fictional, calling to mind an alternate intelligence that manipulates us through our very thoughts—not unlike the universal manipulators Fort suggested. These texts indicate why the work of schizophrenics made for good SF fodder. Psychoanalyst Laurence A. Rickels made similar observations while comparing O'Brien's *Operators and Things* to Philip K. Dick's *Vulcan's Hammer*. Dick's book follows a humanity held captive by the Unity Organization, which like O'Brien's Operators can influence humans' thoughts throughout their lifespan. Writes Rickels:

> Inside the book the last pages advertise other items on the press list: "if you enjoyed *Operators and Things*, you will surely want to read" the series of true eyewitness accounts of contact with extraterrestrial life that is otherwise the specialization of this press. Thus one time zone's Spiritualism is the other era's science fiction. The autobiographical subject of *Operators and Things* sets up schizophrenia as the prehistory of the sci-fi genre.[33]

O'Brien does compare the plight of a schizophrenic to that of an SF author: "Schizophrenics, long before writers dreamed up science fiction, had—as they still have—a consistent way of developing mental worlds filled with Men From Mars, devils, death-ray experts and other fanciful characters."[34]

Indeed, psychological non-fiction sometimes bears hallmarks of SF, functioning as an alternate type of maybe-fiction. The similar stories of Shaver, Rogers, and O'Brien are certainly vast webs of delusion with science-fictional overtones, but other tales from the annals of psychiatry reveal similar SF or maybe-fictional worlds. For example, there is the work by Daniel Keyes, *The Minds of Billy Milligan*, which examines the titular sufferer of multiple personality disorder. While the wide-ranging network of personalities Milligan embodies is an intriguing subject on its own, the book becomes science-fictional when these personalities display superhuman traits. One is an escape artist who can break out of straitjackets and handcuffs with ease; another has immense strength and "the ability to control his adrenaline flow."[35] The SF nature of Milligan's plight was utilized as inspiration for M. Night Shyamalan's *Split* (2016) and *Glass* (2019), both films using the fantastic true story to tell an SF-tinged superhero tale. The complex system of personalities within Milligan, each possessing their own talents and role within Milligan's life, resembles Fort's notion that each organism is part of a larger organism, and each organism has a collection of smaller organisms within it. Perhaps human consciousness is no different. While this was worth a brief note in relation to Palmer and Shaver, these science-fictional, anomalous psychology stories are perhaps the topic for another book, nevertheless relevant to anomalies influencing SF and possibly vice-versa. As Kripal noted, "psychopathology and the paranormal go just fine together," and the paranormal certainly has its place in SF.[36]

Howard Browne, Paul W. Fairman, and the Return of Palmer-esque Amazing Stories

Far from being quelled completely after Palmer left *Amazing Stories* in 1948 to start *FATE*, the maybe-fiction of the Shaver Mystery era simply lay dormant. While Palmer's successor, Howard Browne, moved the magazine to a format more fitting for SF purists, this trend did not last forever. SF historian Mike Ashley notes:

> Rather than ridding himself of the sensationalistic Palmer approach, Browne began to copy it. "Master of the Universe," a so-called history of the future from 1975 to 2575 revealed in a manuscript found off the coast of Spain, was serialized in *Amazing* from April to November 1952, but was tedious.[37]

The maybe-fiction of Palmer-era *Amazing* continued to crop up occasionally with Browne. However, with his successor, Paul W. Fairman, the magazine made an almost full, if short-lived, return to maybe-fiction in the mid-to-late-1950s. In October 1957, Fairman published a special issue of *Amazing* dedicated to flying saucers. Palmer himself attempted to do this shortly before his termination, but the pulp publishing giant Ziff-Davis would not allow him. Now it seemed that the company realized that the subject generated readership. Other big names in the newly born UFO field were featured in the issue, including an article written by Palmer. In his article he reaffirms that Ziff-Davis would not let him publish the flying saucer issue of *Amazing*, writing:

> Here was a story made for *Amazing Stories* and I had an exclusive! Needless to say, a special cover was prepared, and a special edition readied, giving the whole story, photos and all. I will never know why the late Mr. William B. Ziff told me to kill the whole thing. But killed it was. Mr. Ziff was very close to Washington affairs, particularly

air force affairs, because of his tremendously important magazine, *Flying*. Perhaps he knew something I didn't.[38]

Palmer's hint of a conspiracy is another example of the former *Amazing* editor trying to create a mystery, a phenomenon that could continue throughout multiple issues. Of course, the UFO subject was not limited to the pulps; by the time this issue came out, flying saucers were well-entrenched in popular culture.

The man who started the flying saucer craze with the help of Palmer in *FATE*, Kenneth Arnold, contributed to this special issue. He concludes with a declaration of SF fandom before his experience, another member of the SF fandom that eventually saw the fiction become real: "As an early reader of *Amazing Stories*, I was always fascinated by the imaginative powers of its authors, but now I've seen for myself, and it's imagination no longer."[39] Returning to this issue was Richard S. Shaver, who had been relegated to appearing in a few Palmer-edited publications after his stories stopped being printed in *Amazing*. He writes the brief essay "Historical Aspect of the Saucers" in which he connects the flying saucer phenomenon to his omnipresent subterranean torturers. Shaver insists, for instance, that he told *Amazing*'s "readers about flying saucers before anyone else."[40] He further states that most flying saucers are mental projections, "a sort of television broadcast in which a receiver was not necessary." It is in this article that Shaver reveals that he was a reader of Charles Fort, saying that "space travel is older than the pyramids. Other investigators (Charles Fort, as an example) have gathered evidence of this, which you can read for yourself if you are truly interested in the matter that is readily available."[41] The biggest takeaway from Shaver's article, however, is his claim that the saucers originate from his omnipresent caves: "I have seen them. I say also that they come from vast caverns inside the earth."[42] Shaver performs early ancient astronaut theorization, describing numerous anomalies from ancient times which can be connected to his Lemuria mythology. Just as the saucers have always been part of human history, so too have the Teros and the Deros underground. His conclusion is decidedly Fortean:

> They are the products of intelligent races far beyond us in capability. They are not angels in disguise. They are not the spirits of the dead. They are not from another dimension. They are not from heaven or hell. They are other human races far more favored than we, and it is sad indeed to contemplate that it is so.[43]

Shaver's inclusion in this issue came after a long hiatus pushed by editors and the magazine owners, who had grown tired of Palmer's ways as editor. His return would be unprecedented if not for the fact that Fairman clearly brought a return of Palmer-style *Amazing*. Also included was an article by Gray Barker, a regular in Palmer's *FATE* and the man who provided the first comprehensive study into the Men in Black phenomenon, having numerous encounters with MIB himself. His 1956 book *They Knew Too Much about Flying Saucers* explores his and others' experiences with MIB, who seemed to crop up to warn UFO researchers not to investigate the phenomena. Fascinatingly, Barker includes in this book a chapter dedicated to Shaver's experiences entitled "Lemuria." He gives an overview of the Shaver Mystery saga, eventually implying a connection between Shaver's Deros and MIBs as perpetrators of "an ancient and almost unbreakable conspiracy to keep the secret [...] and those who pried into matters that did not concern them were in trouble."[44]

Beyond this special issue, Fairman extended this Palmer-esque editorial style to another Ziff-Davis publication, *Fantastic*, which in July 1958 published a special Shaver Mystery edition of the magazine. This issue came nearly a decade after the initial hold it had on readers. Unsurprisingly, the SF fandom had the same reaction to the Mystery as it did so many years before, "with most readers howling in protest over the issue and regarding it as 'rot.'"[45] Historian Mike Ashley writes that Palmer, and presumably Fairman as well, "pandered to the more fanatical instincts and in doing so degraded the science fiction he published."[46] Whatever the case, with Fairman and (the stricter) Howard Browne continuing to let maybe-fiction exist on the periphery of SF, this connection was allowed to continue. Maybe these works degraded the SF, but they do not seem to ever completely fade away. Whether factual or not, these stories are most certainly damned, and continue to march. While Fort's influence seems more distant in these later pulp maybe-fiction texts, his name still appears in them. He set a precedent for stories of this type to appear in the SF pulps after the posthumous republication of *Lo!* in *Amazing Stories* and his work proves to be a valuable reference point for the research in these later works.

John W. Campbell

Palmer was not the only SF pulp editor to push his writers into the weirder areas of Forteana. John W. Campbell was the editor of *Astounding Science Fiction* from 1937 to 1971, a lengthy amount of time, which allowed him to see future SF greats develop and flourish under his editorship. In non–SF-oriented circles, he is most often recognizable not as an editor, but as the author of the 1938 novella *Who Goes There?* which went on to inspire the movies *The Thing from Another World* (1951) and *The Thing* (1982). Even this story has hints of Fortean leanings, a paranoid, cosmically dreadful tale of Antarctic scientists attempting to evade a hidden and vicious manipulator—a manipulator that can take the form of anyone it kills. Sam Moskowitz writes of the power of Campbell's story: "It is not strange if sometimes readers shake the hypnotic wonder of the wheeling cosmos from their minds and demand: 'Who goes there?'"[47] Andrew May notes Campbell's contribution to Fortean SF by essentially publishing one of its earliest examples, Eric Frank Russell's *Sinister Barrier*: "Campbell made the decision to run the story, not in *Astounding*, but as the lead feature in the first issue of a new Street & Smith magazine called *Unknown*—a kind of crossover between the science fiction and weird fantasy genres."[48] Campbell saw great value in this Fortean story, allowing it to be the main attraction of an inaugural issue of a new pulp. While generally keeping a clear distinction between fact and fiction as opposed to Palmer's blurring, Campbell "had strong Fortean tendencies"[49] resulting in publishing numerous Fortean stories, including Russell's *Sinister Barrier* and Heinlein's early work. While also developing the hyper-rationalist Isaac Asimov, Campbell had a soft spot for more Fortean authors, developing Heinlein and Clarke early on. He wrote of Fort's work as having "not less than one good science fiction plot per page."[50] He reviewed the 1941 edition of Fort's collected works in the August 1941 issue of *Astounding* calling it "a perfectly magnificent source-book and challenge to writers and readers of science fiction, [...] it's not all light reading, but it's a vast mine of fascinating material for either science-fiction or fantasy."[51] While it was F. Orlin Tremaine who published the serialization of Fort's *Lo!* in *Astounding*, Tremaine also picked Campbell to succeed him. Perhaps Tremaine saw in Campbell some great similarities, especially in their admiration of Fort as an SF resource. Both editors developed and published Fortean SF writers, further establishing Fortean tendencies in pulp SF outside of the development of maybe-fiction from Palmer.

Campbell gained a reputation later in life for pseudoscience, an all too familiar result of having a mind so open it closes in on itself. Even the aforementioned Fortean SF writers stopped working with him after this development. Even Heinlein, with all his Fortean and noetic interests (explored in Chapter 7), ended his long friendship with Campbell. Campbell eventually became a proponent of L. Ron Hubbard's Dianetics, publishing Hubbard's initial article in *Astounding*. Calling to mind Vallee's research in *Messengers of Deception*, Hubbard's religious movement seems to motivate humanity to give in to a higher force—an "intellectual abdication" as Vallee says. While still qualifying as maybe-fiction, the medium may call for some type of speculative paradigm shift, but they rarely call for the religious devotion that is inherent in Hubbard's work. Yet it would be impossible to deny Hubbard as continuing this trend of maybe-fiction in SF pulps. Darrell Schweitzer notes that "the original Hubbard *Astounding* article reads like a mix of Shaver and Charles Fort, a breathless mass of illogic and unproven assumptions claiming to be rock-solid fact."[52]

Campbell's shift to this type of work was not well received by his contemporaries. Whereas the author and editor was once a champion of the Fortean mindset of not letting dogmatic rationalism get in the way of real science and "an outspoken critic of entrenched attitudes," he quickly moved away from this mindset to more dangerous areas. This included championing Hubbard's Dianetics, as well as promoting various machines that broke the laws of physics, like the Hieronymus machine (a machine that detected supposed "eloptic radiation") and the Dean Drive ("a reactionless device" that could create energy from nothing).[53] He changed the name to *Analog Science Fact & Fiction* around this time. May writes that "several of Campbell's editorials in the early issues of *Analog* referred to the Dean Drive—not because he was convinced that it could do all the things Dean claimed, but because he felt it deserved more serious investigation than it was being given by the scientific establishment."[54] His reasoning here is more respectable and Fortean in nature than that of the Hieronymus Machine. This device functioned, according to Campbell, by some form of psionics, a term he created to mean psychic electronics. Campbell's reasoning for supporting the Hieronymus Machine recalls Palmer and some of the mystical science revealed in the Shaver Stories. Campbell found that the machine worked whether it was plugged in or not, with the goal of "amplifying subtle radiations from a test sample, resulting in a tingling sensation when a psychically sensitive individual touched the detector plate."[55] This ecstatic reaction to the Hieronymus Machine, which sounds like it could quite possibly be Campbell being affected by the power of suggestion as opposed to psychic sensitivity, is quite different than his reaction to criticism to the Dean Drive. He does not promote the Fortean idea that science should not just casually dismiss any claim that seems too good to be true, but rather seems to have fallen victim to a trick of the mind. While to the present both devices have not been proven to be feasible, Campbell's interest in them and desire to have science examine them further indicates Fortean leanings. Like his writing on Scientology, his judgments seem to have been premature, but not ill-natured. It is also the case that unlike Palmer, his promotion of these machines did not have a questionable, possibly commercial motivation.

It should be noted that true maybe-fiction texts and Fortean mindsets do not involve systems and machines that have been scientifically proven to not work. Rather, they involve unverifiable, anomalous experiences or reports outside the capabilities of scientific testing. Professor Henry H. Bauer considers Forteana to be separate from natural and social sciences, fitting in more neatly into a field of "anomalistics" which require different methods of examination.[56] These are events and concepts that are not provable by established scientific methods. This includes the Shaver Mystery. For all their impossible science, they still outline a strange state of consciousness and rely on storylines more than the science that Shaver attempted to peddle.

The machines that Campbell examined broke the laws of physics or included particles that no one can find evidence for. The Hieronymus Machine would fall under the anomalistics category as it supposedly highlighted "eloptic" energy, a form of energy not yet understood or confirmed by science. While still highly doubtful, if something breaks the laws of physics, it cannot be judged on the standards of those laws. While the Dean Drive broke known laws of physics, its results *could* be measured by these laws, making it capable of being judged by those standards. Regardless, to have such speculative science come from *Astounding* was a major shift away from what the fandom wanted, especially regarding the outcry against *Amazing*. It becomes somewhat ironic that the SF fandom that turned on Raymond Palmer for publishing the "dangerous"[57] Shaver stories so fervently idolized Campbell. Few if any still follow the Shaverism ideology, but many people are Scientologists. Maybe-fiction meant for entertainment is rarely dangerous, but this is not the case with maybe-fiction meant to instruct a populace. Shaver may have intended to promote an ideology, but Palmer's edits were clearly aiming to entertain. Even if towards the end of the Shaver Mystery's run in *Amazing* the line between entertainment and pseudoscience was growing thinner and thinner, this is at times a difficult distinction to keep straight, but it perhaps illuminates why Campbell's decision to run Fortean SF was well-received and his later editorial decisions were not. Something about Forteana strikes readers as more real, perhaps more terrifying. Forteana does not necessarily mean that magic exists but rather that something strange could *conceivably* happen and science would be at a loss to understand it.

With editors of the two most popular pulp SF magazines exhibiting Fortean tendencies, albeit in their own unique ways, Forteana was given a head start in continuing to influence the SF writers of the future. This head start was lucrative, considering the time at which these Fortean stories appeared in the 1940s and '50s, an era that would be instrumental in influencing a large number of SF greats. Of course, these editors' interest in fringe subjects was not viewed with much approval by the SF fandom. Toronto mentions that the two editors were often considered responsible for the "death" of SF in the late fifties. Writer Phillip José Farmer "put Campbell on the rack for his promotion of L. Ron Hubbard's *Dianetics* and, much later, his obsession with psionics."[58] Palmer was held responsible for SF's death because he promoted Shaver Mystery stories, again supposed "fact" making its way into fiction. For many, this had the lasting effect of making the genre worse. The genre did not die—it has remained alive in some form or another to the present day. So too has the Fortean influence continued, in large part because of its prevalence in pulp fiction. Branching into the paperbacks market after the pulp decline, Forteana continues its somewhat hidden existence in numerous SF works.

The Historians and the Futurian Phenomenon

Even if Palmer and Campbell changed what was acceptable in a pulp SF magazine so brazenly, reader reaction was not unanimously positive. Readers eventually grew tired of the Shaver stories and Palmer was ousted from *Amazing Stories*, shuffled safely away to a strictly Fortean publication, *FATE*.[59] Campbell too fell into disregard for his esoteric (and more reprehensible) interests and beliefs. Mike Ashley writes of *Astounding*'s stagnation toward the end of Campbell's run: "Because of the Dianetics uproar, *Astounding* was no longer in a position to dictate trends, and Campbell's prejudices—particularly on issues of sex and race—meant that *Astounding* was unlikely to carry too many taboo-breaking stories."[60] But Palmer and Campbell caused enough of a stir that SF readers can be reminded of their conflation of truth and fiction when reading more contemporary SF authors like Arthur C. Clarke or Philip K. Dick. Campbell especially helped stories influenced by Fort reach a wider audience, even calling Fort's works an excellent SF source-book. How did this influence remain even after it grew admittedly tiresome in the pulps? This continuation is likely because of the phenomena of avid SF pulp readers becoming writers and editors themselves, a concept explored in Damon Knight's *The Futurians*. It is here that the Fortean influence extends even further, evolved but remaining at its core classic Fort. Knight himself is an interesting author to tackle the Futurian phenomenon. Seven years earlier he wrote Fort's first comprehensive biography, *Charles Fort: Prophet of the Unexplained*. The book included an introduction by one of the most famous professed Forteans, R. Buckminster Fuller, and further solidified Fort's influence on SF beyond Sam Moskowitz's observations in *Seekers of Tomorrow*. "Fort's influence on other writers is incalculable," Knight writes. "His ideas have diffused so widely that compiling a list of examples would be a hopeless task."[61] The book included a phrase often attributed to Fort himself, perhaps because it sums up the implications of Fort's work so well: "Do things fall where a universal mind, which may be the mind of an idiot, conceives that they are needed?"[62] Later biographer Jim Steinmeyer and others paraphrase this quotation as "if there is a universal mind, must it be sane?" Knight was very well-versed in Forteana, being an active member of the International Fortean Organization like many other Fort-inspired writers. An article in *The INFO Journal* tells of Knight following up on a report from Fort of a piece of quartz that fell from the sky in a meteoric explosion, eventually being displayed at the Leyden Museum of Antiquities.[63] His attempts to track down the quartz from above were unsuccessful.[64] Knight was also a prolific SF author, appearing in a broad range of pulp SF publications, and he even penned a story that became an episode of *The Twilight Zone* (1950's "To Serve Man").

Before exploring *The Futurians*, it is worth noting that Knight was not the only SF historian to also be a dedicated Fortean. Moskowitz too, whose works on SF history have been important to recording Fortean influence, was interested in Fort and a member of INFO. Moskowitz republished the previously explored Fort proto–SF short story, "A Radical Corpuscle," likely noting its importance as a precursor to the SF stories to come.[65] Moskowitz further discussed Fortean SF in a lengthy profile piece in a June 1965 issue of *Amazing*:

> Fortean concepts have penetrated the main body of science fiction to a considerable extent. A review of the subject would require a tome. The ironic aspect is that the *readers*, while extolling certain individual literary efforts, have literally raged against the trend. The abuse handed out to John W. Campbell for exploring in fiction and articles areas which science "cannot explain" has achieved at times an intensity far beyond polite criticism. It was not completely deserved. He was predominantly trying to get authors out of monotonous ruts.
>
> Science fiction has attracted many crackpots in the past who thought its readers would be fertile ground for their particular obsession. The rejection of cultist, mystical or irrational notions has been almost total whether it was the absurdity of Deros living in caverns under the earth or the "truth" behind the flying saucers. Charles Fort and the Forteans, promoted by authors and editors but never eagerly embraced by the science fiction readers, are headed for the limbo of Richard S. Shaver and the flying saucers.[66]

Though the article's title, "Lo! The Poor Forteans," might suggest a wholesale defense of the Forteans, Moskowitz instead gives a balanced overview of their history in relation to SF. Indeed, Moskowitz explains how Fortean thought could be seen as dangerous when not in relation to fiction. While saying that "there is no evidence that reading Fort unfettered the mind of any scientist enough to contribute as a metal clamp to civilization," he nevertheless agrees that Fortean thought can lead to some dangerous paths:

> If there is any doubt that his viewpoint leads to *wrong thinking*, not clear thinking, one need only review the career of the official organ of the Fortean Society (titled *Doubt* after its tenth issue), and read the views presented.
>
> Fort initially started as the "gadfly" of science, but *Doubt* ranted and raved against the Pope, Jesus Christ, conscription, vivisection, vaccinations, Wasserman tests and Einstein.[67]

While *Doubt* at this point had become a mouthpiece for Tiffany Thayer, who Moskowitz notes laughed at the gullibility of the masses when Sputnik was launched into orbit, Thayer serves as an excellent example of how innocuous Forteans can turn bad. Yet, Moskowitz sees the launch of Sputnik as the "death blow" for the Forteans, which proved to be an inaccurate prediction. He would later become involved in the second incarnation of the Fortean society, INFO, just as Knight did. *The INFO Journal*'s final editor, Michael Shoemaker, says that Moskowitz was "a loyal member of INFO, from its founding until he died." Shoemaker indicates that Moskowitz published an article and several letters in the journal.[68]

Despite their shared interest in Forteana, Moskowitz and Knight never really got along. Knight was a member, unsurprisingly, of The Futurian Society of New York, "a group of hungry young science fiction fans and would-be writers"[69] who did evolve into some of the most influential authors in the genre. As chair of the 1939 World Science Fiction Convention, Moskowitz barred several Futurians from attending, fearing they would disrupt the proceedings by handing out pamphlets critical of the event: "A shrill argument against the convention's organizers, arguing that the event was run by coercion and dictators, was at the bequest of the publishing industry, furthering their own interests."[70] Moskowitz was a member of a rival group, the New Fandom, a group with which Knight himself took issue. Originally made up of five SF fan groups, Knight remarked sardonically on their lack of cohesion: "The membership never exceeded the original five, and since (then) these five promptly split into two factions."[71] Although Knight was often quite critical of Moskowitz, he appreciated his end goal. On Moskowitz's historiography of SF fandom, *The Immortal Storm*, Knight wrote:

> In spite of the author's comic pomposity [...] his innumerable misspellings and grammatical errors, his remarkable talent for the mixed metaphor [...] and his healthy admiration for himself—or perhaps partly because of them—he tells an engrossing story, livelier than ninety-nine per cent of mundane history, and most novels.[72]

In another essay, Knight writes:

> Sam Moskowitz is a man I have disagreed with about as often as he has opened his hundred-decibel mouth. He has many admirable qualities; he's worked as hard for fandom as anyone living; he edited the foredoomed *Science-Fiction Plus*, according to report, with vigor and integrity beyond the call of duty. The only trouble with him, in fact, is his incredible talent for being wrong.[73]

The extent of SF fandom feuds has been carefully examined through numerous other works, but this book is primarily interested in these two SF authors/historians. Whereas nearly every other aspect of SF culture was a differing point between the two, they both agreed on one rather contentious subject within SF: that the works of Charles Fort were valuable to the genre. While not linked to his Fortean interests, Knight's work on the history of the Futurians helps to further explain Fort's longevity as an SF influence.

While the Futurian phenomena could be distilled into a concept affecting only those who were members of the society, the tendency for pulp fans to become writers was not limited to this group. Knight writes of the pulps, *Amazing Stories* in particular, that "it was a snag in the stream of history which a V-shape spread out in dozens and then in hundreds of altered lives."[74] Knight then details an impressive list of names who he credits *Amazing Stories* with influencing, such as Ray Bradbury, Isaac Asimov, Arthur C. Clarke, Roger Zelazny, etc. The list goes on. This phenomenon of pulp fans who become writers and editors illustrates how Fort's influence traveled out of the pulps into contemporary SF even though his outlandish works seemed destined for obscurity. Andrew Milner notes how important the Futurian phenomenon was for the literary merit of SF, saying "there can be no avant-gardes in so unmodernist a field as SF," yet the genre's "history is nonetheless replete with intellectual formations the organization, vocation, and trappings of which bear close resemblance to those of the historical avant-garde."[75] He further states that the Futurians are an "obvious example" of this SF intellectualism which is "especially interesting given (their) close proximity to the pulp milieu."[76] The pulps in this sense were the birthplace for highbrow SF despite their own tendency towards the lowbrow. The fact that Fort's influence survived these transitions seems to imply that Fort's work resonates with SF at its core; whether it is a lowbrow or highbrow story, Fortean thought endures.

The Futurians were most overtly a political movement and a specific collection of authors. Richard Toronto writes how the group was "cerebral and leftist" and "made no bones about their [...] leanings."[77] However, it is one phenomenon associated with the group that matters most to the Fortean trend of SF—the tendency for SF fans to become SF authors and editors. Accordingly, this tendency helped Fort's influence carry on in the genre past when his work was contemporary to the pulps. Writers like Clarke and Dick especially were particularly fervent fans of SF who would become some of the most prominent authors later on. Clarke wrote a book about his fandom called *Astounding Days* (utilized in the following section) and PKD had an immense collection of Campbell-edited SF. The trend for Forteans to be SF fans initially will also become important. John Keel, for instance, at one point wrote and published an SF fanzine. Futurian does not equal Fortean, but a specific facet of the Futurian phenomenon will prove important to Fort's continual influence in SF from the publication of his works to the present: SF fans became creators and editors of both SF and maybe-fiction literature. The influence of Fort survived this transition to influence further eras of SF.

5

Continuation of Cosmic Dread

A Fortean Analysis of Arthur C. Clarke

> *My own attitude towards the paranormal and fringe sciences generally has changed over the years from tentative acceptance to disillusioned skepticism.*
> —Arthur C. Clarke[1]

Arthur C. Clarke's continual interest in Fortean topics has been under-examined even within SF scholarship. Of course, it should be noted that he did not consider himself a Fortean—although SF writers with Fortean sensibilities do not always do so. A quote relevant to this topic appeared in the Clarke biography by Neil McAleer, with the author speaking of the circumstances that brought about the novel *Childhood's End*:

> "When this book was written in the early fifties, I was still quite impressed for what is generally called the paranormal," Clarke said. Today he admits to being "an almost total skeptic." Why? Because he has seen too many claims exposed as fakes. Says Clarke, "it has been a long, and sometimes embarrassing, learning process."[2]

McAleer feels that this shift in attitude matters very little. The paranormal "was a powerfully used theme in *Childhood's End*, and tens of thousands of readers have been emotionally jolted by its implications in the work."[3] In Clarke's formative years, when he did not denounce his ponderings on the paranormal, Fort proved to be an important factor. Not a member of the Futurian Society, but nevertheless a product of the same pulp magazine SF upbringing, Clarke represents a clear example of the Futurian phenomena. This is illustrated by his book *Astounding Days*, which he dubs a "science fictional autobiography," which tracks his fascination with various works appearing in *Astounding Stories*, Fort included. Clarke explains how these stories affected him as a young SF reader and developing writer. This development is a decidedly Futurian process: a pulp SF fan becoming an SF writer. Clarke is passionate about his formative texts even as he recalls them as a much older man. Regarding Fort's work, Clarke displays a complex but ultimately positive relationship with the damned facts:

> Apart from the occasional "fillers," a few of which we have already discussed, the Clayton *Astounding* never published any non-fiction. The new management waited six months, then announced it would start serializing Charles Fort's *Lo!* in the April 1934 issue. It was to run for eight installments, concluding in November. No choice could have been more appropriate for a science fiction magazine, and Fort's writing was to have a tremendous impact on the field.[4]

While acknowledging that he considered most Forteans "ignorant and opinionated science-bashers," he noted that Fort's own "wry sense of humor and refusal to take himself as seriously as did his followers excused many of his faults."[5] Clarke appreciated numerous facets of Forteana and the paranormal without becoming one of these aforementioned disciples. He tells in his autobiography of the importance of Fort's "most fervent advocate in the United States," Eric Frank Russell, who encouraged the young author, and became a mentor of sorts.[6] This beneficial relationship was despite the fact that "on the subject of the Forteans (Russell and Clarke) did not agree," Clarke being more skeptically inclined than Russell. Nevertheless, Clarke praises Fort's work and notes its influence on his own: "I found his eccentric—even explosive—style stimulating and indeed mind-expanding; years later he undoubtedly helped to inspire [...] my two Yorkshire Television productions, *Arthur C. Clarke's Mysterious World* and *Arthur C. Clarke's World of Strange Powers*."[7] An extension of these Forteana TV shows came after the publication of *Astounding Days* with *Arthur C. Clarke's Mysterious Universe* in 1995. All-in-all, there were 52 episodes of Clarke covering Fortean material and, however skeptical he was regarding the veracity of the paranormal phenomenon covered, it illustrates his interest in the subject. In one episode of *Arthur C. Clarke's Mysterious World* (1980), an elderly but lively Clarke, at his Colombo home, plays table tennis with a Sri Lankan man. Clarke asks him about a personal encounter he had with falling fish; the man points out the nearby tree where the fish landed.[8] As is the case with every episode in Clarke's shows, he gives an introduction to the type of phenomenon that will be covered. Various objects falling from the skies (fish, frogs, rocks, etc.) are signature Fortean research material. Later in the episode, Clarke acknowledges Fort, saying that his interest in these specific unexplained phenomena came from reading the works of "a rather remarkable American man named Charles Fort." Clarke goes so far as to read an excerpt of one of Fort's books, which covered a report of little fish falling from the sky near Clarke's location in Colombo. The author's various Fortean television shows illustrate an interest when Clarke was a young and

5. Continuation of Cosmic Dread 99

impressionable reader of *Astounding Stories*—driven to "tentative acceptance" as he calls it. The shows also indicate a continuing interest with Fort's texts far into his existence as more or less a total skeptic. Clarke was the best kind of skeptic when it comes to paranormal phenomena: a skeptic that gives the questionable or unverifiable reports their day in court.

As stated by Clarke himself, *Childhood's End* came at a time when he was still considering the veracity of a paranormal reality. In the prologue to the 1990 edition of the novel, he muses about the disclaimer before the original edition of the book: "When *Childhood's End* first appeared, many readers were baffled by a statement [...] to the effect that 'the opinions expressed in this book are not those of the author.' This was not entirely facetious." Clarke wrote not long before this an "optimistic picture of our future expansion into the universe" but *Childhood's End* seems to paint a darker portrait. Clarke says, "now I have written a book which said 'the stars are not for man.'" Clarke tries to explain away any confusion this might cause readers. He denounces the "bookstores, news-stands, and airwaves [...] polluted with mind-rotting bilge about UFOs, psychic powers, astrology, pyramid energies, etc."[9] This statement is perhaps pointed at publishers such as Ray Palmer who had little discretion in dealing with the paranormal and blurred the line between fiction and non-fiction to sell copies. Clarke, however, has a much more sober approach. He does not discount all paranormal activity and even concedes that life exists elsewhere in the universe.[10]

Childhood's End illustrates an awareness of this distinction between serious study into the paranormal and the pulps' sensationalism. In other words, Clarke separates the maybe-fiction wheat from the chaff, a highly important task if one wishes to be taken seriously. As "The Overlords" begin their time on Earth, hoping to guide human evolution, one of them, Karellen, asks another if he found "anything among all the rubbish" in an extensive library of parapsychology books. The other Overlord responds that while there has been evidence of what he calls a "breakthrough," "the material is so selective [...] that one cannot use it for sampling purposes. And the evidence is confused with mysticism—perhaps the prime aberration of the human mind."[11] Clarke also seems to poke fun at his own position through the Overlords' discussion of Rupert Boyce: "He pretends to be open-minded and skeptical, but it's clear that he would never have spent so much time and effort in this field unless he had some subconscious faith."[12] Indeed, *Childhood's End* illustrates the possible power of paranormal research through its implications: Our research into it is primitive, but the little evidence we have points towards humanity's innate psychical powers. This is a decidedly Fortean conclusion, but it is hard to know if Clarke is expressing genuine belief in this fact or if the conclusion is instead intentionally fantastical for fiction's sake. One must never forget that this is explicitly a work of fiction. However, Kripal makes note of the fact that "Clarke turned to the [...] phenomena in the 1950s and concluded that the behavior of the things in the sky (with impossible speeds and turns that would instantly kill any human occupant) suggested that they were not physical at all." Kripal then quotes John Keel's investigation into Clarke's inspirations: "So (Clarke) looked deeper, into psychic phenomena, philosophy and theology and published his findings as *Childhood's End*."[13] The novel comes directly from Fortean research; as Keel suggests, it illustrates perfectly Clarke's less-scientific interests—illuminating those that are more esoteric. Kripal's quote also demonstrates the continual fascination with those ships in the skies, the damned facts that just will not go away.

As a work of fiction, *Childhood's End* contains various concepts that could easily be applied to the conclusions of Fortean works and maybe-fiction, notably the idea that "the stars are not for man."[14] Such a claim draws up feelings of a Fortean brand of cosmic dread, again reminiscent of the "I believe we are property" adage. This concept is not limited to this novel alone. In both *Childhood's End* and the later work *2001: A Space Odyssey*, Clarke portrays a human race that is being toyed with by some unseen force, helped along in their progression, though the motivations of these unseen forces are often ambiguous. The monoliths in *2001* serve as checkpoints in a cosmic scavenger hunt; when encountered, these checkpoints launch humanity into an evolution, with David Bowman becoming the vastly superior Star-Child. As the conclusion to the book states: "There before him, a glittering toy no Star-Child could resist, floated the planet earth with all its peoples."[15] We are property, as Fort would say; we are playthings to the Gods, as Keel would say. This same sentiment is expressed in *Childhood's End* with the more visible yet highly secretive Overlords who are subjects to a higher race, an "*Overmind* using (them) as the potter uses his wheel."[16] The ramifications of such a statement make the cosmic ecosystem of *Childhood's End* appear like an actualization of Fort's "A Radical Corpuscle": systems within systems within systems. Who is to know where humanity falls within this vast network of higher and lower intelligences? But the Fortean and maybe-fiction concepts in Clarke's work do not end with the concept of being subjects to a higher intelligence. There is also the fact that the Overlords in the novel look indistinguishable from the Devil of the Christian mythos, an idea that relates to Vallee's notion that numerous religious tales and ancient stories thought to be products of human imagination actually have a basis in unexplained phenomena. The Overlords appeared to humanity in earlier days and their image was etched in our memories as supernatural and malevolent beings, perhaps not wrongfully so. There is also the inclusion of a Ouija board session which proves to be a success, but the humans misinterpret the results as a spirit connection. What occurs is more akin to ESP, a product of human evolution at its earliest stages, as the Overlords explain. Clarke's own skepticism comes into play with this sequence: If the novel's implications are to be taken as Clarke's own opinion (which may be a dubious assumption in this case) he acknowledges that unexplained phenomena exist, but there is a frustratingly prominent human tendency to explain it in supernatural terms without truly knowing what is occurring. The Overlords also share this opinion, remarking of the session leader: "Boyce is remarkably obtuse and simple-minded. This makes his attempts to do research in this, of all fields, rather pathetic."[17] Clarke's fictional work clearly exhibits signs of his Fortean influence and, even though he is reluctant to admit the importance of the paranormal in his texts, the ponderings on the paranormal and Fortean are some of the most thought-provoking facets of both *Childhood's End* and *2001*. Whatever the case may be, Kripal calls it "an SF classic that would come to have a major influence on the counterculture of the 1960s and future readings of UFOs."[18] Again, SF and maybe-fiction appear intertwined, and we are left unsure of which is influencing the other.

Even as Clarke grew more skeptical as his career progressed, his various theories never stray too far from Forteana. Note "Clarke's three laws" as derived from his *Profiles of the Future*, a work based on various essays. The three laws, as they are most commonly generalized, include:

1. When a distinguished but elderly scientist states that something is possible, they are almost certainly right. When they state that something is impossible, they are very probably wrong.[19]
2. The only way of discovering the limits of the possible is to venture a little way past them into the impossible.[20]
3. Any sufficiently advanced technology is indistinguishable from magic. (Clarke added this law in a footnote after seeing a French edition of the essay take a line from the end of the piece and credit it as Clarke's second law. He further mentions, in his typically self-aware manner, that "as three laws were good enough for Newton," he has "modestly decided to stop there.")

The third law, which is the most widely known, is a hallmark of Fortean thinking and appears to have been inspired (if not outright borrowed) from Fort. Speaking of an impressive magician he had personally observed, Fort states: "I was a witness of a performance that may someday be considered understandable, but that, in these primitive times, so transcends what is said to be known that it is what I mean by magic."[21] But rather than accuse Clarke of plagiarism, Clarke's three laws need to be examined for what they are: a latter-day variation of a particularly Fortean philosophy. The first law expresses the same distaste Fort had for scientists who attempt to explain away everything and ignore the outliers. Perhaps Clarke sympathized with Fort's frustration—as he saw vast technological advancement take place in his lifetime, the concept of the possible expanding before his very eyes. This leads into the second law, which expresses a Fortean desire to push boundaries and explore the unknown, a task which Fort gallantly spearheaded at the start of the century. The possible Fortean influence in these laws is relevant to this exploration in that these laws have influenced numerous SF authors since their publication. Philip K. Dick ponders the third law in *VALIS*, as will be explored in the next chapter.

Whereas "The Failure of Imagination" can be viewed to a certain extent as an almost Fortean treatise, it is important to note that Clarke never lost faith in the abilities of the scientific community—he merely encouraged it to push what it perceived as boundaries. One of the reasons *2001* is lauded is because of its remarkable portrayal of space travel before it existed outright. Many of his non-fiction writings detailed earnest predictions, many of which turn out to be true. Selections in *Profiles of the Future* describe the necessary advancements for space travel, including attainment of greater speeds, a better understanding of gravity, etc., but his ultimate viewpoint (whether optimistic or pessimistic) mirrors a major theme of *Childhood's End*: "Man will never conquer space. [...] A truth which our forefathers knew, which we have forgotten—and which our descendants must learn again, in heartbreak and loneliness."[22] Much like *Childhood's End*, this statement is a somber proclamation. There is a streak of cosmic pessimism in Clarke's statement, quite reminiscent of a latter-day Wells, viewpoints confined by the technological age in which they were formed. But with this brand of cosmic pessimism, Fort might find himself in agreement albeit for different reasons. Clarke feels man will never conquer space because of the technological impossibilities of doing so. It is important to remember that Clarke disliked dubbing anything impossible. In this instance, the vastness and infinity of space renders it literally unconquerable no matter what technological advancements occur. The human race is more likely to die out before conquering even a fraction of outer space. Fort, however, would likely disagree with this sentiment because space is already conquered, conquered by those damned celestial bodies in the sky.

Clarke mentions Eric Frank Russell as an important component to his interest in Forteana, but Russell seemed to have a direct influence on Clarke as well: "I owe him many debts, for he was my first literary collaborator and my first source of income from writing. Some of his stories used ideas that I provided and he paid me promptly and generously."[23] It is nearly impossible to map specific texts where this exchange of ideas occurred, but even Russell's *Sinister Barrier* (said by one reviewer to be one of the few true examples where Fort's work was used effectively[24]) must be noted as a work similar to Clarke's. One wonders if the influence went both ways, given Clarke's stated indebtedness to Russell as well as the similarities between

5. Continuation of Cosmic Dread   103

the Fortean notion of humanity being "property"—a theme prevalent in both *Sinister Barrier* and *Childhood's End*. Russell's Vitons and Clarke's Overlords seem to overlap. Without spending too much time on speculation, such consistencies are worth noting, especially with the pulp SF community's constant internal dialogue. Clarke speaks often in his autobiography of how important Russell's "help and guidance" was to him as well as other SF authors of the period.[25] The Fortean presence, as usual, is understated but nevertheless seems to permeate the SF world with regularity.

Fort never claimed that the aerial vehicles contained extraterrestrial occupants (as they had been part and parcel of the Earth for eons), but his descriptions of their presence is always ominous. One is reminded of the particularly dark phrasing of the ships in the sky as being "vast black thing(s) poised like a crow over the moon." This phrasing is reminiscent of Clarke's own writing, not so much *Childhood's End* but the cosmic spectacle of *2001: A Space Odyssey*. In the final act of the novel, the content becomes Fortean; more mystical than science-based. In a novel which only calls for a modicum of suspension of disbelief in the first two sections, the final part treads strangely fantastical grounds, grounds most clearly relatable to Fortean phenomena and maybe-fiction in general. It is at this point in the novel that Clarke becomes more ambiguous about the events that occur and the implications of these events.[26] Distinct from *Childhood's End* in which extraterrestrials merely oversee the development of mankind into higher beings, *2001* features an unseen higher force directly propelling humanity into evolutionary jumps, utilizing the monoliths for this task from the dawn of man onwards. Forteana is featured prominently in *Childhood's End* albeit in a more referential sense (with the Ouija board and the Overlords' interest in occult writings as evidence of human learning, knowledge, and evolution). However, the Overlords themselves do not correlate as precisely to Forteana because of how straightforward their presence and purpose is. The correlation is clearer in *2001*—the beings are of a grander scale and align closely with later works of Forteana and maybe-fiction. In addition to the Fortean philosophy of an unseen force guiding humanity in its development, *2001* includes sections that resemble the paranormal phenomenon itself. This phenomenon is gestured at by Fort but explored more concretely by later Fortean researchers.

Vallee includes several instances of UFO witnesses and abductees being given various foodstuffs. These are strange encounters, to say the least, but the fact that there are recurring events is always a notable facet of Forteana. The most astounding instance is possibly the 1961 case of Joe Simonton of Eagle River, Wisconsin. Simonton was given three cakes by three UFO occupants who "had dark hair and skin and wore outfits with turtleneck tops and knit helmets." The case was taken quite seriously, investigated by an Air Force Major and key Project Blue Book employee, J. Allen Hynek. The story is largely a typical UFO encounter apart from the element of food being given to the witness. Their craft was a large, metallic saucer, "brighter than chrome." The ufonauts gave him both food and drink, the cakes being prepared on a "flameless grill of some sort" and the drink being water carried in a jug the same strange metal of the craft. Simonton claimed the cake "tasted like cardboard." The cake was examined by the Air Force who found that "the material was an ordinary pancake of terrestrial origin."[27] Again, the veracity of this story is unknowable, but the Air Force's interest seems to lend some credence to the event. Regardless, the report is a fascinating maybe-fiction vignette.

This ufological tale lines up neatly with a plot element of *2001: A Space Odyssey*. These supposed extraterrestrials seemed to have a grasp on how to make human food, but they did something clearly wrong, like one who observes a behavior and tries to imitate it even though it comes unnaturally. A similar phenomenon occurs after Bowman arrives in the "anonymous hotel suite" after his strange cosmic journey, a room that appears to be a carefully constructed replica of a human creation. After thinking that he might possibly be back on Earth, as unlikely as that seems to him, he gradually realizes that it is a construction by some unseen force:

> It bore, in the familiar type he had seen thousands of times, the name: Washington, D.C. Then he looked more closely; and for the first time, he had objective proof that, although all this might be real, he was not on Earth. He could read only the word *Washington*; the rest of the printing was a blur, as if it had been copied from a newspaper photograph. He opened the book at random and riffled through the pages. They were all blank sheets of crisp white material which was certainly not paper, though it looked very much like it.[28]

Bowman finds that the phone does not work but looks just like a normal phone. The furniture again looks normal, but the drawers are useless and do not open. As in the case explored by Vallee, the entities seem to understand human objects and needs in a superficial sense but fail to understand the inner workings in various ways.[29] Similarly, we have Bowman's encounter with food: "Bowman picked up a carton of a familiar breakfast cereal, thinking as he did so that it was odd to keep this frozen. The moment he lifted the package, he knew that it certainly did *not* contain cornflakes; it was much too heavy."[30] Bowman discovers that the package contains a strange blue substance with the consistency and texture of bread pudding. Each can and package is filled with this material and seems to be basic human nutrients compiled into one food item. The water from the faucet shocks Bowman because it is pure and distilled, tasting nothing like tap water. He concludes that "his unknown host were obviously taking no chances with his health." Bowman appears to be under observation, being either used or guided by an unseen intelligence with motivations unknown. Ignoring other implications of the abduction experience, Bowman's encounter resembles a classic alien

5. Continuation of Cosmic Dread   105

abduction. Before his transformation into a Star-Child, he is placed in this nondescript hotel suite which "his hosts had based [...] upon (terrestrial) TV programs."[31] They try to make him comfortable with this change of scenery, a markedly positive type of abduction experience. Once Bowman falls asleep, he undergoes what can only be described as a cosmic/mystic experience; he is being rapidly aged or evolved. An operation is taking place and it seems to be his hosts' doing. Even after he is transformed, the baby is guided along by yet another monolith, indicating that these hosts, whatever they may be, have had a hand in human development for "three million years." Again, this is a hallmark of the abduction experience, admission of alien intervention. Clarke's final section of *2001* is not completely analogous to an abduction experience, but it does bear many similarities.

It is unclear if Clarke read Vallee's work or other writers of alien encounters, but because of his interest in Fort and constant utilization of Fortean topics, it seems that Clarke had a working knowledge of the phenomenon at large. One hopes that Clarke would not lump in a respectable writer like Vallee with the aforementioned "rotting bilge" of the paranormal publishing world and, given his moderate approval of Fort it seems unlikely that he would. This knowledge works its way into Clarke's writing, leading to a fictional incident that closely resembles the supposedly factual incidents of maybe-fiction. The author prominently displays his scientific interest via consistent conveyance through both his fiction and non-fiction. His less scientific, more esoteric knowledge is on display in these works as well, albeit in a more understated fashion. This interest is always there, as hidden as it gets when Clarke's scientific interests are always pushed to the forefront, but even Clarke's non-fiction, separate from his television shows, has a paranormal component. Kripal mentions, "Clarke would also [...] sponsor three volumes of Fortean anomalies (meaning the TV shows) and write a number of critical essays on the subject of contactees and flying saucers."[32] One such essay in which Clarke boasts (or sometimes laments) such a deep knowledge is "More Last Words on UFOs," written in the 1990s and collected in *Greetings, Carbon-Based Bipeds!* Clarke, at this point a more-or-less total skeptic, comes across as crotchety in some regards as he reminisces about the UFO debate and postulates on why it has not yet been conclusively solved. "I would like to remind the UFO fanatics how earlier widely accepted stories of alien meetings turned out to be ludicrous fabrications," Clarke writes. "Does anyone remember George Adamski's *The Flying Saucers Have Landed*?[33] He reported cities on the other side of the moon, and I believe there was once a lady who made a good living by lecturing about her honeymoon on Venus."[34] He further decries that "one of the chief reasons that I have never been able to take reports of alien contact seriously is that no spaceship ever contains aliens—the occupants are always human!" Clarke says that "genuine extraterrestrials would really be alien—as different from us as the praying mantis, the giant squid, the blue whale."[35] Despite the skeptical intentions of the essay, Clarke, perhaps unwittingly, reveals that he is very well read when it comes to maybe-fiction. He knows the typical facets of alien encounters (particularly the contactees of the 1950s) that appear in these maybe-fiction texts and this is (perhaps inadvertently) revealed via the "Reception" chapter of *2001*, a section which bears several hallmarks of extraterrestrial encounter.

In 1973's *Rendezvous with Rama*, Clarke again displays an intermediary position between science and the unknown early into the narrative. The astronomer Stenton reminisces about H.G. Wells' "The Star" and how Rama could cause a similar apocalypse on Earth:

> He would never forget the images of hurricanes and tidal waves, of cities sliding into the sea, as that other visitor from the stars smashed into Jupiter and then fell sunward past the Earth. True, the star that old Wells described was not cold but incandescent, and wrought much of its destruction by heat. That scarcely mattered; even if Rama was a cold body, reflecting only the light of the Sun, it could kill by gravity as easy as fire.[36]

Clarke's outlook often resembles the cosmic pessimism of Wells himself in this passage and "The Star" is one of Wells' most clearly cosmically pessimistic. The story ponders an Earth ravaged by the cruel game of chance of the universe, swallowed by a rogue sun. The images presented are not entirely different from the eventual fate of the Earth when our sun's time runs out, destroying the planet and extinguishing all life. But Clarke's novel does not solely convey this cosmic pessimism, it again shows hints of a Fortean mindset. Only a page later, Clarke decries the fact that "even by the twenty-second century, no way had yet been discovered of keeping elderly and conservative scientists from occupying crucial administrative positions." He writes of a distinguished astrophysicist whose rationality is sometimes at odds with the reality of the universe:

> Professor Davidson was not much interested in objects smaller than galaxies and never bothered to conceal his prejudices. And though he had to admit that ninety percent of science was now based upon observations from space-bourne instruments, he was not at all happy about it. No fewer than three times during his career, satellites had been launched to prove one of his pet theories and done precisely the opposite.[37]

Again, we see the balance Clarke strikes between promoting the use of science and being at odds with hyper-rationality. This passage echoes his first law which certainly has relevance to Fortean thought. While Clarke illustrates his knowledge of astronomy, he is quite critical of the more Wellsian idea that humans know everything there is to know. He may share some traits of cosmic pessimism, but he also shows some traits of Fort's philosophy while not falling too deeply into it. Clarke is, in a sense, a quite open-minded rationalist.

5. Continuation of Cosmic Dread

Rendezvous with Rama also expands upon themes explored in both *Childhood's End* and *2001: A Space Odyssey*. The more religious member of the *Endeavor* expedition hypothesizes on the possible purpose of Rama in highly Fortean terms. Boris Rodrigo is a member of the Fifth Church of Christ, Cosmonaut, which holds the belief that Jesus Christ was an alien from outer space. Commander Norton notes that Rodrigo's religious beliefs make him a better team member even though he might find him a little eccentric. Especially on the Rama mission, the "Cosmo Christers" believe that it may be a visitation from Christ himself. Rodrigo offers up one explanation to Norton: "I believe that Rama is a cosmic Ark, sent here to save—those who are worthy of salvation."[38] Norton has to admit this is plausible, as he feels that "stripped of its religious overtones, Rodrigo's theory was at least as convincing as half a dozen others he had heard."[39] Like numerous other works of Fortean SF, such as Heinlein's "Goldfish Bowl" or Herbert's "Rat Race," this theory postulates humanity as a sort of useful possession of another species. Others hop aboard the hypothesis that Rama is intending to use or harm humanity's assets which now span across several planets and satellites in the solar system. The president of Mercury nearly succeeds in launching a nuclear missile at Rama for fears of this sort: "It is foolish to pretend that these creatures *must* be benevolent and will not interfere with us in any way. If they come to our solar system, they need something from it."[40] The Hermian president presents the analogy that Ramans are akin to an advanced termite colony:

> Like Rama, its functioning depends upon a whole series of specialized biological machines: workers, builders, farmers—*warriors*. [...] What degree of co-operation or understanding would ever be possible between human beings and termites? When there is no conflict of interest, we tolerate each other. But when either needs the other's territory or resources no quarter is given. Thanks to our technology and our intelligence, we can always win if we are sufficiently determined. But sometimes it is not easy, and there are those who believe that final victory may go to the termites.[41]

Again, Clarke presents a mixture of both cosmic pessimism and the Fortean notion that humanity's assets are somehow useful to a higher intelligence—a notion more aligned with cosmic dread.

In the end, Rama seems wholly uninterested in Earth, simply using the sun as a refueling station for its continual journey. This is not without Fortean implications; much of Forteana considers the indifference of other forces upon the Earth. But Clarke's conclusion most closely resembles Wells' cosmic pessimism: "They would probably never even know that the human race existed. Such monumental indifference was worse than any deliberate insult."[42] This again highlights the balancing act Clarke often performs between Fortean and Wellsian interests, they do not always have to exist in eternal opposition to one another. Just because the universe is indifferent to humanity does not preclude the proposition that some higher intelligence effects humanity, perhaps unknowingly. Fortean phenomena can exist in forces indifferent to humanity as well as those who want to toy with it. There are still Fortean overtones in the Ramans utilizing the sun's energy: While the sun is not in the true possession of humans, it has in many ways been regarded as *our* star. To have another intelligent species utilize it without acknowledging humanity's existence is still a blow to humanity's perceived standing in the universe.

Some of Clarke's short stories also contain this hybridization of hard science and Forteana. The 1953 short story, "The Possessed," (originally published in *Dynamic Science Fiction*) bears the hallmarks of this tendency. A "swarm" of alien parasites traverses the galaxy looking for lifeforms to inhabit, but as their desperation for a host grows, they settle for a primitive form of life on Earth. They hope to push it, as seen in other Clarke stories, towards evolution into an intelligent species. Sadly, they chose lemmings, a species that is popularly believed to commit mass suicide. In "The Possessed," it is revealed that the creatures jump off cliffs as part of the parasitic species' lingering need to be rejoined with the other members of the species who lived on a dying planet. This is not altogether dissimilar from the explanation for lemmings jumping off cliffs which involves migratory instincts rather than intentional suicide. The story is a hybrid of scientific and Fortean thought because of its emphasis on evolutionary science while still being used as a method of explaining Fortean phenomena through fiction. The behavior of lemmings was not entirely understood at the time of publication, as the characters note. One remarks that "no one knows" why the lemmings jump off cliffs, "it's just one of those mysteries."[43] Clarke illustrates a utilization of these mysteries, in line with John W. Campbell's promotion of the unexplained as an SF sourcebook, while still maintaining his scientific standards, opting to use his scientific understanding to create a fantastic tale.

Another short story that reflects this inner turmoil between science and the unexplained is Clarke's 1961 tale, "Dog Star," originally published in *Galaxy*. A moon base employee receives a premonition from his dead dog, Laika, which results in averting total disaster via earthquake. The observatory worker considers both the scientific reasons for this premonition to have occurred:

> It is hardly necessary for me to say that I do not believe in the supernatural; everything that happened has a perfectly rational explanation. The human mind has strange and labyrinth ways of going about its business; it knew the signal that would most swiftly rouse me to the knowledge of danger. [...] There is no mystery about it, no miraculous warning across the gulf that neither man nor dog can ever bridge. Yet sometimes, I wake now, in the silence of the Moon, and wish that the dream could have lasted a few seconds longer.[44]

The scientist is shaken by this experience, seeming to try very hard to rationalize how such an improbable event could have occurred. He notes the fact that Laika saved him from a San Francisco earthquake when she was physically with him and this is a conceivable reason why his brain chose Laika to wake him up during the lunar quake. His attempts to assure himself that nothing supernatural occurred is frantic, implying that he is not entirely certain of his rational explanations.

Put simply, Clarke is a markedly scientific minded SF writer, a self-described skeptic, who sometimes branches into Fortean thought. Likewise, his opinion of Fort is not entirely one of reverence:

> Despite his avowed skepticism, he continually promotes the theory—totally absurd in the 1930s or even in the 1830s—that the stars and planets are really quite close, and the earth is surrounded by some kind of shell from which material occasionally falls. If Fort had lived to see men walk on the moon (well, he would have been only 95...) he would have had to eat a good many of his sarcastic words about astronomy. Skepticism is one thing; stupidity is another. But then, everyone is stupid about *something*.[45]

Nevertheless, Clarke displays both an interest in and a utilization of Fortean topics throughout his works in both literature and electronic media. What is one to make of this apparent contradiction? Perhaps Clarke is a prominent example of the consistent internal war regarding the veracity of paranormal claims and the skepticism of the scientific community (which sometimes branches into cynicism when distinguished but elderly scientists are involved). He then is very much like your humble author, highly doubtful of many of the claims, but because of the outright enjoyment which many of these maybe-fiction texts produce, a peculiar sort of faith lingers. The stories do not have to be true, but they leave lasting impressions on their readers. This is not unlike the paradigm shift that reading a work like *Childhood's End* could stir; a fiction altering the real world, creating a renewed and more paranormal form of reality. No, the stories do not have to be true. But their implications always seem to have some resonance with reality. It was not full-blown reverence, but it would be untrue to say that Clarke did not hold the Forteans in high regard at times. Kripal quotes Clarke's *The Fountain of Paradise* in an epigraph: "A dear friend, a great scientist, now dead, used to tease me by saying that because politics is the art of the possible, it appeals only to second rate minds. The *first*-raters, he claimed were only interested in the *impossible*."[46] Clarke also features a section in *Astounding Days* where he does some Fortean cataloguing of his own, perhaps the most fitting way to illustrate his connection to Fort with finality: "A letter to the editor from Richard McKim of Oundle, Peterborough reports a 'mysterious incident involving a Canada goose. The farmer reported that he had seen a flash from the sky; the goose had been struck in flight and fallen in a nearby river.' The goose—which had a hole clean through it—was put in deep-freeze and later examined by a professor of veterinary medicine, who had decided from the state of the unlucky bird's heart that it had been killed by an electric shock." There is no satisfactory explanation given for this event, scientists claiming at once that a meteorite was responsible or "some unusual form of atmospheric electricity." Clarke notes that the scientists' ultimate "confession of ignorance […] would have provoked a scornful comment from Fort."[47] Clarke illustrates that even skeptical, scientifically-minded authors can possess such a cynicism regarding these accounts, but still enjoy the stories behind Fortean phenomena. Clearly, the impossible is interesting—the only necessary justification for the enjoyment or utilization of maybe-fiction.

6

Forteana and Religious Experience

A Fortean Analysis of Philip K. Dick

> *I have now finally read Arthur C. Clarke's* Childhood's End. *What I wanted to do was find out if any details resembled details of my 3-74 et al. experience. Generally, no. All I can say is that his story is compatible with my experience; I mean, if my experience were so, his book could grow out of it; or, if his book were true my experience could grow out of it.*
> —Philip K. Dick[1]

Religious scholar Jeffrey J. Kripal lists both Philip K. Dick and Arthur C. Clarke among authors who write "explicitly about their spiritualist, psychical, paranormal, and occult interests and experiences." He further says that "such occult experiences were hardly tangential to such authors. They were integral components of the creative process."[2] Kripal also points out that these interests permeate SF and even literature at large, as will be explored later. As we have learned, there is scarcely a modern-day occult/paranormal conversation that is disconnected from Fortean thought. He firmly planted himself as the unshakably permanent influence on any maybe-fictional, anomalous, or, often, esoteric reference that appeared after his books. However, whereas Clarke is a perfect example of an SF writer directly interested and in conversation with Fort's writings and subject, Philip K. Dick's Fortean influence came not only from Fort directly but also from experiencing Fortean phenomenon firsthand. It was Dick's personal paranormal experience which made him develop a philosophy remarkably like Fort's. It is with Dick that, again, SF seems infected by a religious bent, recalling the days of Fort's emergence when science's insufficiencies were brought to the forefront. Dick's work oftentimes is more invested in the fantastical or religious than it is hard science, differentiating him from both the strict evolutionary science of Wells and the more balanced approach of Clarke. Dick's writing in the novel *VALIS* is more like a confessional of someone grappling with their own sanity than it does an SF novel. However, because of the presence of a choice few SF elements in the work, it can retain this label.

Dick's awareness of Fort is not well-documented, but Fort is mentioned in the 1953 short story "The Indefatigable Frog," a piece whose very title suggests a semblance of a connection with Fort given his penchant for falling frogs. Though the plot is largely about scientists comically arguing about Zeno's Paradox,[3] a character refers to the situation of a frog hopping into the room as having "shades of Charles Fort."[4] The story itself is not particularly Fortean, but Dick's illustration of a partial knowledge of Fort is relevant to this exploration. Even so, Dick would not necessarily have to know about Fort to write Fortean fiction, especially given his history of experiencing the paranormal firsthand. Dick is often listed as an author who was a fan of Fort, but little accessible documentation of such a claim exists. His former wife, Tessa B. Dick, confirms that PKD both "read and admired Fort's work." Beyond this, he seems to have read about Fort himself:

> Phil used to talk about all the strange events that Fort wrote about. [...] Frogs falling from the sky comes to mind. [...] Phil said that Fort had a box full of newspaper clippings about strange events, but one day he threw it out. He realized that he did not have a plan, was not organized, so he had to start over. So Phil must have read about Fort, in addition to reading Fort's work.[5]

The brief mention of Fort in Dick's short story as well as the revelation that Dick read Fort's work *and* background material on Fort himself serves as a fitting beginning to a deeper analysis of Dick's work for possible Fortean influence or, at the very least, an overlap in Fortean philosophy.

PKD corresponded with Fortean author Brad Steiger shortly after the publication of Steiger's book, *Gods of Aquarius*, finding connections between the text and his paranormal experience. It seemed that Dick resonated with Steiger's "Star People" hypothesis, or "individuals who feel that they bear within their genes awareness acquired by extraterrestrial interaction with humans in prehistoric or ancient times and who have now been activated by DNA memory to fulfill a mission in assisting others in their spiritual and evolutionary advancement." Steiger wrote of the correspondence at length in a 2007 *Alternate Perceptions* magazine article:

> Sometime after the book's publication, I received a letter from Philip K. Dick, who told me that he suspected that he was such an individual as those whom I had profiled in the book. He had first realized this in 1974 when his own "DNA memory packet" began to fire within his psyche.
>
> At that time, he told me, he was shown in a vision, "more properly, an inner hologram," the cover of my book, *Revelation: The Divine Fire* (Prentice-Hall, 1973). A feminine voice told him that this book would help him to understand what was occurring to him. He was also told by the voice to get in touch with me.

6. Forteana and Religious Experience

Although Dick said that he did read the book and that he did receive the requisite information and comfort that he was promised during the vision, he was reluctant to contact me until he read of my research with those individuals whom I had given the name of Star People. Dick said that he was about to publish a novel (*VALIS,* 1981) that would advance numerous similar concepts.

"I wish to hide behind the veil of fiction," he wrote. "I can claim that I made the whole thing up. The revelations that I received were so astounding that it has taken me five years to arrive at a place where I will even put forth the concept as fiction."[6]

Even though it has proven difficult to find copies of the alleged correspondences between the International Fortean Organization and Philip K. Dick, his interaction with Steiger, a regular Fortean himself, makes this claim viable.[7] This is especially pertinent in relating his "experience" to Forteana, as he sought answers from the Fortean community and even admitted to having to write of his experience under the guise of fiction, not unlike the claims seen before in various maybe-fiction texts (e.g., Shaver). Dick was an enormous fan of the very pulps that influenced Clarke and others. He had a "precious pulp collection, which included complete runs of *Unknown, Unknown Worlds,* and *Astounding* (*Stories*) back to 1933."[8] Dick is another writer exemplar of the Futurian phenomenon of SF writers being avid pulp readers in their formative years. It also shows that he had complete collections of *Astounding Stories,* which would have included the reprinting of Fort's *Lo!,* and *Unknown,* which would have contained Eric Frank Russell's *Sinister Barrier.* Dick writes in his *Exegesis*:

> We are as in an ocean to them, and we are like lower life forms whom they are trying to contact. But they are very different from us. Thus although they are ETIs they are not from another planet, star system, etc., but are right here (except in a 5-D world; they can see us but we can't see them).[9]

Kripal notes that "Dick is voicing a common theme in paranormal literature," a theme of another intelligence altering our world as it appeared in Palmer's SF pulps, which was "in turn [...] deeply influenced by (Charles Fort)." PKD's passage is an extension of Fortean thought, although more reminiscent of later Forteans such as Keel who "have since identified the [...] mysteries as extradimensional as opposed to extraterrestrial."[10]

Dick's reading of Fort may have influenced his worldview more than Dick himself knew. If the possible correspondences with INFO, the actual correspondence with Brad Steiger, and the various facets of Dick's experience are considered, it is clear that Dick was a bit of a Fortean thinker. He would outline theories reminiscent of both a computer-simulated reality and a latter-day version of Fort's own ponderings on whether humanity was akin to cattle for some higher force. Even more like Dick is a later Fortean, John Keel, who was also a prominent member of INFO. Keel says of humanity:

> We are biochemical robots helplessly controlled by forces that can scramble our brains, destroy our memories and use us in any way they see fit. They have been doing it to us forever. We are caught up in a poker game being played with marked cards. Yet, in the closing years of this century, we are like the inveterate gambler who, when informed that the game is crooked, shrugs and says, "I know.... But it's the only game in town!"[11]

Later, he would go on to declare that "Earth will be a free lunch counter for a long time to come."[12] Keel is notably pessimistic about the higher forces at play but also tackles the proposition with a sense of humor, much as Dick seemed to. To write like a Fortean and to think like a Fortean, as Dick certainly does, is to be a Fortean. Background into Dick's knowledge of Fort and related topics is simply historical context which is not necessarily required to analyze his work for Fortean inclinations. It could just be that, as others have suggested, there is hardly an original SF plot that was not first established by Fort's research. Dick's *VALIS* does at many points read like a technologically updated rendition of Fort's theories. However, for many SF authors, the connection to Fort was much closer and these plots and concepts do not just appear by chance. Dick was aware of Fortean research and the fact that he sought Brad Steiger's help after his experience lends some credence to the fact that *VALIS*'s Fortean relation is not mere happenstance.

Like the previous chapter on Clarke, this exploration hopes to look beyond the more commonplace themes in Dick's writing—which often tend to be political—and examine Dick as a writer more heavily influenced by the thinking of maybe-fiction and Forteana. Dick's reputation in mainstream culture does little to acknowledge the inherent esotericism of Dick's work and persona. As his career progressed, his works became more invested in drug addiction and philosophical questions than simple SF storylines. Works like *A Scanner Darkly* (1977) and *VALIS* (1981), for instance, find a basis in semi-autobiographical content stemming from both his drug addiction and subsequent paranormal/mystical experiences that may or may not have been linked to his drug usage. Dick said that drugs did not directly influence his writings, simply the culture surrounding them.[13] While it would be easy to categorize works like *VALIS* as drug-induced ramblings, Dick insisted that his fiction was inspired by actual external intelligences influencing his life. To say that his writing is nothing more than a drug-addled brain's attempt at making sense of hallucinations does not give enough credit to how real the experiences were for Dick. An addict (as Dick admits he was, completely dependent on amphetamines following his divorce) sometimes does not know how to distinguish reality from hallucination, but Dick insists he never took hard drugs.[14] Even if his VALIS experience was a hallucination, its effects are more far-reaching and all-consuming. While this book in no way condones

6. Forteana and Religious Experience

the use of psychoactive drugs, hallucinogens have been used for centuries in order to produce mystical-type experiences. Many will have a knee-jerk reaction to Dick's drug usage and condemn *VALIS* and similar works unfairly, but such usage in no way discredits his experience.

Dick has mentioned what interests him most and invariably creeps into his fiction: "What is reality?" and "What constitutes the authentic human being?"[15] This exploration is clearly more interested in the former, which bears the most resemblance to Fortean thinking. This prior quote comes from an undelivered speech Dick had written in 1978 which is closely connected to the same mindset that produced *VALIS* but is largely more accessible. In it, he discusses the first story he published which follows a dog that sees the garbage men taking food from the family (a full garbage bin) and concludes that eventually the garbage men will eat the family. Dick follows this observation by pondering the nature of reality:

> Of course, the dog is wrong about this. We all know that garbagemen do not eat people. But the dog's extrapolation was in a sense logical—given the facts at his disposal. [...] And that led me to wonder, if reality differs from person to person, can we speak of reality singular, or shouldn't we really be talking about plural realities? And if there are plural realities, are some more true (more real) than others? What about the world of a schizophrenic? Maybe, it's as real as our world. Maybe we cannot say that we are in touch with reality and he is not, but should instead say, his reality is so different from ours that he can't explain his to us, and we can't explain ours to him. The problem, then, is that if subjective worlds are experienced too differently, there occurs a breakdown of communication ... and there is the real illness.[16]

Andrew May notes the connection of Dick's work to Gnosticism: "Some of Dick's fictional works dramatize the Gnostic idea of a 'fake universe' by positing a sub-universe that is even more fake. For example, the novels *Eye in the Sky* (1957) and *A Maze of Death* (1970) both portray a group of characters thrust into a counterfeit, mentally projected reality."[17] This gnostic thinking certainly plays into *VALIS* where it seems Dick wonders if he is creating his own false reality or piercing the veil to see the universe as it really is. The question of what reality is plagued Dick throughout his life, so it should come as no surprise that once he experienced mystical visions, the reality question haunted him even more.

"There is a streak of the irrational in the universe," wrote Dick. "We, the hopeful trusting Rhipidon Society,[18] may have been drawn into it, to perish."[19] Like Fort, Dick also agreed that there seemed to be an irrationality to the world. Unlike Fort, Dick sought to explain it through what he considered a variety of religious experiences and theological ponderings. Dick wrote his highly philosophical and practically feverishly delusional work, *VALIS*, in 1981. As referenced in the text, just seven years earlier, he experienced the same religious experiences as the book's protagonist, Horselover Fat. In many respects, *VALIS* implies that Dick is conveying his own experiences through the text as a means through which to process them more lucidly: "I am Horselover Fat, and I am writing this in the third person to gain much-needed objectivity."[20] As explained later, "'Philip' means 'Horselover' in Greek, lover of horses. 'Fat' is the German translation of 'Dick.'"[21] Horselover Fat serves as a fractured alternate persona of Dick with delusions of a God (named Zebra in the text) speaking to him. This is not far from what Dick perceived as reality. "In his own precise terms," Kripal says, "Dick was 'resynthesized' or 'reprogrammed' by a pink beam emanating from a vast super consciousness that he called VALIS an acronym for vast active living intelligence system."[22] Dick's *Exegesis* documents his internal struggle as he came to terms with his experience and the implications of it. Sections of *The Exegesis* appear verbatim in *VALIS* through Horselover Fat's struggle, a proxy for Dick to discuss it in the semi-fictional work. The experience is well summed up by Kripal:

> On February 20, 1974, the doorbell rang at Dick's apartment in Fullerton, California. The author was feeling a bit woozy from some sodium pentathol he had been given at the dentist's office for an oral surgery to remove two impacted wisdom teeth. A young woman was at the door. She was delivering a packet of Darvon for the pain. Dick was struck by her dark hair, her eyes, and her beauty. He was also attracted to her gold necklace, which featured the fish sign used by the early Christians as a symbol for Christ. This golden symbol [...] somehow triggered a two month series of remarkable experiences in the author, including various memories of past lives.[23]

The depth of Dick's pondering on what was happening to him is intensive. His *Exegesis* is nearly 1,000 pages long and even the condensed form of it in *VALIS* illustrates that he grappled heavily with the question of what to make of his experience—he struggled constantly over just *what* was behind the visions he was receiving. He considered the possibility that it was "his beloved dead sister Jane speaking to him from beyond the grave through the right hemisphere of his brain" or even "the possibility that he had encountered the living God, Christ, the Logos, or Jung's collective unconscious."[24] The main point of Dick's endless self-investigation was "the beam of pink light fired at (his) head" which he "believed deep down underneath, not God but technology, and technology from the future at that."[25] A similar experience occurred to Robert Anton Wilson which will be examined later, but others have noted the similarity to Richard Shaver. An acquaintance of Shaver, Tal Levesque, said that he "think(s) that Shaver was a normal guy that had data downloaded into his brain."[26] This data download is not uncommon amongst paranormal and religious experiences and highly resembles some SF plots; William Gibson's "Johnny Mnemonic," for instance. Even the religious scholar, Kripal, had a similar experience in Calcutta in 1989. Finding himself "paralyzed, like a corpse, more or less exactly like the Hindu god Shiva as he is traditionally portrayed in Tantric art." Kripal says that his brain "felt as if it had suddenly hooked up to some sort of occult Internet and that billions of bits of information were being downloaded into its neural net."[27] Clearly, Dick was not alone in some aspects of his religious experience and *VALIS* relates closely to that experience. The work is rendered comparable to a maybe-fiction text, teetering into non-fiction at points. The experience forever altered his life, and like many maybe-fiction texts, the conventional reality of the event means very little as it *was* real to Dick. As in maybe-fiction, the implications are the same regardless of whether or not the experience is definable in traditionally "real" terms. As Kripal says, "*VALIS* was no mere literary conceit for Dick. Nor was the pink light. Both were autobiographical facts of immense power and immeasurable, really infinite significance."[28] Much of the narrative of *VALIS* can be tracked directly to *The Exegesis* with only a choice few plot points being added, but even these additions seem to have the purpose of furthering Dick's analysis of the experience.

Advancing from the earlier Gnostic thinking which both Kripal and May point out, Dick seems to sympathize with Fort mostly with regards to his monistic tendencies even though he never addresses Fort directly. While the experience is indeed religious in nature, it expands the notion of Gnosticism and moves towards a more paranormal or Fortean philosophy—one not all that different from Clarke's higher intelligences guiding human progress or Fort's notion that humans are the property of some higher force. What is different about *VALIS*, it must be reiterated, is that this narrative was *real* to Dick. May, for instance, compares Dick to Richard Sharpe Shaver as writers who dealt with fabrication. His assertion that Shaver "never questioned his own view of reality, while Dick did so to the point of obsession"[29] is a fair comparison, quite accurate in the case of *VALIS*. Dick is certainly no Shaver, who took every voice in his head as reality. Dick is obsessive and questions his sanity because of the experience; he even ponders whether reality itself is a possible construct which is standard Dick fare. What Dick seems certain of is the reality of the experience itself. He questions certain aspects of it and obsesses over its meaning, but the event always definitely occurred to him. Dick pushes SF into an even tighter relationship with maybe-fiction. In the case of *VALIS*, it is hard to say whether it is one or the other.

Parallels between Dick's *Exegesis*/*VALIS* and the works of Fort are common. "Someone is playing a board game with time, someone we can't see," Dick writes.[30] Similar to Fort's theories regarding humanity, the idea that "we are property" again comes to the forefront, especially in the sense that the higher intelligence in Dick's work is seen as controlling the course of humanity, more along the lines of a God figure. The twist, in contrast to most traditional religion, is that Dick feels that this higher intelligence is possibly insane: "If the whole universe were irrational, because it was directed by an irrational—that is to say, insane—mind, whole species could come into existence, live and perish and never guess."[31] Of course, Dick (or Fat) also believes that there is yet another higher intelligence beyond the irrational mind controlling our universe. His belief seems to resemble some of Fort's thinking. Again, the short story "A Radical Corpuscle" seems to be prophetic proto–SF.

Dick even ponders Clarke's first law in *VALIS* when he is wondering if the more magical visions he is seeing are some form of advanced technology.[32] Of course, VALIS *is* an advanced technology to Dick, technology that some maybe-fiction might argue exists. As indicated by the epigraph of this chapter, Dick saw some overlap in his encounter with the fiction presented in *Childhood's End*. *VALIS* indicates such an overlap as well: "I did not think that I should tell Fat that I thought his encounter with God was in fact an encounter with himself from the far future. Himself so evolved, so changed, that he became no longer a human being."[33] Dick illustrates how SF can be influenced by the paranormal and vice versa as Dick's conclusion about Fat's encounter resembles a mashup between concepts found in both *2001: A Space Odyssey* (some from the book and some from the film) and *Childhood's End*. These are general SF tropes yet to Dick they were a reality.

Specific passages of *VALIS*, in the end, seem to matter less to its Fortean analysis than the strange conditions under which the book was written. It is more closely related to a book like Whitley Strieber's *Communion*[34] wherein the author conveys a paranormal or supernatural experience they had as the truth, rather than a typical SF book as would be written by Arthur C. Clarke. Unlike Strieber, however, *VALIS* is a maybe-fiction while also being an SF novel, a peculiar combination but one that exemplifies the tight relationship between SF and Fortean material. It is undoubtedly a spectrum, worthy of a chart of some sort, where one could plot where SF is at its most science-fictional and maybe-fiction at its most maybe-fictional. But once one of the two categories veers close to the center of this hypothetical chart, one category starts to influence the other. At the very center might be a work like *VALIS* which is both at the same time.

Readers might have mistaken Dick's masking of a personal experience in a book marketed as fiction as an indication that the book truly was fiction. However, the author was quite vocal about this experience, beyond just his friends. Dick let the world know this in a speech given at an SF conference at Metz, France:

> One thing I really want you to know: I am aware that the claims I am making—claims of having retrieved buried memories of an alternate present and to have perceived the agency responsible for arranging that alteration—these claims can neither be proved nor can they even be made to sound rational in the usual sense of the word. It has taken me over three years to reach the point where I am willing to tell anyone but my closest friends about my experience beginning back at the vernal equinox of 1974.[35]

6. Forteana and Religious Experience

It is important to note how carefully Dick makes these claims. For an intelligent thinker and popular author like Dick, claims such as these can ruin a career. For this exploration, the above passage is not proof that Dick was too "crazy" to care about the implications—fully schizophrenic and now without filter. Quite the contrary. This paranormal event that he experienced was real enough and important enough to him that he needed to tell the public. Anyone who is about to tell a friend, a loved one, or even a professional about a strange experience they had will preface their statement much in the way that Dick did in this speech. Perhaps one day the paranormal will be taken with less reproach and accepted as just a facet of the irrational reality which Dick saw and attempted to explain.

7

A Hard-Headed, Commonsensical Fortean
A Fortean Analysis of Robert A. Heinlein

> *One man's "magic" is another man's engineering. "Supernatural" is a null word.*
> —Robert A. Heinlein[1]

Much has been written about the work of SF maverick Robert A. Heinlein, a figure who has been greatly lauded for his work and simultaneously criticized for the militarism that appears in certain texts. Among these is the popular novel *Starship Troopers*, a book which still appears on U.S. military reading lists. A *Popular Mechanics* article even suggests that the novel has become the modern military's version of Sun Tzu's *Art of War*.[2] Even though his other most famous work, *Stranger in a Strange Land*, tackled free love and utopianism as opposed to militarism, these themes still have little to do with the Fortean SF pertinent to this book. However, while Heinlein's work may not have much concern with Forteana upon first glance, he was supposedly one of the most active practicing Forteans. Heinlein was purportedly a member of INFO (International Fortean Organization) from 1965 to his death in 1988, although verification of his membership has been conflicting. According to rumor, his membership checks were displayed on the walls of the INFO offices. Dr. Stephen Webb finds this fact "strange given the hard-headed common sense possessed by many of Heinlein's characters."[3] This is a fair observation; the bulk of Heinlein's work is certainly not preoccupied with Fortean topics, most of the time the works deal with present-day social issues through the lens of an SF story. When compared with the previous works discussed, a novel like *Starship Troopers* seems as far away from Fortean SF as one can get, a primary source when examining the militaristic bent of SF. However, with the Cold War era, the paranoia that permeated every nook and cranny of America also found its way into Heinlein's stories, often resulting in tales

7. A Hard-Headed, Commonsensical Fortean   121

which could be considered as containing Fortean paranoia in addition to Cold War paranoia. It is indeed strange that one of the writers most visibly active in a Fortean organization shows the least amount of influence in his stories. However, this chapter intends to examine many Heinlein works where this influence, whether conscious or not, is prominent.

While expressing his disappointment that Heinlein was a Fortean, Webb admits that "some of Heinlein's best early short stories were Fortean in tone."[4] Among these, Webb examines "They," a story featuring a man who believes he is one of the few real people left on Earth. In true Fortean fashion, the delusion extends to believing that some grand manipulator has created the universe. Webb notes the question that this story raises: "The universe could be there in order to fool us—and if it is, how could we know?"[5] This story illustrates clear Fortean philosophy from Heinlein—that humans are some kind of property of another entity. As many Fortean SF stories go, this entity has possibly created our universe as a form of fiction, an idea that is explored later on in Heinlein's World as Myth stories. Webb also briefly examines Heinlein's 1942 short story "The Unpleasant Profession of Jonathan Hoeg" which again deals with the fictional nature of reality. The story begins as an offbeat detective thriller following a man who does not remember his profession before the plot devolves quickly into an almost meta-fictional commentary. The man finds his profession to be an art critic of Earth—an art project created by some unseen force. As Webb notes, the parallels to "They" are noticeable, both stories question reality as a possible creation of some higher intelligence, very much in line with Fort's work. The common trend of Fortean SF early on is the concept of Earth being utilized by another force for some unwitting purpose. This is seen in these Heinlein stories as well as those of Eric Frank Russell and Edmond Hamilton. But other Heinlein short stories also contain Fortean conceits and these will be explored here: "Goldfish Bowl," "Year of the Jackpot," and "Project Nightmare."

Heinlein first started publishing in *Astounding Science Fiction*, edited by John W. Campbell, a familiar name in Fortean SF. They corresponded regularly and like Eric Frank Russell, Heinlein was "another of Campbell's favorites." However, it would be dangerous to overstate Campbell's influence on Heinlein. According to his wife, Virginia, in the posthumous publication of his letters, *Grumbles from the Grave*, Heinlein "did not admire (Campbell's) writing style and objected strenuously to the various changes JWC made in his stories." Virginia Heinlein adds, however, that "Robert learned much about the art of writing from John."[6] There is also the fact that Campbell did not immediately accept one of Heinlein's most blatantly Fortean stories, "Goldfish Bowl." This short story's very title is based on a Fortean notion, according to Heinlein biographer William H. Patterson, Jr., of "picturing aliens so far above us intellectually that they might not even interact with human beings—any more than we interact with goldfish in a bowl." Campbell's initial rejection letter expressed that the story "lacks point" and "simply has no punch."[7] Heinlein did not want the title of the story to be "Goldfish Bowl" because he felt that it would give away the gist of the story, but it was eventually accepted by Campbell and published in the March 1942 issue of *Astounding* under this title. It follows a military science team investigating a massive pillar of water in the ocean, showcasing Heinlein's experience serving in the Navy. The story includes not only a Fortean notion of being tiny specks to greater, vastly more intelligent organisms but also includes a weather phenomenon that Fort was particularly fond of cataloguing, waterspouts or pillars of water, which appear in the beginning and are the illustration on the story's first page.[8] Fort covers this phenomenon and others like it in *Lo!*, for instance, this report of Australian weirdness: "Not rain, but columns of water fell near the town of Avoca, Victoria, and, in the *Melbourne Argus*, the way of accounting for them was to say 'a waterspout' had burst here. There were wide floods in Tasmania. Fields turned to blanks that were then lumpy with rabbits."[9] Though these reports could be explained away by known weather phenomenon, Fort is consistent in focusing on the strange nature of their occurrence. Fort notes the strange weather patterns he followed from May 1889 reports which involved weird objects falling from the sky or columns of water pummeling the earth following droughts:

> Deluge and falls of lumps of ice, throughout England. France deluged. Water dropped from the sky, at Lausanne, Switzerland, flooding some of the streets five feet deep. It was not rain. There were falling columns of water from what was thought to be a waterspout. The most striking of the statements is that bulks dropped. One of them was watched. Or some kind of vast, vaporous cow sailed over a town, and people look up at her bag of water. Something that was described as "a large body of water" was seen at Coburg, Ontario. It crossed the town, holding its bag-like formation.[10]

While the Fortean reports clearly describe an occurrence stranger than a waterspout, the go-to explanation is almost always a waterspout. In fact, Fort notes that many of the strange falls, be it of animals, rocks, blood, etc., are often explained away by waterspouts picking them up and flinging them long distances. In "Goldfish Bowl," the events are so Fortean it is possible that the waterspout in the beginning is a reference to Fort. The possibility is compounded by the fact that beyond the waterspout, the story results in humans being made captive like goldfish by higher intelligences who exhibit slight misunderstandings of human behavior akin to Clarke's *2001*.

Other hints of Fortean philosophy are found throughout the story. While still speculating on the nature of the pillars, a phenomenon called the LaGrange fireballs come up in conversation. One of the two scientists of the story, Graves, is revealed as having the Fortean notion that "all the odd phenomena turned up in the past few years can be hooked together into one smooth theory with a single, sinister cause."¹¹ He expands on this theory further:

> I see in these several phenomena, the Pillars, the giant fireballs, a number of other assorted phenomena which should never have happened, but did—including the curious case of a small mountain peak south of Boulder, Colorado, which had its tip leveled off "spontaneously"—I see in these things evidence of intelligent direction, a single conscious cause. [...] Call it the "X" factor. I'm looking for X.¹²

One will note the obvious Fortean nature of the phenomena described. The phenomena, and the Colorado incident specifically, could have been plucked directly from Fort's books. Likewise, calling the force behind the phenomena the "X factor" is reminiscent of Fort's original title for *The Book of the Damned* which was going to be X followed by its sequel Y. Graves' postulation that all strange phenomena stems from a single force is also markedly Fortean, connecting unlike data with any inherent strangeness. Furthermore, the strange nature of people disappearing after fireball events connects two Fortean topics as being related; Fort was interested in both strange disappearances and fireballs in the sky. While the beings in "Goldfish Bowl" that capture and keep earthmen as pets may treat them as goldfish more than cattle, the trend of early SF works placing humans in the hands of powerful manipulators continues. It is not unlike Eric Frank Russell's works, which categorize Earth as a cosmic farm or cosmic insane asylum. "Goldfish Bowl" is also a precursor to the abduction events in Clarke's *2001: A Space Odyssey*. When Graves and Eisenberg are kept as pets by whatever force is behind the great pillars of water, they are left in an indescribably bare place and given food of sorts: "The first was an amorphous lump of nothing in particular, resembling a grayish cheese in appearance, slightly greasy to the touch and not appetizing." The second type is round globes of water that are somehow suspended as spheres. The food turns out to be "sour, nauseating (and) unpleasant." In the Clarke chapter, we see Bowman kept captive by a similar ultra-intelligent force that understands the basics of human needs, but not the intricacies. Like the captives of Heinlein's short story, Bowman is given a strange blue substance as sustenance. In both cases, this emphasizes how unlike humans these higher beings are. While Heinlein makes clear through parallels that Graves and Eisenberg are kept like goldfish, Clarke does not make this notion explicit, but it is nevertheless implied. As illustrated by Vallee in the Clarke chapter, these types of events are not limited to the fictional realm, pancakes that taste like cardboard were offered to a human by beings from a UFO in 1961.

Eventually, both of the captive scientists die, and their bodies are deposited back on Earth like old playthings that have outlived their entertainment value. Eisenberg marks his body with the message

"BEWARE—CREATION TOOK EIGHT DAYS" as a warning to the captain of the expedition, but the cryptic message is lost on the captain. His attempt to warn others of the pillar-beings only becomes another bit of Forteana. Easily readable, Heinlein's "Goldfish Bowl" serves as an excellent introduction to Fortean SF, covering almost all facets of the genre in a concise word count. The work is rivaled only by the stories of Eric Frank Russell and Edmond Hamilton as the most boldly Fortean in nature. While clearly interested in Fort, his other stories do not feature Fortean philosophy so plainly, but nevertheless illustrate Heinlein's familiarity with the subject matter.

Another of Heinlein's short stories contains Fortean overtones but its themes are decidedly apart from the common Fortean cosmic horror, existing within the realm of a less specific variety of cosmic horror. "The Year of the Jackpot" initially appeared in *Galaxy Science Fiction* in 1951 but was later republished in the collection *The Menace from Earth* along with "Goldfish Bowl" in 1959. The story's protagonist, Potiphar Breen, is a statistician who compiles seemingly disparate data from news reports. In the beginning of the story, he ignores a lady undressing on the side of the street to go through various newspapers while in a drugstore booth. He pays no mind to the major stories, instead opting for the seemingly more mundane ones such as "the maximum and minimum temperatures in Brownsville, Texas," and "the closing prices of three blue chips and two dogs on the New York Exchange."[13] Most notable are the stranger items he finds in the papers:

> Among them a publicity release in which Miss National Cottage Cheese Week announced that she intended to marry and have twelve children by a man who could prove that he had been a life-long vegetarian, a circumstantial but wildly unlikely flying saucer report, and a call for prayers for rain throughout Southern California. Potiphar had [...] written down the names and addresses of three residents of Watts, California, who had been miraculously healed at a tent meeting of the God-is-All First Truth Brethren by the Reverend Dickie Bottomley, the eight-year-old evangelist.[14]

These peculiar tidbits and the fastidious cataloguing by Potiphar Breen are highly reminiscent of Fort's work. Breen's scrapbooking from newspapers takes place throughout the short story, not unlike the bundles of tiny handwritten notes that Fort made out of anomalous reports in newspapers and scientific journals. Like Graves in "Goldfish Bowl," Breen in "The Year of the Jackpot" finds that a certain kind of "X factor" is the root cause of all these strange happenings. He concludes that the population of Earth is going through a manic cycle—the newspaper reports lead Breen to believe that humanity is at the mercy of some unchangeable cosmic rhythm. "It means we're lemmings," Breen says, explaining to his romantic interest, Meade Barstow. Breen can see the inevitability of a "jackpot" or a crest in data he puts together that indicates the pinnacle of collective madness for humanity.[15] While the story

7. A Hard-Headed, Commonsensical Fortean   125

does not imply that some form of consciousness is behind these rhythms, the hints of Forteana are clear in the odd data that Breen collects and the conclusion that all anomalous events stem from a single source. The influence of Fort is not as clear in "The Year of the Jackpot" when compared to the blatantly Fortean "Goldfish Bowl," but Heinlein nevertheless includes certain Fortean ideas and even possible references to Fort himself. The latter is merely speculative, but the former is undeniable: Earth's anomalies have a single source and, regardless of whether these events occur because of some alternate form of consciousness or a natural cycle, the results are terrifying.

"Project Nightmare" features a world where people with Fort's "wild talents" exist, primarily ESP and telekinesis. While this short story continues the trend of Heinlein's militaristic fiction, its main themes are more militaristic than the Fortean ones that were prominent in "Goldfish Bowl." The story follows the military's attempts to utilize psychics to find nuclear bombs planted in the United States by Russia. This interest in Fortean "wild talents" would extend later into Heinlein's life as illustrated by his membership to the Institute of Noetic Sciences, a topic to be explored later in this chapter. The short story serves as an excellent example of Heinlein using telepathy in a story, a subject that he seemed to believe truly existed. As Heinlein would write to IONS, noetic subjects were the second major theme in his work beside space travel. Even in stories thematically distant from Forteana, there are still hints of his interest in the subjects that fall into this very category.

Heinlein's *The Puppet Masters* is both a representation of Cold War paranoia and a representation of Fortean paranoia, sometimes merging the two together. As will be explored in the following chapter, fellow Fortean SF writer Robert Anton Wilson mentions the book in his theory on the 23 Phenomenon, which tracks a variety of synchronicities connected to the number 23. The moment Wilson is most interested in mentions the pertinent numbers of 23 and 17. The Old Man, a leader of a covert U.S. security team, briefs his team on their situation: "Seventeen hours [...] and twenty-three minutes ago an unidentified space ship landed near Grinnell, Iowa. Type, unknown. Approximately disk shaped and about one hundred and fifty feet across."[16] Beyond RAW's thoughts on this moment, the usage of the Fortean phenomena of UFOs is not unfamiliar in SF. However, the ideas explored in the text lend themselves to a dual reading, perhaps indicating that the use of UFOs is more significant. One reading sees the invading parasites as analogous with communism, expressing Cold War anxieties. Another reading sees the text as possibly Fortean in nature, the titular puppet masters as an unknown force that uses humanity for its own devices, not unlike Fort's postulation that we are property of a complex intelligence. Speculatively, of course, perhaps Heinlein even chose the location Grinnell because of its proximity to Lynnville, Iowa, which experienced a strange event in Fort's *The Book of the*

Damned. Fort reports that in 1896, two railroad postal clerks on a train coming from Trenton, Missouri, saw "in the darkness of a heavy rain, a light that appeared to be round, and of a dull-rose color, and seemed to be about a foot in diameter. It seemed to float within a hundred feet of the earth, but soon rose high, or 'midway between horizon and zenith.' The wind was quite strong from the east, but the light held a course almost due north."[17] The light followed the train to Lynnville and disappeared behind the train depot. Fort, as usual, lists the many natural explanations for the light, namely ball lightning. However, he also includes a strange addition from one of the postal clerks, C.N. Crotsenburg, who introduces the event by calling it "so strange that I should never have mentioned it, even to my friends, had it not been corroborated … so unreal that I hesitated to speak of it, fearing that it was some freak of the imagination."[18] Was Heinlein influenced by this Fortean tidbit, noting its resemblance to modern day UFO phenomena? It is impossible to confirm, but there is a strange synchronicity in the fact that the two towns sound phonetically similar and are a mere 15 miles away from one another. But Fortean texts almost always put one in a conspiratorial mindset. Regardless of whether this work was directly influenced by Fort, *The Puppet Masters* contains themes which are markedly Fortean.

The investigating earthlings eventually discover that the parasites hail from Saturn's moon Titan, a planet that is uninhabitable by most standards. However, the moon possesses Earth-like features, like liquid seas and a clear atmosphere, and could harbor life beneath its surface. Heinlein could have chosen this celestial body because life seems possible on Titan, but there are other possible implications. In Greek mythology, Titans are the primordial godlike beings who are as terrifying as they are powerful. Famous for dining on the body of Dionysus, some interpretations imply that humanity sprung from dead Titans. The parasites are referred to as Titans after their home satellite is ascertained, implying that they are a force that is greater than humanity, though they are not quite total gods, having some elements of humanity inside them. This interpretation sees the Titans not so much as communist infiltrators as in the Cold War reading of *The Puppet Masters*, but rather a force that is omnipresent and utilizes humanity for its own devices. Likewise, Titan has made appearances in ufological literature as being the home planet for star people. In Jacques Vallee's *Messengers of Deception*, he explores the case of Jacques Bordas, who encountered a being he was told was from Titan. Bordas was a sickly child until the age of 12 when "he saw some metallic, triangular devices, similar to miniature planes; three of them landed near him. They measured less than nine feet, and one of them opened like a fan."[19] A man dressed in white emerges and tells Bordas that he is going to make him strong and protect him. After this, "the strange messenger gave him a dark, square candy and instructed him to eat it completely, warning that if he did so, he was beginning a new life."[20] Bordas woke up with his mouth tasting of tar, but forever changed, no longer weak or unhealthy. He continued to live an extraordinary life with numerous other alleged contact experiences. Vallee insists, however, that even "the charming and mystical tales of the contactees also had more sinister connotations."[21] One cannot confirm Bordas' experience, but again, even in maybe-fictional literature, Titan's possible symbolic value comes into play. If we were to treat the experience as a form of literature, similar conclusions to Heinlein's *The Puppet Masters* can be drawn. As in Fortean thought, the inclusion of Titan calls to mind a higher, devious intelligence that pulls the strings of humanity in both fact and fiction.

The Cold War reading and the Fortean reading of *The Puppet Masters* need not always be at odds. Again, looking at Fortean researcher Jacques Vallee, the language of UFO cults and even the purported messages of the contacts contain communist paranoiac overtones. He notes that of some of the themes, included are intellectual abdication, or "the widespread belief that human beings are incapable of solving their own problems, and that extraterrestrial intervention is imperative to save us 'in spite of ourselves.'" Vallee notes that this makes "its believers dependent on outside forces and discourages personal responsibility."[22] If the Titans of *The Puppet Masters* can be equated to a form of communism, then said communism would resemble this intellectual abdication as opposed to a more idealized form. The parasites function similarly, "riding" unwitting humans by sending them into a kind of painless stupor. Personal responsibility gives way to the complete control of the manipulating aliens. The philosophy of the "communist" Titans very much resembles that of UFO cults and contactee messages. Vallee further notes that another contactee theme is social utopia, involving "fantastic economic theories, including the belief that a 'world economy' can be created overnight, and that democracy should be abolished in favor of Utopian systems, usually dictatorial in their outlook."[23] Again, these themes that appear in UFO literature are all too relevant to Heinlein's *The Puppet Masters*. The book is a tale reminiscent of Cold War–era paranoia of communist invasion. However, this paranoia could not only be attributable to totalitarian communism, but also to a more cosmic paranoia with similar themes and language that appears in Vallee's research. In short, the messages of the Titans and the messages from purportedly true tales of alien contact are not that different.

Heinlein also created a concept which he called "World as Myth" which proposed that SF stories created new realities. Thomas D. Clareson and Joe Sanders use a passage from Heinlein's *The Cat Who Walks Through Walls* to describe it in their book, *The Heritage of Heinlein*:

> The universe is not logical but whimsical, its structure depending solely on the dreams and nightmares of non-logical dreamers.... If the great brains had not been so hoodwinked by their shared conviction that the universe must contain a consistent and log-

ical structure they could find by careful analysis and synthesis, they could have spotted the glaring fact that the universe—the multiverse—contains neither logic nor justice where we, and others like us, impose such qualities on a world of chaos and cruelty.[24]

Perhaps no other Heinlein quote better expresses such Fortean leanings: It both denotes the universe as irrational and "the great brains" as self-assured fools. Clareson and Sanders say that "this sense of the universe's fundamental, perhaps malleable, chaos may make Heinlein sound like an avant-garde writer dissatisfied with the fictional techniques of realism."[25] This is true, but given Heinlein's Fortean associations, he might also be expressing a questioning of scientific authority's claims on the nature of reality. "World as Myth" propounds an SF multiverse where every story creates its own physical universe, dependent on "the dreams and nightmares of non-logical dreamers." Heinlein, Fort, and even Dick strangely align when it comes to the irrational nature of reality. Heinlein had a strange relationship with Dick, Stephen Webb saying that "in their writings and outlook, Heinlein and Dick seem in many ways to have been polar opposites" but that Heinlein "took an interest in the countercultural Dick."[26] Webb quotes Dick's introduction to *The Golden Man* where Dick says that he considers Heinlein his spiritual father, despite their disparate political ideologies. Heinlein called Dick when he was ill, bought him an electric typewriter, and loaned him money when he owed great sums to the IRS.[27] With "World as Myth" and other Fortean leanings, Dick and Heinlein may have not been so at odds in their fiction, despite their political views being at odds.

Fascinatingly, despite Heinlein's reputation as a hard-nosed SF author with little room for Fortean nonsense, he personally explored the fringe areas of science that approach Forteana later in his career. Already noted was his purported membership with the International Fortean Organization—a membership that was surprisingly lengthy, with Heinlein keeping his membership from its inception to his death. He was not involved with any Fortean media like Clarke or RAW, but his personal letters illuminate some of his more esoteric interests. In addition to INFO, Heinlein and his wife became members of the Institute of Noetic Sciences very shortly after the Institute's inception, in 1973. Created by astronaut Edgar Mitchell, the Institute's goal is to explore parapsychological phenomena, a study which seems averse to the hard-headed military man that Heinlein is often characterized as. In fact, Heinlein engaged in correspondence with Mitchell directly, paying for a membership for himself and Virginia while making note for the group to only send one copy of the newsletter to their residence. Among these letters to Mitchell and IONS, Heinlein reveals that he believes in some form of telepathy. While explaining his own experience in noetics he says that nothing "of any evidential value to anyone else" has occurred in his life but he has had experiences that have "quite a bit of strong evidential value to (him) personally."²⁸ He goes on to report several fascinating claims:

> Ginny and I make limited use of telepathy between ourselves. I have both experienced and seen some minor telekinesis. I have had numerous and surprisingly accurate forerunners as to my own future. I have, on several painful occasions, been aware of the deaths of persons close to me before the news reached me through ordinary channels—and on three of those occasions the event involved death by accident of persons in good health. I have encountered idiot savants with "wild talents." And none of this is worth a hoot as scientific evidence.²⁹

Heinlein seems aware of the discrepancy between science and personal paranormal experience in this excerpt, while still affirming a belief in these phenomena. He is mildly frustrated by this discrepancy, seemingly trying to balance between the supposedly irrational events he has experienced and his belief in the scientific method. Like Fort, he expresses some disappointment that science has not fully mediated the paranormal questions that plague believers. Of Virginia, he writes that while she had enough experience in noetics "to make her very receptive," she had no experience "of evidential value by the strict rigor of methodology required by science." Heinlein's use of the phrase "wild talents" may stem from his knowledge of Fort's work, especially given that the topic at hand describes the same varieties of phenomena which Fort explored in the book of the same name. Heinlein also connected his fiction to his noetic interests, writing to Captain Mitchell:

> If you are familiar with my fiction (no reason why you should be, but some astronauts are), you may have noticed that the two recurring themes in my stories are: (a) space travel, and (b) all of the subjects you gather together as "noetics" and defined in [...] the Institute's brochure.³⁰

Heinlein partially admits to Fortean themes running throughout his works in this instance. Noetics are not an entirely different beast, focusing on medical mysteries and working to find a scientific basis for forms of consciousness generally considered to be bunk science. Fort himself outlines numerous cases of synchronicity bordering on telepathy, special powers that humans have sometimes exhibited, and much more. His membership in INFO and IONS illuminates Heinlein as a writer with great interest in Fortean subjects—even if his fiction does not feature it as actively as other authors examined.

Heinlein is a fascinating author of Fortean SF because his characterization by most scholars seems so averse to Fortean leanings. He was a military man whose main characters often had the strong-willed and no-nonsense attitudes of military men; Forteana does not seem to fit neatly into this stereotype. Yet Heinlein has numerous stories that have Fortean leanings—even his ideology at times indicates an author who is more curious about the unexplained than might be suggested through his most popular stories. Take the epigraph from this chapter as an example: "Magic is another man's engineering. Supernatural is a null word." This quote comes from Heinlein's character Lazarus Long, a figure who exemplifies the hardheaded archetype that Heinlein often utilized. Yet, this phrase does not discount the existence of anomalies and Fortean phenomena—it merely suggests that humanity is not examining these events correctly.

8

Conspiracy and Forteana
A Fortean Analysis of Robert Anton Wilson

> *Of course, we do not like to think of ourselves as hallucinators. We prefer the more soothing term, "misperception," for cases like this. Only the mentally "ill" are hallucinating, we think.*
> —Robert Anton Wilson[1]

Robert Anton Wilson is a bit of an anomaly not only in this exploration into the world of Fortean SF, but also the world of SF in general. At times, his work hardly seems SF but for a few instances of advanced technology and a fantastical nature that often pushes the stories into the genre of fantasy. However, Wilson, or RAW, is seen as primarily an SF author, and this book will examine him as such, especially because of his relationship to Fortean thought. Awash in conspiracy theories and endless paranoia, RAW's work is intriguing yet often difficult to decipher—reminiscent of the obscure nature of the Illuminati. *The Illuminatus Trilogy*, for instance, is a decidedly postmodern tome, with controversial psychologist Timothy Leary (who makes several appearances in the book) calling it "more important than *Ulysses* or *Finnegans Wake*."[2] For perhaps the best introduction to this exploration's next subject, *The Illuminatus Trilogy* (coauthored by Robert Shea) includes a facetious self-degradation of itself in its first installment:

> The authors are utterly incompetent—no sense of style or structure at all. It starts out as a detective story, switches to science-fiction, then goes off into the supernatural, and is full of the most detailed information of dozens of *ghastly* boring subjects. And the time sequence is all out of order in a very pretentious imitation of Faulkner and Joyce. Worst yet, it has the most raunchy sex scenes, thrown in just to make it sell, I'm sure, and the authors—whom I've *never* heard of—have the supreme bad taste to introduce real political figures into the mishmash and pretend to be exposing a real conspiracy.[3]

This self-description of the trilogy is quite apt. Shea and Wilson's work skirts the outright experimental while maintaining a grounding sense of humor and self-deprecation throughout. The work is often stream-of-consciousness and written in a manner quite challenging to the reader, calling to mind the structure of Fort's own works. Fort would often jump from case to case with little apparent organizational backbone before slipping into his own theories, also often given in a self-deprecating manner. Wilson was well-versed in Fortean thought and beyond technical similarities between the two, there is also a great amount of overlap in the philosophy of Fort and the disjointed philosophies put forth in Wilson's various writings. This examination will consider all of these factors. Though clouded in a haze of drugs and sex, of all the authors examined in this book, the work of RAW most clearly resembles Fort's writing style. In *The Illuminatus Trilogy*, Wilson's fastidious collection of research into the origins and existence of an Illuminati conspiracy is automatically reminiscent of Fort's own obsessive cataloging of anomalous phenomena. Wilson is also similar in tone; theories are treated as half-baked and ludicrous even by their theorizers. *The Illuminatus Trilogy* is primarily a comedy based around the ridiculous conditions necessary for a New World Order–type conspiracy to even function as it is supposed to.

In order to give the work a Fortean analysis, it must be made clear how conspiracy theories play into the world of maybe-fiction. Often these works are frowned upon because of their clearly partisan nature, especially in the present political climate where conspiracy theorists are most closely associated with political extremism and the theories themselves clog the arteries of knowledge production. It is dangerous territory to examine. For the purposes of this book, conspiracy theories will be treated as maybe-fiction only in the sense that they often mash together factual information with that which is unprovable or unknowable. Conspiracy theories can sometimes fall within the realm of maybe-fiction, perhaps explaining why belief in UFOs is often equated with a belief that the moon landing was faked. It can even be said that conspiracy theories and the paranormal share a similar, often maligned space in literature. Fort himself never got into Illuminati-esque conspiracy territory but it is undoubtable that he sensed some grand conspiracy in "dogmatic science's" attempts to keep his damned facts from being discovered or explored. The famous "we are property" statement seems to indicate a similar conspiracy, not related to any government or human organization but one perpetuated by some higher beings up in Magonia who love to mess with the lowly human race. As maligned as conspiracy theories are (even by the author of *this* book) they have an undeniable relationship to Fortean thought, maybe-fiction, and SF. In many of these works, there is a grand scheme at work that people cannot see and often the suggestion that it is being intentionally hidden. However, by the definition I have set forth previously, only conspiracy theories with science-fictional elements can be considered maybe-fiction.

8. Conspiracy and Forteana

RAW and Shea's book also includes maybe-fictional source material amongst its fictional plot, frequently citing very real books and magazines in order to draw a vast and complicated web of conspiracy. For instance, Wilson quotes from *Flying Saucers in the Bible* by Virginia Brasington to outline the seemingly supernatural origin of the eye in the pyramid symbol. This book was indeed real, published by a Nazarene minister in 1963 via Saucerian Press[4] and recently rereleased by Timothy Green Beckley's Inner Light Global Communications. The excerpt Wilson gives us is pure maybe-fiction, referring to a supposed incident between Thomas Jefferson and a cloaked man:

> Asked how he got the plans, Jefferson told a strange story. A man approached him wearing a black cloak that practically covered him, face and all, and told him that he (the stranger) knew that they were trying to devise a Seal, and that he had a design which was appropriate and meaningful.... After the excitement died down, the three went into the garden to find the stranger, but he was gone.[5]

This was Brasington's claim on how the Great Seal of the United States was created, by an ominous, cloaked figure lurking in Jefferson's garden. The claim can of course be disputed; a booklet from the State Department on the seal suggests it originated from the mind of Pierre Eugene du Simitiere, a consultant to the founding fathers. However, given the vast conspiracy that theorists believe is at play, a pamphlet from the State Department can easily lie. Keel also referenced this supposed incident in 1970's *Operation Trojan Horse*, which connects the tale with Men in Black encounters throughout history.[6] The incident does not have the direct political implications that Jefferson's MIB encounter had, yet a conspiracy could surely be manufactured from this footnote of history. RAW was aware of Keel's writings, as he was with many maybe-fiction authors, which will be explored later. He references a Keel-written *FATE* article in *The New Inquisition*, covering a 1966 midwestern UFO flap.[7]

As Shea and Wilson's investigation into the Illuminati gets deeper, a character named Simon Moon gets consumed by numerology, finding endless synchronicities regarding the number 23 and 17. Speaking on his research into 23, Moon finds an instance of numerical synchronicity in Charles Fort's work,[8] specifically citing a case from *Lo!*:

> A case that is mysterious, and that may associate with other mysteries, was reported in the London newspapers (*Daily Mail*, April 2; *Daily News*, April 3, 1923). It was at the time that Lord Carnarvon was dying, in Cairo, Egypt, of a disease that physicians said was septic pneumonia, but that in some minds, was associated with the opening of Tut-Ankh-Amen's tomb. Upon Lord Carnarvon's estate, near Newbury, Hampshire, a naked man was running wild, often seen, but never caught. He was first seen, upon March 17th, Lord Carnarvon fell ill, and died upon April 5th. About April 5th, the wild man of Newbury ceased to be reported.[9]

In *The Illuminatus Trilogy*, Simon Moon makes special note of the dates that mention 17, 23, and even 5, which supposedly have a special role in Illuminati numerology. What all these numbers mean is never made abundantly clear although there are implications that it is some sort of elaborate code indicating which events the Illuminati have a hand in. Whatever the case, Moon makes a point of illustrating how often these numbers crop up together, citing Charles Fort in the process. Even the example taken from Fort implies a synchronistic relationship between two events that may be very much unrelated. Many of the numerical synchronicities can be explained through simple chance or the Baader-Meinhof phenomenon, which explains how once someone is made knowledgeable of some subject, that subject will appear everywhere they look. Simon even notes seeing the phenomenon in an SF work we have examined previously, Heinlein's *The Puppet Masters*. He says that he bought the book, "thinking the plot might parallel some Illuminati operations. Imagine how I felt when Chapter Two began, '23 hours and 17 minutes ago, a flying saucer landed in Iowa...'"[10] Clearly Shea and RAW are acknowledging how SF and maybe-fiction seem to inform one another with the examination of these synchronicities.

Regardless, Robert Anton Wilson did some Fortean journalism with the 23 phenomenon later when his article on the subject appeared, unsurprisingly, in the 23rd issue of the *Fortean Times*. This article explores the subject in a strictly non-fiction capacity and even reveals a PKD-esque experience which Wilson had only a year before PKD:

> On July 23rd, 1973, I had the impression that I was being contacted by some sort of advanced intellect from the system of the double-star Sirius. I have had odd psychic experiences of that sort for many years, and I always record them carefully, but refuse to take any of them literally, until or unless supporting evidence of an objective nature turns up. This particular experience, however, was especially staggering, both intellectually and emotionally, so I spent the rest of the day at the nearest large library researching Sirius. I found, among other things, that July 23rd is very closely associated with that star.[11]

The common trend of getting so involved in some sort of psychic event now seems commonplace among Fortean SF writers. Of course, like PKD, Wilson was greatly occupied with mind-altering drugs, but this does not necessarily eliminate the realness of the experience. For some Forteans, drugs simply open people up to paranormal experiences more than they would be without them. However, this is largely a topic for a different book. Wilson spoke on Dick's experience in another *Fortean Times* interview:

> One of Phil's therapists suggested that sexual abuse by his grandfather might have been the root of his problems, so this ties Phil in with current theories of the abduction phenomenon. But Phil had a much more developed mind than some of these victims and drew a whole cosmology out of it—one of the most fascinating world views

I've ever studied. I often think his ideas make more sense than Christianity or Hinduism, or atheism or Forteanism, and then I think "this is the ravings of a madman, how did I get sucked into this!" But then I read more, and start to wonder again....[12]

Wilson is quite level-headed about Dick's experience for someone who has had similar mystical experiences—agnostic as ever, but also curious as ever.

The *Illuminatus Trilogy* was well-regarded by the reviewers at the *Fortean Times*, who wrote that "though Fort has only one fleeting mention that I can remember, the authors are fully aware of the Fortean philosophy, and indeed, the scope of the book is a brilliant exercise in Fortean flexibility, and an outrageous mirror of modern folly."[13] The *Fortean Times* is perhaps where RAW's relationship with Forteana existed most clearly. In addition to the article about the 23 phenomenon, Wilson had an article about James Joyce appear in the Spring 1983 issue. *Cosmic Trigger* was reviewed in issue 25, making RAW an outlier in the publication's book reviews section which mainly focused on Fortean non-fiction. No other SF author was so clearly involved in or revered by the Fortean community; RAW is in many respects *the* Fortean SF writer despite his fiction often not following directly in line with Fortean thought, as earlier pulp stories did. The *Fortean Times* work written by RAW is not the only instance of Wilson indulging in Fortean research or non-fiction. His book *The New Inquisition: Irrational Rationalism and the Citadel of Science* is a book perpetuating the Fortean cause. As the title suggests, Wilson used the book to decry scientific dogmatism, a familiar venture in Forteana. The section which quotes Fort is perhaps the most enlightening for the purposes of this exploration:

> Some of you recall that Charles Fort collected over 300 cases of these falls of segregated living organisms. Motivated by the same desire to liberate humanity from dogma as I am—or motivated by the same blasphemous desire to subvert and corrupt, the Citadel will tell you—Fort published these cases in four huge books that annoyed Martin Gardner so severely that he decided that Fort was "sinister." I predict that Mr. Gardner will say the same about me.[14]

Clearly from this sample, Wilson not only admired Fort but also felt united in the cause. This is not to say that Wilson never deviates from Fort's philosophy—Wilson says that he is more "conservative" than Fort and would not blame a "God" for the happenings. He concedes that if he were to humor the idea of God, he would "prefer to guess that somebody has been monkeying around with the Big Bang and we are in one of the Imperfect Universes."[15]

Wilson quoted Fort more extensively in his autobiographical follow-up to *The Illuminatus Trilogy*, the 1977–1995 trilogy *Cosmic Trigger*. This work begins the expansion of Wilson's work into maybe-fiction territory, the whole book being geared toward the maybe-fiction genre as opposed to being relegated to specific sections as these subjects were in *Illuminatus*.

Key to this text is his PKD-esque experience in 1973 with psychic messages from Sirius, an incident which RAW explores with a considerable amount of composure. With regards to his paranormal experiences and reality in general, he willfully employs "neurological model agnosticism—the application of the Copenhagen Interpretation beyond physics to consciousness itself." This model, according to RAW, "allows one to escape from certain limits of mechanical emotion and robot mentation that are inescapable as long as one remains within one dogmatic model or one imprinted reality-tunnel."[16] This model agnosticism intends to create personal realities whilst still accepting that there is probably one true reality that no one is able to comprehend; each person unsuspectingly has their own personal reality tunnel and the true reality cannot be "observed" without personal interference from whoever observes it. With this theory, RAW proves himself to be operating on a remarkably different wavelength than the average person, not unlike PKD. RAW recalls meeting Dick: "My impression was that he was worried that his experience was a temporary insanity and was trying to figure out if I was nutty, too. I'm not sure if he ever decided."[17] Where the two writers diverge in their experiences and writings is that RAW's seems markedly less religious in nature, opting for a more scientific, but no less complex, reading. Perhaps this is owing to RAW staying true to his professed agnosticism. Yet, Erik Davis notes that *Cosmic Trigger* skirts darker, more mystical territory even in pushing scientific boundaries: "Even the discovery of the deeper patterns that organize the world cannot be separated from the baffling abyss that frames them—an abyss that, sometimes, stares back, and even whispers."[18]

Beyond Fort, RAW had a particular fondness of futurist R. Buckminster Fuller, himself a Fortean granted a life fellowship to the Fortean Society by Tiffany Thayer.[19] This fondness is unsurprising given Fuller's own beliefs that "everything we see is inside our heads," a notion which RAW references at the very beginning of *The New Inquisition*.[20] Fuller seems to exist on the same wavelength as RAW, experiencing or being interested in altered states of consciousness and the nature of reality:

> "Out-of-body experiences," "astral projection," contact with alien (extraterrestrial?) "entities" or with a galactic Overmind, etc., such as I've experienced, have all been reported for thousands of years, not merely by the ignorant, the superstitious, the gullible, but often by the finest minds among us (Socrates, Giordano Bruno, Edison, Buckminster Fuller, etc.).[21]

In both *The New Inquisition* and *Cosmic Trigger*, RAW utilizes Fuller's hypotheses to develop his own theories on the nature of reality. RAW too was a futurist in many respects, using the works of Fort to decry the stagnation of science. For him, the only way forward was for science to eliminate any taboos and expand the boundaries of what scientists consider fruitful research.

8. Conspiracy and Forteana

In an interview with the *Fortean Times* in 1995, Wilson spoke about various Fortean subjects, from Whitley Strieber to Aleister Crowley to supposed radio signals coming from the Sirius star system. The interview reveals his interests in Forteana in a much more concise manner than his novels and non-fiction, illuminating his basic thoughts. "Not believing in anything, not disbelieving in anything—that may be one of the most important of the ideas in my books, though I hardly invented it," Wilson says. "It's characteristic of modern physicists to have that attitude. It also ties in with Fort's notion that the products of minds are not acceptable as subject matter for belief—except temporarily."[22] RAW has also written blurbs for some more prominent works of Fortean journalism. Of John Keel's *Disneyland of the Gods*, he wrote: "Keel's books never fail to astound and delight me."[23] This is unsurprising given that Keel's thesis in this work is all too similar to RAW's own in *The New Inquisition*, calling for an end to scientific dogmatism if just to keep the broad field of scientists honest. Of Jacques Vallee's *Messengers of Deception*, Wilson uses notably fiction-oriented terms to describe the work of non-fiction: "As suspenseful as a Hitchcockian Thriller, brilliantly argued [...] a smashing achievement."[24] In this book by Vallee, the research follows UFO cults and the overall psychological implications of the phenomenon on cultures. RAW may have been particularly interested in the grand conspiracy Vallee attempts to uncover behind the U.S. government's preoccupations with UFOs. In *Cosmic Trigger*, Wilson notes how "UFOlogists, including Jacques Vallee and John Keel, have noted that the majority of Contactees eventually became embroiled in mystical or occult groups, sometimes even as the founders of Messianic new cults."[25] Regardless, Wilson also recognizes in this short blurb how maybe-fiction can function like fictional literature despite being non-fiction, an idea explored in a later chapter. RAW's connections to Fortean researchers goes beyond just a familiarity with Keel and Vallee. Prominent cryptozoologist Loren Coleman also had a lasting friendship with Wilson, "correspond(ing) with Wilson [...] from the 1970s through the early 1990s, until his health and his in-and-out self-exiles moved him near-and-far from many people."[26] Speaking about the recently passed Wilson, Coleman explains just how important the author was to him:

> Had RAW's writings in the late 1970s impacted me? Well, let me just mention this one piece of my private life. When I married my second wife (now ex-) in 1980, after we both read *Cosmic Trigger*, we picked (to the strange surprise of our friends and families) a Friday. Why? Because we wanted to get married on May (2+3 = 5), 23rd, two 23s, in honor of Robert Anton Wilson's book or more properly, its concepts and Fortean linkages.[27]

With so many acquaintances in the Fortean community, RAW is more than just an SF author greatly influenced by Fort. In addition, he seems a valid Fortean researcher in his own right, accepted by the community as one of their own. In this blog post, Coleman bids Wilson a fond farewell saying, "I'm sure someplace, Bucky Fuller, Timothy Leary, Charles Fort, and Robert Anton Wilson are deciding whether it's time to play supercheckers or Texas hold 'em."[28] Perhaps the true Fortean heaven.

This paradise (to some) is exactly what Wilson might deserve. In this exploration into Charles Fort's influence on SF, RAW serves as perhaps the best example, fitting into the mold completely where other authors only fit partially. Wilson uses Fortean themes in his fictional work, much like Clarke, but he also has witnessed Fortean phenomena firsthand in a manner like PKD's experiences. As if he were not already a model Fortean SF writer, he goes a step further and does his own Fortean research, sometimes blending it into his otherwise fictional works. In *Cosmic Trigger*, Wilson argued for an overarching agnosticism, not only with regards to religion but for every facet of life. He writes that while the threatening and omnipresent "New Inquisition" tries to halt exploration into the unknown and poorly understood, one should keep an agnostic mindset to weather out the storm. Almost a personal form of civil disobedience, RAW says that "agnosticism is both honest and becomingly modest."[29] One likes to think that Coleman was correct in saying that RAW and Fort are friends in the afterlife. They both illustrate a consistent willingness to battle the status quo of the scientific community without being too self-serious about it. Fort likewise displays a certain agnosticism with his "no one is correct" attitude, mostly directed at Christian fundamentalists who would use his tirades against science as proof that they are correct. It is then fitting that Robert Anton Wilson is the last Fortean SF author with a chapter dedicated specifically to him, for he is perhaps the author that is most like Fort himself. He is equal parts Fortean researcher and fiction mastermind to an extent not reached by others in this exploration, but he held such a status proudly.

9

A Procession of the Damned
Fortean Footnotes

"*Battalions of the accursed, captained by pallid data that I have exhumed, will march. You'll read them—or they'll march. Some of them livid and some of them fiery and some of them rotten. Some of them are corpses, skeletons, mummies, twitching, tottering, animated by companions that have been damned alive. [...] But they'll march.*"
—Charles Fort[1]

Introduction

The following examination deals with Fort's influence showing itself in a variety of SF literature and other mediums. These vary widely. Sometimes they show that an author has only a casual working knowledge of Fort and mentions him in their work. At other times, his influence is more pronounced and involves not only knowledge of Fort but an exhibition of the characteristics of Fortean thought. Others are simply an extension of Fortean phenomena popping up in SF which can be tied more indirectly to Fort. The threads may be thinner in some places and more pronounced in others, but Fort's influence remains. Other sections examine Fort as he is referenced in modern popular culture, sometimes fleetingly, but still offering the opportunity to examine the works as possible vessels for Fortean thought. It appears the ominous march of Fort's damned facts and hypotheses continues to this very day.[2]

Secular Interest: William Gibson and "The Gernsback Continuum"

William Gibson, one of the most prominent present-day SF authors, is mostly known for his cyberpunk novel *Neuromancer*, but early in his career, he wrote a short story that at once seems like a love letter to the golden age of SF pulps while simultaneously being a scathing indictment, and more often the latter than the former. Nevertheless, the story contains multiple instances of Forteana, perhaps as an ode to all the anomalous reports that found their way into the SF pulps. The photographer protagonist is given an assignment to take photographs of retro-futurist architecture, the kind of designs based on what America thought the future would be like. Of course, this future never came. The photographer says that it was "relentlessly tacky: ephemeral stuff extruded by the collective American subconscious of the Thirties, tending mostly to survive along depressing strips lined with dusty motels, mattress wholesalers, and small used-car lots."[3] Despite this dislike of the aesthetic, the photographer encounters a strange aircraft straight out of a pulp cover and takes the photograph to his friend Merv Kihn. Gibson characterizes Kihn as a "free-lance journalist with an extensive line in Texas pterodactyls, redneck UFO contactees, bush-league Loch Ness monsters, and the Top Ten conspiracy theories in the loonier reaches of the American mass mind."[4] Kihn dismisses the photographer's sighting as "a semiotic ghost," clarifying that the visions of the aircraft stem from the photographer's exposure to futurist designs, comparable to how pulp SF colored contactees' encounters with extraterrestrials. "I could buy aliens," he says, "but not aliens that look like Fifties' comic art."[5] Again, Forteana is used as an example by Kihn, citing the airship sightings of the 1800s. Kihn's dismissal has a somber effect on the photographer: After he finishes the photography assignment, he sees the same ship "but there was something tenuous about it, as though it were only half there." He then gets a newspaper and immerses himself in disasters, continuing to live in his "near-dystopia."[6]

This short story is an interesting take on Forteana, as an escape from a harsh reality rather than the cosmic dread we see so often in other Fortean SF. Gibson seems to be well-versed in maybe-fiction, as he invents his own cryptozoological creature/extraterrestrial entity for the story. Kihn interviews a teenager who had been attacked by a "*bar hade*." He explains further: "A bear head. The severed head of a bear. This *bar hade*, see, was floating around on its own little flying saucer, looked kind of like the hubcaps on cousin Wayne's vintage Caddy."[7] A 2010 tweet from the author revealed this to be completely his creation, not based on any source; Gibson's "affectionate approximation of a certain flavor of paranormal folk motif."[8] Gibson would also declare himself a Fortean at a book reading:

> Oh, I'm totally a Fortean! I've been a Fortean since I was … actually I'd have to find out. I've been a Fortean ever since Ace Books republished Charles Fort's three [*sic*] great weird philosophical books about strange shit that he'd found in old […] newspapers. And I continue to be. […] That's Charles Fort for those of you who don't know him. If you wanna have a really strange experience go find *The Book of the Damned*

by Charles Fort which was published in the 1920s and has two sequels. It's kind of the mother of all *X-Files* stuff.⁹

The importance of Ace Books' publication of the works of Charles Fort was seen earlier with author Jack Womack, and seems to have made impressions on several different SF and maybe-fiction figures.

Perhaps due to this similarity in Fortean outlook, Gibson wrote an introduction to Womack's collection of UFO books, named after the Donald Keyhoe book of the same title, *The Flying Saucers Are Real!* The book outlines the many examples of strange maybe-fiction that Womack collected over the years and displays the kooky illustrations that accompanied them. In his introduction to the collection, Gibson provides further insight into his familiarity with Fortean topics. He reminisces on his mother's experience seeing a flying cigar-shaped object and how such a sighting caused his young mind to imagine more fantastic features to the craft. Gibson now holds a somewhat skeptical position on his mother's sighting: "I believe she had been infected, in her loneliness, her anxiety, by what we now think of as a meme."¹⁰ Nevertheless, he acknowledges the power maybe-fiction holds in addressing Womack's collection, saying that "the truth, all these years, hasn't, as *The X-Files* had it, been out there, but rather was in here. Within these peculiar volumes, these testimonials to certain human needs."¹¹ Gibson realizes that the unprovable (or sometimes even improbable) veracity of these tales is of little import. They speak to some sort of desire that humans have, a want for a world that is stranger than commonly accepted. As "The Gernsback Continuum" suggests, it is acceptable to get lost in a maybe-fiction reverie, even without wholehearted belief.

Frogs Continue Falling: Fort in Military SF

While Fortean phenomena might show up in recent SF with somewhat consistent regularity, Fort himself is referenced more rarely. In 2015, Hank Davis helped to amend this when he wrote a military SF story where a professed Fortean is included as a character. It is featured in an anthology Davis edited, *Future Wars ... and Other Punchlines*, dedicated to David Drake, a fellow SF author and "dean of military science fiction" who Davis says, "has been known to express antiestablishment Fortean tendencies."¹² The brief story, "Into Each Life, Some Periwinkles Must Fall," follows a military colonel who enlists the help of a "verticologist," a person who studies anomalous falling objects, after a collection of bayonets falls from an empty sky. Throughout the investigation, other military objects, including grenades and tanks, fall from the sky, leading the duo to assume that "something" is dropping outdated paraphernalia that it assumes the military "needs" after the president initiated "huge cutbacks in the defense budget."¹³ This leads them to be highly concerned about nuclear warheads being dumped onto the country after the president announces a cutback in the national stockpile. The humorous tale deftly places Fortean anomalies within the context of military SF, even though military SF does not seem like a genre that would be often interested in Forteana. Even David Drake, whose Fortean interests have been displayed more prominently in his personal life than in his military SF, bears hallmarks of this influence in his fiction.

In Drake's most well-known work, the original collection of short stories in the "Hammerverse," *Hammer's Slammers*, his Fortean influence is subtly hinted at. In a brief interlude describing the history of the titular mercenary group's favored weapon, the powergun, some passages resemble the cataloguing of oddities prevalent in the works of Fort:

> Thirty thousand residents of St. Pierre, Martinique, had been killed on May 8, 1902. The agent of their destruction was a "burning cloud" released during an eruption of Mt. Pelee. Popular myth had attributed the deaths to normal volcanic phenomena, hot gases or ash like that which buried Pompeii; but even the most cursory examination of the evidence indicated that direct energy release had done the lethal damage.[14]

The mention of this incident is unassuming amidst the collection of classic military SF stories, but Drake seems to have drawn directly from Fort's reporting on the matter. Fort covered the eruption of the Caribbean volcano Mt. Pelee in *Lo!* and implies that something more than a classic volcanic eruption occurred; he postulated that there were alternate warning signs and coincidences that were ignored by the "deadly cult" of scientists. These included various catastrophes occurring in other parts of the world, electrical storms, and "soot and water, like ink," falling from the sky in France.[15] There was a greater force at work, and the people of St. Pierre are complicit in the resulting death toll: "May, 1902–30,000 persons, who perished properly—blackened into cinders, with academic sanction. They turned into ashes, but the principles of orthodoxy were upheld."[16] Charles Fort has had a tangible influence on military SF, as minor as it might be, illustrating that Forteana is conducive to nearly any SF, even that which is interested primarily in military affairs, a topic seemingly far-removed from Fort's own writings. Perhaps it is, as Hank Davis noted, the antiestablishment tendencies of Forteana that weaves its way into the genre, which often examines the ethical and moral questions of military action through an SF lens.

Minor Mentions in Pop Fiction: Charles Fort in Stephen King Novels

Among other contemporary authors with Fortean influence, the most popular and widely read is Stephen King, who namechecks Fort in his novels

Firestarter (1980) and *It* (1986). In *Firestarter*, specifically, the father of the pyrokinetic child, Charlie reads Fort's *Lo!* as a bedtime story along with another work of maybe-fiction, Frank Edwards' *Stranger Than Science*, both of which frighten the young girl.[17] While King is primarily a horror writer, it is notable that this clearly Fort-influenced work leans toward SF, involving government experiments that result in its subjects developing psychic powers. *It*, while markedly less SF in nature, does contain plot elements that are slightly Fortean, with the evil entity being a product of some cosmic terror far older and vastly superior in every respect to humanity. In the novel, the entity of the cosmic "turtle" which created the universe calls to mind the Fortean notion of Earth being but a microcosm of a larger advanced macrocosm that humans could never comprehend. Another SF novel of King's, *The Tommyknockers* (1987), is also influenced by Fortean phenomena—its title coming from supernatural beings that would cause mischief in underground mines, often making the sound of "knocking" in the caverns. The book is a much deeper foray into SF, although the plot has a limited relationship to Fortean phenomena besides the existence of a vastly more intelligent alien species. This species, however, does not hold the cosmic, indescribable power over humans that would mark the novel as truly Fortean.

Fort in Young Adult Literature: Blue Balliett's Chasing Vermeer

While far removed from SF, Fort even makes an unlikely appearance in young adult literature. In Blue Balliett's 2004 YA novel, *Chasing Vermeer*, a character reads and is fascinated by Fort's *Lo!* with the book even being visible on the cover. Likely utilized to introduce children to radically different ways of thinking about the world, the inclusion of Fort renders the man and his work endearing and intriguing:

> Fort was an extraordinary thinker. He looked fearlessly at occurrences that no one could explain. Even better, he looked everywhere for patterns. Calder understood the man's fascination with connecting things that didn't seem related, and he admired the way Fort challenged the experts.[18]

Perhaps stressing the value of Fort's work to adolescent intellectual development, Balliett also includes an epigraph taken from Fort's *Wild Talents*: "One can't learn much and also be comfortable. One can't learn much and let anyone else be comfortable."[19] If they were around to witness it, many of Fort's early critics would be horrified that the author is now being taught in schools. Yet Balliett illustrates just how Fort can be valuable, pushing young readers to think differently about the world, as basic as it may seem to an adult reader. Fortean thinking ultimately leads to the protagonists having the ability to solve the story's grand mystery. It's worth noting that Balliett initially was a Fortean writer, writing two books about "unexplainable events" and "ghost stories," making her yet another example of a maybe-fiction author also having an interest in fiction.[20]

Fort in Film: Paul Thomas Anderson's Magnolia

Outside of SF, references to Fort appear continually in other forms of media, including the critically acclaimed Paul Thomas Anderson film *Magnolia* (1999) which ends with a markedly Fortean phenomena: a rain of frogs. Anderson's standpoint on Fort illustrates how remarkably enduring Fort's influence continues to be, even within contemporary culture:

> Anderson said he really loves "how Fort was skeptical of any scientific explanation. He thought it shouldn't be explained or that there was a far better explanation. He believed in a place called 'Megonia,' [sic] a mythical place above the firmament where stuff would go up to and hang out before dropping back down to earth. 'Magnolia' is a little tribute to that. And it sounds funny, but he believed that you can judge a society by the health of its frogs. That doesn't seem too crazy to me because our frogs are getting all deformed and dying."[21]

While Anderson's admiration seems a little tongue-in-cheek in this excerpt, the influence is still undoubtedly there. However, Mr. X, a frequent contributor to Fortean publications like *The INFO Journal*, notes that Anderson's knowledge of Fort seems largely superficial, pointing to factual errors in the opening prologue to Anderson's film:

> Given the opportunity to publicize his film, Anderson and his supporters were not willing to admit how superficial their knowledge of Fort's books actually was. Anderson apparently never read much more than a paperback copy of *Wild Talents*; then, he wrote the screenplay. Fort wrote: "In the *New York Herald*, Nov. 26, 1911, there is an account of the hanging of three men, for the murder of Sir Edmund Berry Godfrey, on Greenberry Hill, London. The names of the murderers were Green, Berry, and Hill. It does seem that this was only a matter of chance. Still, it may have been no coincidence, but a savage pun mixed with murder."[22] If he had bothered to research Fort's source article, my website, or "Edmund Berry Godfrey," he would have discovered that the murder of Sir Godfrey occurred in 1678 (not in 1911, the date of the *New York Herald* article about coincidences). [...] P.T. Anderson is an entertainer (exploiting Fort's writing and reputation, and, really, not a Fortean).[23]

Mr. X's observations are important when considering Charles Fort's influence on popular culture. Although his work appears referenced in numerous places, it is preferable to make the distinction between something being truly Fortean and a cultural product being influenced by only a cursory knowledge of Fort.

Fort in Comic Books

A fictional interpretation of Charles Fort appeared in comic book form in 2001 as one of the protagonists of *Necronauts*, a backing feature of the comic series *2000 AD*. As "a collector of facts relating to the arcane and unusual," he is sought out by a fictional Harry Houdini, H.P. Lovecraft and Sir Arthur Conan Doyle to explain the sudden dark visions that all are experiencing. This version of Fort is more outwardly vocal about his views, as opposed to the timid character presented by biographers: "I have spent a lifetime cataloguing the obtuse and arcane, those damnable awkward facts that science cannot explain. [...] These things are real, gentlemen. They occur. And the world is not the safely rational place we wish it to be."[24] Fort utilizes his "we are property" line, but uses it to refer to Lovecraft's Dark Gods, the antagonists in the tale. The plot development is fitting given the similarities already developed between Lovecraft's mythos and Fortean thought. The tale is certainly ridiculous given Fort's actual personality; beating Lovecraft's Tcho-Tcho people with a cricket bat does not correspond with the temperament that gave him the moniker "the hermit of the Bronx." Yet, Fort has proven to be a semi-popular figure to return to in comic books, even being granted his own miniseries in the following year.

Fort: Prophet of the Unexplained follows Fort attempting to solve a bizarre murder case, again joined by H.P. Lovecraft, in this instance a much younger version. Like his *Necronauts* variant, Fort's biographical details are changed to suit the role of the occult detective he plays in the comic. This Fort is a librarian by day, alien hunter by night, who rides a steampunk motorcycle. His research into the bizarre murders leads to the discovery of a Lovecraftian alien creature nesting in the Statue of Liberty. He manages to save future president Theodore Roosevelt and kill the creature with the aid of an extraterrestrial doctor.[25] This depiction of Fort is not nearly as vitriolic against the scientific establishment as he appears in *Necronauts*, instead the comic focuses on crafting a Fort more akin to a Van Helsing–esque character. Some indications of Fort's dislike for scientific dogma are still included, such as when an alien device cures the mortally wounded friendly ET. The fictional Fort responds to young Lovecraft's exclamation "it's a miracle!" with: "Advanced science, young man. No use trying to debunk it.... Or so I've learned."[26]

Beyond these more major appearances, Fort also served as the narrator to Doug Moench's *The Big Book of the Unexplained*, a 1997 collection of anomalies in comic format. A fictionalized version played a small role in the 1996 Caliber Comics series *The Searchers*, a proto–*League of Extraordinary Gentlemen* of sorts, following the adventures of the descendants of famous writers. Fort served the role of finding a book which made writers' visions a reality, leaving their descendants living in a world populated by what should be fiction. It is fitting that Fort served the role of opening a Pandora's box to make the world stranger. His presence in comics may be limited, but Fort appears quite often for a relatively obscure writer. Even with fictional versions of him put aside, Kripal notes books that involve "flying saucers and aliens, [...] just about all [...] rely in some way on the four weird books of Charles Fort, the amazing stories of Ray Palmer, and the aftermath of those still unexplained events that swirled around Kenneth Arnold."[27] Indeed, just as Fort left his mark on the SF that followed him, he left a mark on the often similar genre of comic books.

10

Afterthoughts

My only guide has been the persistent feeling that science had offered no answer to some basic needs in our hearts, and perhaps the present loneliness of man, echoed in the great mysteries of times past, had provided most of the emotional power, most of the intellectual quality, mobilized in that unreachable goal: Magonia—a place where gentle folks and graceful fairies dance, and lament the coarse world below.

—Jacques Vallee[1]

After reading my work, more than a few readers and editors have said to me: "You should write fiction." To which I immediately reply: "But that's what my critics say I've been writing all along."

—Jeffrey J. Kripal[2]

Our Haunted Planet

In a bit of my own Fortean research, I stumbled across a UFO report near Delphos, Kansas, in 1971, which left behind unusual physical evidence. Ronald Johnson, a 16-year-old farm boy, walking his dog

> suddenly saw [...] a mushroom-shaped object, illuminated by multicolored lights over its entire surface and hovering twenty-five yards away, within two feet of the ground. Its diameter was about nine feet. The glow from the object was such that Ronald could see no details, and it was making a sound like "an old washing machine which vibrates." Then it brightened at the base and took off. The witness reportedly became temporarily blind. During all this the dog was "very quiet."[3]

After this evening sighting, the object left a strange luminescence in a ring upon the ground and in nearby trees. The ring was dry and "crusty" and could apparently repel water despite the ground around it being damp. It made Ronald's mother's fingers go numb, rendering her unable to take the pulse of patients in her occupation as a nurse. Perhaps most terrifying of all was the fact that Ronald was plagued by physical symptoms and nightmares following the encounter. According to Vallee, "he had the same dream, night after night, in which human-like creatures were looking into his window from the outside. Two or three times, when coming into his bedroom, his parents found him screaming, standing by the window."[4]

Elsewhere in Kansas, witnesses of the strange do not receive nightmares from their experiences, but rather enlightenment. Two hours away from Delphos, Dr. Scott Corder ran his medical practice in Ottawa, a town about an hour southeast of Kansas City. Starting as an investigator of the phenomenon in the late '70s, Corder encountered Donna Butts, a resident of Russell, Kansas. Butts gave Corder her entire story: "On a car trip in central Kansas in 1980, she saw a spaceship. Then, four years later, she began getting regular visits from a celestial being who called himself Cephas, but he was actually the Apostle Peter." Corder became enveloped in these strange happenings, eventually receiving a visit himself. As Corder "wolfed down a hamburger at the Sonic Drive-In one night, none other than the Apostle Peter, returned from a distant solar system to hasten Earth's new age, had caught his eye and winked at him."[5] Corder coauthored a contactee book with Butts in 1983 entitled *UFO Contact, the Four*, a text filled with various prophecies Butts channeled from these extraterrestrials. Because of Corder's involvement in the subject matter and eventual eccentric religious fervor, state medical authorities attempted to stop him from practicing medicine. The story even appeared in the sensationalist half-truth news rag, *The Weekly World News*, in a shockingly none-too-sensational article.[6]

One county eastward of Dr. Corder, in Lyndon, Steven L. Gibbs purportedly travels through time via a device he created called a Hyper Dimensional Resonator. A former Nebraska farmer, he was given the instructions to build the machine from a future version of himself. As strange as this may sound, Gibbs has created a following by selling HDR units. A paranormal researcher named Patricia Griffin Ress has written books following Gibbs's time travel experiments and exploits entitled *Stranger Than Fiction: The True Time Travel Adventures of Steven L. Gibbs—The Rainman of Time Travel*, and more recently, *Why I Believe the HDR Unit Works and Time Travel is Possible!* Despite its dated website design, the website hdrusers.com continues informing people about Gibbs' machine. Not breaking with the tradition of maybe-fiction texts interacting with one another, Ress alludes to the aforementioned Corder and Butts book:

> Indeed, even Donna Butts, the famous abductee / contactee of the UFO Butts-Corder case, said that she had been told by a group of aliens calling themselves the Americans that a "transmutational channel" had opened over Nebraska and Kansas. […] It is no coincidence that Steve Gibbs is from Nebraska and so is author Kathleen Keating, who sees the Biblical rapture occurring in a manner not inconsistent with the workings of Steve Gibbs [sic] time machine.[7]

Albert S. Rosales, a researcher who has compiled an enormous database of anomalous humanoid encounters, uncovered a report from an undisclosed location in Central Kansas. Originally reported by famed ufologist J. Allen Hynek, it happened on a summer night in 1972. A witness was driving on an isolated road when he saw "bright lights in a field" and assumed that they were those of a tractor. Upon further inspection: "He came upon a humanoid figure, described as having four arms, tall, well-built and wearing a tight-fitting black coverall and black skullcap. He also wore white gloves and a white belt. His facial features were not quite human; his eyes were large and round." Bizarrely, he spoke English and told the witness that "he was fourth in command of the nearby vehicle, which the witness was unable to see due to the glare." The humanoid told the witness that he was repairing the object and that he was a "miscreation" from another planet. The witness somehow persuaded the humanoid to let him on board the craft, but "went into a trance-like state" and recalled nothing except arriving at what seemed to be a "space station." He says that he stayed in this place for two weeks, where he was "given a translator" and saw "libraries" and "large glass-like buildings." Eventually, he was dumped in the same spot of isolated road where the journey began and saw the craft leave silently.[8]

Sightings of these aerial vehicles have taken place in Kansas since the days of Fort. In 1897, "a prosperous and prominent farmer" named Alexander Hamilton witnessed such a ship, well before the term "flying saucer" was in the popular vernacular. Researcher Frank Edwards reports on the claims of Hamilton:

> Every part of the vessel which was not transparent was of a dark reddish color. We stood mute with wonder and fright. Then some noise attracted their attention and they turned a light directly upon us. Immediately on catching sight of us they turned on some unknown power, and a great turbine wheel, about thirty feet in diameter, which was revolving slowly below the craft, began to buzz and the vessel rose lightly as a bird. When about three hundred feet above us it seemed to pause and to hover directly above a two-year-old heifer, which was bawling and jumping, apparently fast in the fence. Going to her, we found a cable about half an inch in thickness made of some red material fastened in a slip knot around her neck and going up to the vessel from the heifer tangled in the wire fence. We tried to get it off but could not, so we cut the wire loose to see the ship, heifer and all, rise slowly, disappearing in the northwest.[9]

The event seems to predict a phenomenon that would become common in the mostly rural state: cattle mutilations. In other instances, farmers will find their cattle dead in their pastures, drained of blood and missing vital organs. Fort wrote about these occurrences in *Wild Talents*, specifically a case in 1903 Staffordshire, though he puts forth the idea (as usual, semi-seriously) that "slashers and rippers of cattle may be throw-backs to the ape-era."[10]

In Southeast Kansas, amongst limestone quarries and abandoned lead mines, an air of mysteriousness shrouds the area, somewhat undefinable yet palpable upon viewing the mounds of toxic dust left behind from decades of lead mining in Treece, Kansas, a ghost town near the Oklahoma border that has been bought out by the EPA for cleanup. Amongst the toxic dust, something unsettling and possibly Fortean lurks. The nearby town of Scammon makes a strange appearance in Ben Mezrich's 2016 book *The 37th Parallel*. Mezrich recounts Debbie Zukowski's investigation into a UFO sighting as a member of MUFON's Star Team, a group that responds as quickly as possible to reports. The report was of a craft that looked like "a big mobile home in the sky," bright but without definite shape.[11] The sighting was nothing extraordinary, even for such an astonishing phenomenon like UFOs, but Zukowski's experiences after interviewing the witness are notably strange. The police department will not give her a copy of the report, even though one was made. She finds herself followed by black cars with tinted windows and government plates. The FBI becomes somehow involved with the case, Zukowski finds them talking to a police officer in a local restaurant where she seems to cause great suspicion. Another squadron of black vehicles follows her on a six-hour drive all the way back to her St. Louis home. Kansas seems to house its own version of *The X-Files*; FBI men following UFO researchers, time travelers, a doctor finding religion in UFOs, etc.

Not to be outdone by the Gobi Desert or Arrakis, a wormlike cryptid supposedly takes residence in Kansas' Lake Inman, the largest natural lake in the state. Bearing the name Sinkhole Sam because of the deep water area of the lake in which he was spotted, the entity is described as being "a very large snake-like creature, about 15 feet long and the diameter of an automobile tire."[12] Perhaps Sam is a marine variant of the Mongolian Death Worm, but it is unknown how he ended up in a Kansas lake. Maybe to promote tourism for the tiny town, supposed experts were brought in after the initial 1950s sighting, and presented findings akin to a carnival sideshow. They declared "that Sam was a 'Foopengerkle,' one of a species thought to be the 'extinctest' creatures ever to inhabit the Kansas Plains. This must be where he became Sam rather than Samantha, because (the experts) maintained that no female 'Foopengerkles' ever existed. Their final report urged caution, since Sam did not seem to realize he was extinct."[13] Sightings of Sam have been conspicuously sparse since this initial flurry of attention.

Kansas did not escape Fort's fastidious cataloging; he finds an 1882 report of an 80-pound mass of ice falling from the sky in Salina.[14] A flying serpent appeared in Fort Scott in 1873, among other places in the country, marking a continuation of "the very worst case of delirium tremens on record."[15] The most frightening piece of Kansas Forteana that Fort uncovers is the case of the Koett family of Ellinwood, who quickly moved after their "house had been bewitched—pictures turned to the wall—other objects moving about—their pet dog stabbed with a pitch fork, by an invisible."[16] Perhaps this was the case of an extremely nasty intruder, or maybe something dark and unknowable lurks on the Kansas prairie. Growing up in the state, there are times when the darkness seems darker and the silence seems louder, but the mind can play tricks. Maybe all these cases were the result of the paranoia that seeps into the minds of residents of isolated communities. I leave this open to the reader.

Closing Remarks

Here I have attempted to utilize some brief Fortean research of my own to illustrate how SF continues to "read like a series of imaginative riffs, with techno-realistic pictures now, on Charles Fort," as Kripal writes. The stories have evolved from being the loosely connected collections of anomalous data from Fort's time, now comfortably populating a variety of spaces, from the fringes to popular culture. But the science-fictional nature of our reality remains a consistent theme. Each of these cases occurred within my original home state of Kansas, but anyone can find a similar treasure trove of SF plots in their own backyard. In my later home of St. Louis, I continued to find these reports that sound like the beginnings of an SF novel. In the suburb of Kinloch in 1968, a bigfoot-like creature attempted to abduct a child from a backyard.[17] In 2000, St. Clair County (on the Illinois side of the metropolitan area) had numerous witnesses come forward to report a sighting of a triangle UFO, including a police officer.[18] In my current home of Pittsburgh, the so-called "Pennsylvania Roswell Incident" of 1965 occurred thirty miles east in Kecksberg. Witnesses saw a bright fireball crash to the surface of the Earth, some reporting seeing an "acorn-shaped spacecraft half buried in a gully." A model of the craft built for the incident's recreation in the television show *Unsolved Mysteries* is now displayed by the town's fire department.[19] The list could go on. I mostly ignore classifying these stories as "true" or "hoax" to retain the mode of entertainment they create. This literature, maybe-fiction, is entirely indebted to Fort. He popularized works of anomalous reports and influenced similar researchers to follow. Maybe-fiction continues to have an interlocked relationship with SF as the fact and fiction exist often indistinguishable from one another. Fort's mark on our lives and literature remains, although his name is somewhat forgotten in the madness of strange lights and phenomenal people that make up both our reality and our fiction. Whether our SF resembles our reality, or our reality resembles our SF, Fort had a hand in the development of both literary forms.

Unlike many maybe-fiction authors and even SF authors, I have never had a paranormal experience. Even the brilliant religious scholar and invaluable source Kripal had a paranormal experience in 1989, which he credits for the inception for the book *Mutants and Mystics*. The closest incident resembling such an experience was when I thought that some dark force followed me home from a small, rural Kansas graveyard I visited while exploring the backroads of the southeast portion of the state. Placed there was a gravestone for a baby less than a year old who had died in the 1950s. I was immediately overcome by a sense of eerie dread—I was plagued by nightmares for the next few nights and could not shake the horror of them even in waking hours. I chalked this up to circumstances that easily built up a paranoid state. Perhaps it was the paranormal non-fiction I read—perhaps they are that powerful. Not only does maybe-fiction entertain us, they can generate belief and experience, forming a cycle; belief (or suspension of disbelief) and experience are exactly the two necessary components for maybe-fiction. Yet neither of these components is required to enjoy maybe-fiction. In the previous chapters, I have gestured toward an understanding of the maybe-fiction genre as a type of "real" SF that functions similarly narratively but relies on a modicum of suspension of disbelief to be enjoyed fully. My interest in maybe-fiction did not originate from my own paranormal experience, but from reading the texts conveying others' experiences. I read these as a child, when my ability to recognize the difference between reputable and questionable texts was undeveloped. Yet I still read these works and enjoy them today whilst others scoff at them. At times, finding the stories amusing is an understandable response, but, in general, maybe-fiction lacks the respect that it deserves as a literary medium. Some might read these stories for a laugh at the expense of "crazy people." I do not think that Fort would laugh at them; he would somehow see a way in which their experiences or hypotheses were valid, no matter how much they seem to resemble fiction. As he said, there is no such thing as an absolute fictionist. Without immediately questioning an author's credibility and writing their works off as make-believe, maybe-fiction can be read as fascinating texts, gripping commentaries on our own reality. The texts can reveal a world that functions like an SF novel and creates experiences that frequently color our fiction. There is often the suggestion from Fort and others that our reality is being written, resulting in metatextual implications that are even more extreme.

Kripal appeared in the 2017 documentary *Love and Saucers*, a character study of David Huggins, a man who claims to have had numerous experiences with extraterrestrials and lost his virginity to an alien grey. The film gives great sympathy to its subject, setting out neither to disprove nor confirm the experiences of Huggins—who seems to be quite sane despite his claims, which some would find outlandish. Kripal offers his thoughts on Huggins' assertions. He treats the man much as the film itself does, with the careful respect he deserves, when it would be overwhelmingly easy to

10. Afterthoughts

dismiss him as mentally ill. But Kripal also provides an insight into the very relationship between SF and the paranormal:

> Some of the best and most popular science fiction writers of all time had jaw-dropping paranormal experiences and that's why they wrote the stories they wrote. It's the paranormal that produces the science fiction and then the science fiction loops back and influences the paranormal.[20]

I believe Kripal is completely correct in this statement. The symbiotic relationship between SF and the paranormal has given rise to the very existence of what I have termed maybe-fiction—works that exist somewhere in between the realms of fiction and non-fiction—including a broad swath of work from such unlike authors as Richard Sharpe Shaver and Jacques Vallee. This symbiotic relationship is not limited to specific kinds of work within the SF realm either, affecting such unlike works as Clarke's *2001: A Space Odyssey* and Shea and Wilson's *The Illuminatus Trilogy*. Why this influence is evident throughout SF is likely because of one simple fact: The unexplained has always fascinated us.

Another religious scholar, Brenda Denzler, wrote that the field of "ufology is a modern-day response to the lure of the edge—both a popular scientific inquiry teetering on the cutting edge of discovery and a manifestation of a 'lunatic fringe' living at a conceptual boundary beyond which there be monsters."[21] While this "lure of the edge" can most certainly be applied to the sciences, it can also be applied to the arts—especially literature. I believe it is this "lure" that made Fort's work appeal to SF authors, editors, and readers. All authors within this work found some facet of Fort's work that resonated with them. The result is a varied subset of literature, including both SF and maybe-fiction, that reveals the boundless speculation and creativity that comes from one man's quest to catalogue the unexplained. Fort himself likely felt such a lure, fastidiously attempting to pose explanations for the unexplainable. This lure is nearly omnipresent in all the literature examined in this work—SF authors as well as maybe-fiction authors are drawn to the topics on the fringes, though the latter is sometimes forced to reckon with the edge through no fault of their own.

In this book, I have attempted to illustrate how Charles Fort was an integral factor in bringing the real, albeit strange, world we inhabit into SF, but also how SF itself may have influenced later Fortean events and anomalous experiences. This consistent relationship continues to this day, continually going back-and-forth between fiction and non-fiction until determining what is real and what is not becomes an ambiguity-ridden and increasingly unattainable task. In December 2017, *The New York Times* featured a cover story revealing that the United States Defense Department spent 22 million dollars searching for answers regarding UFOs. Backed by "black money" and with the blessing of Senator Harry Reid, the program investigated sightings of aircraft that seemed to defy the traditional laws of physics. Concrete answers to these sightings were not achieved, but a frightening realization of unknowing was dredged up: "A 2009 Pentagon briefing summary of the program prepared by its director at the time asserted that 'what was considered science fiction is now science fact,' and that the United States was incapable of defending itself against some of the technologies discovered."[22] One such quote sounds exactly like the kind of newspaper clipping that Fort would include in his books:

> The program collected video and audio recordings of reported U.F.O. incidents, including footage from a Navy F/A-18 Super Hornet showing an aircraft surrounded by some kind of glowing aura traveling at high speed and rotating as it moves. The Navy pilots can be heard trying to understand what they are seeing. "There's a whole fleet of them," one exclaims.[23]

As further investigations into the phenomena continue, and as the phenomena continue daily, I hope that people are reminded of Charles Fort. I hope they remember the man who first catalogued all those lights in the sky and forever melded facts and fiction, greatly complicating the very definition of SF in its earliest stages. Though Fort may be long gone, the phenomena he documented have never ceased. Without rhyme or reason, but seemingly eternal nevertheless, the damned facts continue their march, still taunting us with their lack of explanation, still influencing our culture and haunting our art.

Chapter Notes

Introduction

1. Fort, Charles. *The Books of the Damned: The Collected Works of Charles Fort.* New York: Tarcher/Perigree, 2008: 225.
2. Vallee, Jacques. *Passport to Magonia: From Folklore to Flying Saucers.* Brisbane: Daily Grail Publishing, 2014: 9.
3. *Ibid.*, 23.
4. Kripal, Jeffrey J. *Mutants & Mystics: Science Fiction, Superhero Comics, and the Paranormal.* Chicago: University of Chicago Press, 2015: 101.

Chapter 1

1. Keel, John A. *The Mothman Prophecies.* New York: Tor, 2002: 9.
2. Wells, H.G. *The Time Machine.* New York: Airmont, 1895: 81.
3. *Ibid.*, 113–114.
4. Wells, H.G. *The War of the Worlds.* London: Houghton Mifflin Harcourt, 1898: 273–274.
5. Partington, John S. "The Death of the Static: H.G. Wells and the Kinetic Utopia." *Utopian Studies* 11, no. 2 (2000): 96.
6. Bowler, Peter J. *Evolution: The History of an Idea.* Berkeley: University of California Press, 2003: 319–320.
7. Wells, H.G. *The Time Machine.* New York: Airmont, 1895: 125.
8. *Ibid.*
9. Croce, Paul Jerome. "Science and Religion." *Encyclopedia of American Cultural and Intellectual History.* New York: Scribener's, 1999.
10. Kripal, Jeffrey J. *Authors of the Impossible: The Paranormal and the Sacred.* Chicago: University of Chicago Press, 2010: 40.
11. Fort, Charles. *The Books of Charles Fort.* New York: Henry Holt and Company, 1941: 40.
12. *Ibid.*, 48.
13. *Ibid.*, 59.
14. *Ibid.*, 919.
15. Fort, Charles. *The Booked of the Damned: The Collected Works of Charles Fort.* New York: Tarcher/Perigree, 2008: 3.
16. *Ibid.*, 11.
17. Steinmeyer, Jim. "Introduction." *The Book of the Damned: The Collected Works of Charles Fort.* New York: Tarcher/Perigree, 2008: viii.
18. *Ibid.*, viii.
19. Fort, Charles. *The Booked of the Damned: The Collected Works of Charles Fort.* New York: Tarcher/Perigree, 2008: 1019.
20. *Ibid.*, 24.
21. Steinmeyer, Jim. *Charles Fort: The Man Who Invented the Supernatural.* New York: Tarcher/Penguin, 2008: 255–256.
22. Kripal, Jeffrey J. *Mutants & Mystics: Science Fiction, Superhero Comics, and the Paranormal.* Chicago: University of Chicago Press, 2015: 85.
23. Fort, Charles. *The Book of the Damned: The Collected Works of Charles Fort.* New York: Tarcher/Penguin. 2008: 163.
24. *Ibid.*, 163.
25. Knight, Damon. *Charles Fort—Prophet of the Unexplained: A Biography of the American Iconoclast Who Dared to Explain Centuries of Strange Occult Phenomena.* Point Pleasant, NJ: New Saucerian Press, 2017: 70.
26. May, Andrew. *Pseudoscience and Science Fiction.* New York City: Springer International Publishing, 2017: 13. (Though I do take mild issue with May's decision to use the term "pseudoscience" as an all-

encompassing term for various paranormal topics, his book has been invaluable as a source and is recommended reading. Additionally, May qualifies that "for the most part, this book takes a non-judgmental attitude to the pseudoscientific topics it deals with. Whether they are right or wrong is irrelevant to the book's main purpose" [page ix].)

27. Fort, Charles Hoy. *The Book of the Damned: The Collected Works of Charles Fort*. New York: Tarcher/Penguin, 2008: 14.

28. Kripal, Jeffrey J. *Authors of the Impossible: The Paranormal and the Sacred*. Chicago: University of Chicago Press, 2010: 129.

29. Keel, John A. *Disneyland of the Gods*. Seattle: New Saucerian Press, 1988: 77.

30. Steinmeyer, Jim. *Charles Fort: The Man Who Invented the Supernatural*. New York: Tarcher/Penguin, 2008: 182.

31. *Ibid.*, 183.

32. Knight, Damon. *Charles Fort—Prophet of the Unexplained: A Biography of the American Iconoclast Who Dared to Explain Centuries of Strange Occult Phenomena*. Point Pleasant, NJ: New Saucerian Press, 2017: 47.

33. *Ibid.*, 168.

34. *Ibid.*, 184. (Aaron Sussman was a mutual friend of Thayer and Fort and helped found the Fortean Society.)

35. *Ibid.*

36. Kripal, Jeffrey J. *Mutants & Mystics: Science Fiction, Superhero Comics, and the Paranormal*. Chicago: University of Chicago Press, 2015: 89.

37. *Ibid.*, 90.

38. Tremaine, F. Orlin, editor. "Table of Contents." *Astounding Stories*. New York: Street & Smith, April 1934: 3.

39. *Ibid.*, 11.

40. Langford, Dave. "SF Books of the Damned." *Fortean Times Weird Year 1996*. London: John Brown Publishing, 1996.

41. Kripal, Jeffrey J. *Mutants & Mystics: Science Fiction, Superhero Comics, and the Paranormal*. Chicago: University of Chicago Press, 2015: 89.

42. *Ibid.*, 90.

Chapter 2

1. Steinmeyer, Jim. *Charles Fort: The Man Who Invented the Supernatural*. New York: Tarcher/Penguin, 2008: 139.

2. Vallee, Jacques. *Messengers of Deception: UFO Contacts and Cults*. Brisbane: Daily Grail Publishing, 1979: 244–245.

3. Miller, R. Dewitt. *Impossible—Yet it Happened!* New York: Ace Books, 1973: 103.

4. *Ibid.*, 10.

5. Gould, Rupert T. *Oddities*. New York: Paperback Library, 1969: 11.

6. Miller, R. Dewitt. *Impossible—Yet it Happened!* New York: Ace Books, 1973: 11.

7. *Ibid.*, 11.

8. *Ibid.*, cover page.

9. Gould, Rupert T. *Oddities*. New York: Paperback Library, 1969. Cover page.

10. O'Brien, Barbara. *Operators and Things*. New York: Ace Books, 1958. Cover page.

11. Nodelman, Perry. "The Cognitive Estrangement of Darko Suvin." *Children's Literature Association Quarterly* 5, no. 4 (Winter 1981): 24.

12. Fort, Charles. *The Books of Charles Fort*. New York: Henry Holt and Company, 1941: 864.

13. *Ibid.*, 3–4.

14. Kripal, Jeffrey J. *Mutants and Mystics: Science Fiction, Superhero Comics, and the Paranormal*. Chicago: University of Chicago Press, 2015: 5.

15. Kripal, Jeffrey J. *Authors of the Impossible: The Paranormal and the Sacred*. Chicago: University of Chicago Press, 2010: 122.

16. Kripal, Jeffrey J. *Mutants and Mystics: Science Fiction, Superhero Comics, and the Paranormal*. Chicago: University of Chicago Press, 2015: 26–28.

17. Pasulka, D.W. *American Cosmic: UFOs, Religion, Technology*. New York: Oxford University Press, 2019: 121.

18. *Ibid.*, 122–123.

19. *Ibid.*, 131.

20. *Ibid.*, 135.

21. Davis, Erik. *High Weirdness: Drugs, Esoterica, and Visionary Experience in the Seventies*. London: Strange Attractor Press & The MIT Press, 2019: 1.

22. *Ibid.*, 9.

23. *Ibid.*, 3–4.

24. *Ibid.*, 41.

25. *Ibid.*, 14.

26. Britt, Ryan. "Meet the UFO Expert Who Doesn't Believe in Aliens." *Inverse*, Full Stack Media Inc., 13 September 2016, https://www.inverse.com/article/20857-ufos-flying-saucers-jack-womack. (William

Gibson's introduction to Womack's book is explored in Chapter 9.)

27. Womack, Jack. "Jack Womack: Going, Going, Gone." Forum post at Inkwell.vue. 1 August 2001. https://people.well.com/conf/inkwell.vue/topics/118/Jack-Womack-Going-Going-Gone-page01.html#post23

28. Womack, Jack. "Jack Womack: Going, Going, Gone." Forum post at Inkwell.vue. 2 August 2001. https://people.well.com/conf/inkwell.vue/topics/118/Jack-Womack-Going-Going-Gone-page02.html#post27 (This post also includes a somewhat extensive list of topics that appear in the collection, most of them maybe-fictional: Beginning with Advertising, going on through Amusements, Animals [in relation to people], Anthropology, Archeology, Architecture, Art, Assassinations, Astronomy, Atrocities, Bibliographic, Bibliophilic, Cannibalism, Cities, Comics, Cranks, Crime, Cryptobotany, Cryptozoology [including sea & lake monsters, yetis, yowies, bunyips, Surrey panthers, ghostly mongeese, Owlman—Mothman falls under UFOs], Cults [including Scientology, People's Temple, Elvis], Death [including Forensics and Funerals], Disasters, Disappearances, Drugs, Eccentrics, Fairies (traditional sort), Film, Forteana, Frauds, Gastronomy, History, Hoaxes, Holocaust, Japan, Kentucky, Literature [outré/puzzling/incomprehensible], Lost Continents, Lycanthropy, Magic [stage, cultural], Manias, Medicine, Military Blunders, Mind [altered states], Music, Nature, Nazis, Occult, Pets, Photography, Popular Culture, Propaganda, Racism, Rumors, Russia, Satanism [pro and con], Science [so-called, i.e., Tesla et al.], Sea Mysteries, Sex, Skepticism, Stripping, Subcultures, Teeth, Teratology, Transgender, Travel, UFOs & related [cattle mutilation, crop circles etc.], Vampires, Witches, Women [badly behaved], Zombies.)

29. Shaeffer, Robert. "The 'Transformation' of Whitley Strieber." *BASIS*, the Bay Area Skeptics Newsletter. November 1988. Reproduced at http://www.debunker.com/texts/strieber.html

30. Kripal, Jeffrey J. *Mutants and Mystics: Science Fiction, Superhero Comics, and the Paranormal*. Chicago: University of Chicago Press, 2015: 326.

31. *Ibid.*, 299.

32. *Ibid.*, 87. (Kripal also includes a third "Dominant" that reflects a more Fortean "totalizing system": "The New Dominant" of what he calls Intermediatism, which he associates with the way of knowing called expression or acceptance and the professionalism of a new brand of individuating wizards and witches with various "wild talents"—in essence, superpowers.)

33. Nickell, Joe. "Charles Fort: Purveyor of the Unprobed." *Skeptical Briefs*, Vol. 18.3. Amherst: Committee for Skepitcal Inquiry, Winter 2008/2009. https://skepticalinquirer.org/newsletter/charles_fort_purveyor_of_the_unprobed/

34. *Ibid.*

35. Gardner, Martin. *Fads and Fallacies in the Name of Science: The Curious Theories of Modern Pseudoscientists and the Strange, Amusing and Alarming Cults That Surround Them. A Study in Human Gullibility*. New York: Dover Publications, 1952: 49.

36. Shaver, Richard S. "I Remember Lemuria!" *Amazing Stories*. Chicago: Ziff-Davis, March 1945: 15.

37. Nichols, Preston B., and Peter Moon. *The Montauk Project: Experiments in Time*. Westbury, NY: Sky Books, 1992: 12.

38. Heitman, Danny. "Fiction as Authentic as Fact." *The Wall Street Journal*. New York: News Corp, 11 January 2013. https://www.wsj.com/articles/SB10001424127887323936804578227971298012486

39. Gavin, Michael. "Real Robinson Crusoe." *Eighteenth-Century Fiction* 25, no. 2 (Winter 2012–13): 305.

40. *Ibid.*, 303.

41. Keel, John A. *The Mothman Prophecies*. New York: Tor, 2002.

42. Knight, Peter. *Conspiracy Theories in American History: An Encyclopedia*. Santa Barbara: ABC-CLIO Inc., 2003: 704.

43. Kelleher, Colm A. and George Knapp. *Hunt for the Skinwalker: Science Confronts the Unexplained at a Remote Ranch in Utah*. New York: Pocket Books, 2005.

44. Sutton, David. *Fortean Times*, Issue 302. London: Dennis Publishing, June 2013.

45. Boeche, Ray W. "Where's Steve McQueen When You Need Him?" *Journal of the Fortean Research Center*. Lincoln: Fortean Research Center, April 1986: 5.

46. Foster, Mike. "Batboy led U.S. troops to Saddam… Gotcha!" *Weekly World News*. New York: American Media, 13 January 2004: 24–25.

47. Alexander, Jack. "UFO Expert Warns Earthlings: Space aliens will invade if

Notes—Chapter 2

we lay one finger on 'em!" *Weekly World News*. New York: American Media, 2 March 1993: 6.

48. Strieber, Whitley. *Communion: A True Story*. New York: Avon Books, 1987: 227.

49. *Ibid*.

50. Menger, Howard. *Authentic Music from Another Planet*, Slate Enterprises, 1957. LP record.

51. Phillips, Graham, and Martin Keatman. *The Green Stone*. London: Panther Books, 1983.

52. LaChance, Steven, and Laura Long-Helbig. *The Uninvited: The True Story of the Union Screaming House*. Woodbury, MN: Llewellyn Publications, 2008.

53. Morehouse, David. *Psychic Warrior*. New York: St. Martin's Press, 1996.

54. Kripal, Jeffrey J. *Authors of the Impossible: The Paranormal and the Sacred*. Chicago: University of Chicago Press, 2010: 143–144.

55. *Ibid*., 144.

56. *Ibid*., 180–181.

57. Churchward, James. *The Lost Continent of MU*. New York: Paperback Library, 1970: 12.

58. *Ibid*., 5.

59. Gardner, Martin. *Fads and Fallacies in the Name of Science: The Curious Theories of Modern Pseudoscientists and the Strange, Amusing and Alarming Cults That Surround Them. A Study in Human Gullibility*. New York: Dover Publications, 1952: 170.

60. Regal, Brian. *Pseudoscience: A Critical Encyclopedia*. Santa Barbara: ABC-CLIO, 2009: 81. (Regal also notes how Charles Fort was a precursor of hidden history literature, continuing the trends explored in Chapter 2.)

61. Other alternative history proponents that fit these categories are Ignatius Donnelly, Immanuel Velikovsky, and even Stanislav Szukalski's Zematism.

62. Baratta, Anthony. "WonderCon 2008: Day 2—Part 1!" at *Comingsoon.net*. 24 February 2008. https://www.comingsoon.net/movies/features/42310-wondercon-2008-day-2-part-1#0DgyWWXeljPO0PzR.99 (Emmerich also directed *The Day After Tomorrow*, based on a book by two prominent personalities in maybe-fiction: Art Bell and Whitley Strieber's 1999 work *The Coming Global Superstorm*.)

63. *Prometheus* drew inspiration from *Chariots of the Gods* while *Scooby-Doo! Mystery Incorporated* borrowed from Sitchin's Nibiru mythos.

64. Feindt, Carl W. *UFOs and Water: Physical Effects of UFOs on Water Through Accounts by Eyewitnesses*. Bloomington: Xlibris Corporation, 2010: xxix.

65. Rogo, D. Scott, and Raymond Bayless. *Phone Calls from the Dead*. New York: Berkley Books, 1979: 176.

66. May, Andrew. *Pseudoscience and Science Fiction*. New York City: Springer International Publishing, 2017: viii.

67. Brunwald, Jan Harold. *Too Good to be True: The Colossal Book of Urban Legends*. New York: W.W. Norton & Co., 1999: 19.

68. Fort, Charles. *The Books of Charles Fort*. New York: Henry Holt and Company, 1941: 864.

69. *Ibid*.

70. Matheny, Joseph. *The Incunabula Papers: Ong's Hat and Other Gateways to New Dimensions*. Self-published, 1999.

71. Kinsella, Michael. *Legend-Tripping Online: Supernatural Folklore and the Search for Ong's Hat*. Jackson: University Press of Mississippi, 2011: 68.

72. *Ibid*., 11.

73. Moss, Stephanie. "*Dracula* and *The Blair Witch Project*: The Problem with Scientific Empiricism." *Nothing That Is: Millennial Cinema and the* Blair Witch *Controversies*. Eds. Sarah L. Higley and Jeffrey Andrew Weinstock. Detroit: Wayne State University Press, 2004: 197.

74. *Ibid*., 212.

75. Rock, Ben. "Re: Blair Witch and Forteana." Message to author. 10 July 2019. Facebook message.

76. *Ibid*. (Rock is perhaps referring to Jim Woodman's 1977 work *Nazca Journey to the Sun*.)

77. *Ibid*.

78. Grundy, Benjamin, and Aaron Wright. "17.05." *Mysterious Universe*, season 17, episode 5, 2017. https://mysteriousuniverse.org/2017/02/17-05-mu-podcast.

79. Webster, Ken. *The Vertical Plane: The Mystery of the Dodleston Messages—A Bizarre Record of Communication Through Time*. London: Grafton, 1989.

80. Senkowski, Ernst. *Instrumental Transcommunication*. (Translated from German) http://www.worlditc.org/c_07_

senki_f_38.12.11.htm Originally published 1995.
81. *Ibid.*
82. Vallee, Jacques. *Messengers of Deception: UFO Contacts and Cults.* Brisbane: Daily Grail Publishing, 1979: 263–264.
83. Clark, Jerome. *Extraordinary Encounters: An Encyclopedia of Extraterrestrials and Otherworldly Beings.* Santa Barbara: ABC-CLIO Inc., 2000: 16.
84. Keel, John A. *The Mothman Prophecies.* New York: Tor, 2002: 13.
85. Clark, Jerome. *Extraordinary Encounters: An Encyclopedia of Extraterrestrials and Otherworldly Beings.* Santa Barbara: ABC-CLIO Inc., 2000: 95–97.
86. Conroy, Ed. *Report on Communion: The Facts Behind the Most Controversial True Story of All Time.* New York: Avon Books, 1989: 18–19.
87. Knight, Peter. *Conspiracy Theories in American History: An Encyclopedia.* Santa Barbara: ABC-CLIO Inc., 2003: 120.
88. Johnston, Mike. "Getting to the Bottom of Mel's Hole." *The Kittitas County Daily Record.* 31 March 2012. Accessed 15 July 2019. https://www.dailyrecordnews.com/news/getting-to-the-bottom-of-mels-hole/article_d72b6a68-7ac2-11e1-b3ce-001a4bcf887a.html
89. *Ibid.*
90. Harvey, Doug. "Hole Story." *Aspects of Mel's Hole: Artists Respond to a Paranormal Land Event Occurring in Radiospace.* Ed. Doug Harvey. Santa Ana: Grand Central Press, 2008: 7.
91. *Ibid.*, 9.
92. Vida-Spence, Judith E. "What's Missing?" *Aspects of Mel's Hole: Artists Respond to a Paranormal Land Event Occurring in Radiospace.* Ed. Doug Harvey. Santa Ana: Grand Central Press, 2008: 31.
93. Tucker, Brian. "An Awfully Deep Hole." *Aspects of Mel's Hole: Artists Respond to a Paranormal Land Event Occurring in Radiospace.* Ed. Doug Harvey. Santa Ana: Grand Central Press, 2008: 92–93.
94. Harvey, Doug. "Hole Story." *Aspects of Mel's Hole: Artists Respond to a Paranormal Land Event Occurring in Radiospace.* Ed. Doug Harvey. Santa Ana: Grand Central Press, 2008: 7.
95. Clarke, Arthur C. *Astounding Days: A Science Fictional Autobiography.* New York: Bantam, 1989: 118.
96. *Ibid.*
97. Dolan, Richard M. *UFOs and the National Security State: Chronology of a Cover-up 1941–1973.* Charlottesville: Hampton Roads Publishing Co., 2002: 89. (Dolan's work is one of the few comprehensive surveys of the culture of UFOs from an insider's perspective. While his personal views may come under fire, as many such maybe-fiction texts do, Dolan falls under the same umbrella as Jacques Vallee as a researcher. This work is most valuable when viewed as a book about the development of ufology as opposed to the UFOs themselves.)
98. Keel, John A. "The Flying Saucer Subculture." *The Journal of Popular Culture* 8, no. 4 (Spring 1975): 875.
99. Keel, John A. "The Man Who Invented Flying Saucers." *Fortean Times.* No. 41, Winter 1983. Accessed 14 July 2019. http://www.thejinn.net/man_who_invented_flying_saucers.htm
100. Keel, John A. *The Mothman Prophecies.* New York: Tor, 2002: 267.
101. Strieber, Whitley, and Jeffrey J. Kripal. *The Super Natural: Why the Unexplained Is Real.* New York: TarcherPerigree, 2016: 70.
102. Vallee, Jacques. *Passport to Magonia: From Folklore to Flying Saucers.* Brisbane: Daily Grail Publishing, 1969: 170.
103. Fort, Charles. *The Books of Charles Fort.* New York: Henry Holt and Company, 1941: 638.
104. Vallee, Jacques. *Messengers of Deception: UFO Contacts and Cults.* Brisbane: Daily Grail Publishing, 1979: 168.
105. *Ibid.*, 229.
106. Hynek, J. Allen, and Jacques Vallee. *The Edge of Reality: A Progress Report on Unidentified Flying Objects.* Chicago: Henry Regnery Company, 1975: 230–231.
107. Jeffrey, Adi-Kent Thomas. *Parallel Universe.* New York: Warner Books, 1977. Front cover
108. *Ibid.*, 47.
109. Fort, Charles. *The Books of Charles Fort.* New York: Henry Holt and Company, 1941: 902.
110. Roberts, Anthony, and Geoff Gilbertson. *The Dark Gods.* London: Rider/Hutchinson, 1980: 204.
111. *Ibid.*
112. Putnam, Robert. *Bowling Alone: The Collapse and Revival of American Commu-*

nities. New York: Simon and Schuster, 2000: 21.

113. Hansen, George P. *The Trickster and the Paranormal*. Bloomington: Xlibris Corporation, 2001: 213.

114. Almeida, Rafael Antunes. "UFOs, Ufologists, and Digital Media in Brazil" in *Believing in Bits: Digital Media and the Supernatural*. Eds. Simone Natale and D.W. Pasulka. New York: Oxford University Press, 2019.

115. Suvin, Darko. "On the Poetics of the Science Fiction Genre." *College English* 34, no. 3 (December 1972): 380.

116. Drake, David. "Re: Various INFO Issues." Message to author. 14 November 2018. Email. (Drake also gave an interesting insight into his own views on using Forteana in SF: "Early on I thought that Fort's data would be a great source of story ideas, but I quickly learned that an idea isn't a story, true or not. I don't think that any of those notions ever saw print." Such a viewpoint is notable given Drake's prominence in both Forteana and SF; Drake seems to separate the two despite being highly interested in both. His most popular works are of military SF, with the Hammer's Slammers series and other works set in the same universe. Nevertheless, he tells me that some of his 1970s short stories, "'The Last Battalion" and "Children of the Forest," are directly inspired by Fortean studies [UFOs] and Sasquatches respectively. The latter story appeared fittingly in a special Damon Knight issue of *The Magazine of Fantasy and Science Fiction* in November 1976. Further exploration into Drake's Fortean tendencies are explored in Chapter 9.)

117. "International Fortean Organization." *Wikipedia*, Wikimedia Foundation, 5 Sept. 2018, en.wikipedia.org/wiki/International_Fortean_Organization. (The entry has inaccurate dates for Bob Rickard's founding of *The Times*, which would eventually become *Fortean Times*, further clouding the possibility that the source of this entry is to be entirely trusted.)

118. Webb, Stephen. *All the Wonder That Would Be: Exploring Past Notions of the Future*. New York City: Springer International Publishing, 2017: 154.

119. Shoemaker, Michael. "Re: Charles Fort Inquiry." Message to author. 17 November 2018. Email.

120. *Ibid*. (According to numerous correspondents, the same purveyor of this possible misinformation has created great friction within the group for numerous reasons. I do not wish to name this person out of respect to the correspondents who made it clear that they did not want them named either. I only wish to express my sadness at seeing the remains of the International Fortean Organization, fragmented and largely out of contact. This was a group that I would have liked to have joined, had events not turned out as negatively as they have. I also know that it was a joy to correspond with many of these members and I am disappointed that the forum that was once INFO no longer brings them all together apart from a small convention held once a year.)

121. Rickard, Bob. Reply to "Help Finding a Source About INFO." Forteana.org forums, 24 May 2019. https://forums.forteana.org/index.php?threads/help-finding-a-source-about-info.64640/

122. Knight, Damon. *Charles Fort—Prophet of the Unexplained: A Biography of the American Iconoclast Who Dared to Explain Centuries of Strange Occult Phenomena*. Point Pleasant, NY: New Saucerian Press, 2017: 202.

123. Abrahams, Brad, director. *Love and Saucers*. Curator Pictures, 2017.

124. *Ibid*., 157.

125. *Ibid*., 158.

126. Roberts, Andy. "John Keel R.I.P." *Sott.net*, 2 Sept. 2009, www.sott.net/article/-192949-John-Keel-R-I-P. Interview originally appeared in *UFO Brigantia* Newsletter 53/54, 1992.

127. Keel, John A. *The Lunarite*. Issue 1, 1946. Scan at http://www.johnkeel.com/?p=48

128. Keel, John A. "Was PKD a Flake?" *Philip K. Dick Society Newsletter #15* (ed. Paul Williams). Philip K. Dick Society, 1987: 5.

129. Coleman, Loren. "Mothman Illustrator Frazetta Dies." Web blog post. *Cryptomundo*. 10 May 2010. Accessed on 13 July 2019.

130. Kripal, Jeffrey J. *Authors of the Impossible: The Paranormal and the Sacred*. Chicago: University of Chicago Press, 2010: 167.

131. Vallee, Jacques. *UFOs: The Psychic Solution* (originally published as *The Invisi-*

ble College). Frogmore, Hertsfordshire: Panther Books, 1975: 213.
132. Vallee, Jacques. *Messengers of Deception: UFO Contacts and Cults*. Brisbane: Daily Grail Publishing, 1979: 224–225.
133. Strieber, Whitley. *Communion: A True Story*. New York: Avon Books, 1987: 10.
134. *Ibid*., 24.
135. *Ibid*., 24–25.

Chapter 3

1. Campbell, John W. "Review of *The Books of Charles Fort*." *Astounding Science Fiction*. New York: Street & Smith, August 1941: 147.
2. Lovecraft, H.P. "The Descendant." www.hplovecraft.com/writings/texts/fiction/de.aspx.
3. Wetzel, George T. *Collected Essays on H.P. Lovecraft and Others*. Rockville, MD: Wildside Press, 2015: 13.
4. *Ibid*.
5. Steinmeyer, Jim. *Charles Fort: The Man Who Invented the Supernatural*. New York: Tarcher/Penguin, 2008.
6. Josiffe, Christopher. *Gef! The Strange Tale of an Extra-Special Talking Mongoose*. London: Strange Attractor Press, 2017: 360.
7. Redfern, Nick. *The Slenderman Mysteries: An Internet Urban Legend Comes to Life*. Newburyport, MA: New Page Books, 2017: 80–85.
8. Tyson, Donald. *The Dream World of H.P. Lovecraft: His Life, His Demons, His Universe*. Woodbury, NY: Llewellyn Publications, 2010: 34.
9. Holloway, James. "H.P. Lovecraft and the Horror of History." *Fortean Times*. Issue 369, August 2018: 32.
10. *Ibid*., 39.
11. Lovecraft, H.P. "To Fritz Leiber 15 November 1936." *Selected Letter V: 1934–1937*. Sauk City, WI: Arkham House, 1976: 352–353.
12. Lovecraft, H.P. "To Fritz Leiber 9 November 1936." *Selected Letter V: 1934–1937*.: 343.
13. Wilson, Colin. *The Strength to Dream: Literature and the Imagination*. London: Abacus, 1976: 16.
14. Moskowitz, Sam. *Seekers of Tomorrow: Masters of Modern Science Fiction*. New York: The World Publishing Company, 1966: 143.
15. Russell, Eric Frank. "Sinister Barrier." *Unknown*. New York: Street & Smith, March 1939: 10.
16. *Ibid*.
17. *Ibid*., 11.
18. Russell, Eric Frank. *Sinister Barrier*. New York: Paperback Library, 1966: 67.
19. *Ibid*., 75.
20. *Ibid*.
21. Fox, Gardner. *Showcase* #61. New York: National Periodical Publications, 1966. Cover page. (Perhaps unsurprisingly, Gardner Fox was a prolific pulp SF author before his tenure as a highly influential comic book writer for DC Comics. He possibly had some say in the cover art, as both the cover and title are referential to Russell's *Sinister Barrier*.)
22. Russell, Eric Frank. "Sinister Barrier." *Unknown*. New York: Street & Smith, March 1939: 10.
23. Russell, Eric Frank. "The Creeping Coffins of Barbados." *Fantastic*. New York: Ziff-Davis, April 1958: 87.
24. Thayer, Tiffany. *Doubt*. Issue 61. New York: The Fortean Society, 1931: 66.
25. Knight, Damon. *Charles Fort—Prophet of the Unexplained: A Biography of the American Iconoclast Who Dared to Explain Centuries of Strange Occult Phenomena*. Point Pleasant, NY: New Saucerian Press, 2017: 200.
26. Langford, Dave. "SF Books of the Damned." *Fortean Times Weird Year 1996*. London: John Brown Publishing, 1996.
27. Moskowitz, Sam. *Seekers of Tomorrow: Masters of Modern Science Fiction*. New York: The World Publishing Company, 1966: 75.
28. *Ibid*.
29. *Ibid*., 144.
30. Steinmeyer, Jim. *Charles Fort: The Man Who Invented the Supernatural*. New Yorker: Tarcher/Penguin, 2008: 207.
31. *Ibid*., 213–214.
32. Moskowitz, Sam. *Seekers of Tomorrow: Masters of Modern Science Fiction*. New York: The World Publishing Company, 1966: 76.
33. Gernsback, Hugo. "Foreword to *The Space Visitors*." *Air Wonder Stories*. Mt. Morris, MI: Stellar Publishing Corporation, March 1930.
34. Moskowitz, Sam. *Seekers of Tomorrow: Masters of Modern Science Fiction*. New

York: The World Publishing Company, 1966: 134–135.

35. Hamilton, Edmond. "The Earth-Owners." *Weird Tales*. Indianapolis: Popular Fiction Publishing, August 1931: 140.

36. May, Andrew. *Pseudoscience and Science Fiction*. New York: Springer International Publishing, 2017: 9.

37. Fort, Charles. *The Books of Charles Fort*. New York: Henry Holt and Company, 1941: 534.

38. *Ibid.*, 914.

39. deFord, Miriam Allen. "Slips Take Over." *The Magazine of Fantasy and Science Fiction*. New York: Mercury Press, September 1964: 31–32.

40. Russell, Eric Frank. *Sinister Barrier*. New York: Paperback Library, 1939: 66.

41. Willis, Paul. "Obituary" in *The INFO Journal: Science and the Unknown*. Vol. 4, No. 3. Arlington: International Fortean Organization, May 1975: 29.

42. Steinmeyer, Jim. *Charles Fort: The Man Who Invented the Supernatural*. New York: Tarcher/Penguin, 2013: 257–258. (Fort perceived that Shipley found his work to be a kind of non-fiction fiction, a notion highly resonant with this book.)

43. Willis, Paul. "Editorial" in *The INFO Journal: Science and the Unknown*. Vol. 4, No. 4. Arlington: International Fortean Organization, March 1976. Inside cover.

44. Shoemaker, Michael. "Re: Charles Fort Inquiry." Message to author. 17 November 2018. Email

45. Leiber, Fritz. *H.P. Lovecraft: A Symposium*. Folcroft Library Editions, 1972. Sponsored by the Los Angeles Science Fantasy Society: 4

46. Sapiro, Leland. *H.P. Lovecraft: A Symposium*. Folcroft Library Editions, 1972. Sponsored by the Los Angeles Science Fantasy Society: 4

47. Lovecraft, H.P. "To Fritz Leiber 15 November 1936" in *Selected Letters V: 1934–1937*: 354.

48. Webb, Stephen. *All the Wonder That Would Be: Exploring Past Notions of the Future*. New York: Springer International Publishing, 2017: 154–155.

49. *Ibid.*, 153.

50. Leiber, Fritz, and Bernard C. Gilford. *You're All Alone / The Liquid Man*. Medford, OR: Armchair Fiction, 2010: 10.

51. *Ibid.*, 22.

52. *Ibid.*, 82.

53. Herbert, Frank. "Rat Race." *Astounding Science Fiction*. New York: Street and Smith, July 1955: 90. (In the original printing, Herbert spells Fort's name as "Forte" but it is unclear if this is an error on the author's part or the editorial board. The error is corrected in subsequent reprintings of "Rat Race.")

54. *Ibid.*, 95.

55. *Ibid.*, 108.

56. Andrews, Roy Chapman. *On the Trail of Ancient Man: A Narrative of the Field Work of the Central Asiatic Expeditions*. New York: The Knickerbocker Press, 1926: 103.

57. Herbert, Frank. "Sandworms of Dune." *The Maker of Dune: Insights of a Master of Science Fiction*. New York: Berkeley Books, 1987: 122.

58. *Ibid.*, 123.

59. Palmer, Raymond A. "The Observatory." *Amazing Stories*. Chicago: Ziff-Davis Publishing, October 1946: 6.

60. *Ibid*

61. Sherman, Harold M. "The Green Man." *Amazing Stories*. Chicago: Ziff-Davis Publishing, October 1946: 157. (As a brief aside into the Fortean nature of *Amazing* in this era, while Shaver material is limited to the discussion section of the issue [a man reportedly receives a letter from a "dero" setting the record of the Shaver stories straight] strange science and unexplained mysteries still abound. Just under the ending of *The Green Man*, there is a snippet about "the onion cure," covering experimental studies where onions were used to cure infections in animals. Included are older reports of onions curing dropsies and a call for further research into onions as a cure for ailments.)

62. Gross, Loren E. *Charles Fort, The Fortean Society, and Unidentified Flying Objects*. Fremont, CA: Privately published, 1976: 71.

63. *Ibid*.

64. Fort, Charles. *The Books of Charles Fort*. New York: Henry Holt and Company, 1941: 629.

65. Wilkins, Hubert and Harold M. Sherman. *Thoughts through Space: A Remarkable Adventure in the Realm of the Mind*. New York: Creative Age Press, 1942: 382.

Chapter 4

1. Shaver, Richard S. "A Witch in the Night." *The Hidden World*. Mundelein, IL: Palmer Publications, Spring 1961: 15.

2. Johnson, Robert Barbour. "Charles

Fort: His Objectives Fade in the West." *IF: Worlds of Science Fiction*. Buffalo: Quinn Publishing Company, July 1952: 134.
   3. Kripal, Jeffrey J. *Authors of the Impossible: The Paranormal and the Sacred*. Chicago: University of Chicago Press, 2010: 97.
   4. Kripal, Jeffrey J. *Mutants & Mystics: Science Fiction, Superhero Comics, and the Paranormal*. Chicago: University of Chicago Press, 2015: 91–92.
   5. *Ibid.*, 94–95.
   6. *Ibid.*, 96.
   7. *Ibid.*, 98–99.
   8. *Ibid.*, 99–100.
   9. *Ibid.*
   10. *Ibid.*, 100.
   11. *Ibid.*, 101.
   12. Toronto, Richard. *War over Lemuria: Richard Shaver, Ray Palmer and the Strangest Chapter of 1940s Science Fiction*. Jefferson, NC: McFarland, 2013: 118.
   13. *Ibid.*, 119.
   14. *Ibid.*
   15. *Ibid.*
   16. *Ibid.*, 141.
   17. *Ibid.*, 145.
   18. Palmer, Raymond A. "The Observatory." *Amazing Stories*. Chicago: Ziff-Davis, July 1946: 6.
   19. *Ibid.*
   20. *Ibid.*, 129–130.
   21. Toronto, Richard. *War over Lemuria: Richard Shaver, Ray Palmer and the Strangest Chapter of 1940s Science Fiction*. Jefferson, NC: McFarland, 2013: 6.
   22. Rogers, Margaret (as D.C. Rogers). "Wow! Don't Stop Here!" *Amazing Stories*. Chicago: Ziff-Davis, September 1946: 177.
   23. *Ibid.*, 178.
   24. *Ibid.*
   25. Rogers, Margaret. "Action for Mrs. Rogers!" *Amazing Stories*. Chicago: Ziff-Davis, December 1946: 162.
   26. Rogers, Margaret. "I Have Been in the Caves." *Amazing Stories*. Chicago: Ziff-Davis, January 1947: 10.
   27. *Ibid.*, 23.
   28. *Ibid.*, 23–24.
   29. Rogers, Margaret. "Action for Mrs. Rogers!" *Amazing Stories*. Chicago: Ziff-Davis, December 1946: 164.
   30. Reyna, L.J. "Prefatory Note." Barbara O'Brien's *Operators and Things: The Inner Life of a Schizophrenic*. Los Angeles: Silver Birch Press, 2011: 19.
   31. O'Brien, Barbara. *Operators and Things: The Inner Life of a Schizophrenic*. Los Angeles: Silver Birch Press, 2011: 199.
   32. Tausk, Victor. "On the Origin of the 'Influencing Machine' in Schizophrenia." *Journal of Psychotherapy Practice and Research* 1, no. 2 (Spring 1992): 186.
   33. Rickels, Laurence A. *I Think I Am: Philip K. Dick*. Minneapolis: University of Minnesota Press, 2010: 186.
   34. O'Brien, Barbara. *Operators and Things: The Inner Life of a Schizophrenic*. Los Angeles: Silver Birch Press, 2011: 165.
   35. Keyes, Daniel. *The Minds of Billy Milligan*. New York: Bantam, 1981: xi–xii.
   36. Kripal, Jeffrey J. *Mutants & Mystics: Science Fiction, Superhero Comics, and the Paranormal*. Chicago: University of Chicago Press, 2015: 100.
   37. Ashley, Michael. *Transformation : The Story of the Science-Fiction Magazines from 1950 to 1970*. London: Liverpool University Press, 2005: 48.
   38. Palmer, Raymond A. "Is the Government Hiding Saucer Facts?" *Amazing Stories*. New York: Ziff-Davis, October 1957: 70.
   39. Arnold, Kenneth. "The Saucers Still Patrol Our Skies." *Amazing Stories*. New York: Ziff-Davis, October 1957: 82.
   40. Shaver, Richard S. "Historical Aspect of the Saucers." *Amazing Stories*. New York: Ziff-Davis, October 1957: 96.
   41. *Ibid.*, 97.
   42. *Ibid.*, 99.
   43. *Ibid.*, 101.
   44. Barker, Gray. *They Knew Too Much about Flying Saucers*. New York: University Books, 1956: 65.
   45. Ashley, Michael. *Transformations : The Story of the Science-Fiction Magazines from 1950 to 1970*. London: Liverpool University Press, 2005: 184.
   46. *Ibid.*, 185.
   47. Moskowitz, Sam. *Seekers of Tomorrow: Masters of Modern Science Fiction*. New York: The World Publishing Company, 1966: 46.
   48. May, Andrew. *Pseudoscience and Science Fiction*. New York: Springer International Publishing, 2017: 13.
   49. Webb, Stephen. *All the Wonder That Would Be: Exploring Past Notions of the Future*. New York: Springer International Publishing, 2017: 154.
   50. May, Andrew. *Pseudoscience and Science Fiction*. New York City: Springer International Publishing, 2017: 16.

51. Campbell, John W. "Review of *The Books of Charles Fort*." *Astounding Science Fiction*. New York: Street & Smith, August 1941: 147.
52. Schweitzer, Darrell. *Windows of the Imagination: Essays on Fantastic Literature*. Berkeley Heights, CA: Wildside Press, 1999: 18.
53. May, Andrew. *Pseudoscience and Science Fiction*. New York: Springer International Publishing, 2017: 99–101.
54. *Ibid*., 115.
55. *Ibid*., 100.
56. Bauer, Henry H. *Science or Pseudoscience: Magnetic Healing, Psychic Phenomena, and Other Heterodoxies*. Chicago: University of Illinois Press, 2001.
57. Toronto, Richard. *War over Lemuria: Richard Shaver, Ray Palmer and the Strangest Chapter of 1940s Science Fiction*. Jefferson, NC: McFarland, 2013: 141.
58. *Ibid*., 201.
59. *FATE* magazine is a fascinating publication that continues to this day—an antecedent to *Fortean Times*. Printed in the same style as the cheap, pulpy SF paperbacks, *FATE* is the longest-running journal of Fortean occurrences. Palmer was an editor for the magazine's first seven years. The work helped establish some of the most prominent Forteans, such as John A. Keel and Jerome Clark, but also included an editorial staff from earlier pulp SF such as *Amazing*'s Chester S. Geier, who was on staff during the Shaver Mysteries. The magazine's first issue in 1948 was headlined by the writings of Kenneth Arnold whose sighting of flying saucers while piloting a plane near Mount Rainier, Washington is generally considered the sighting that sparked the UFO craze. This was not Palmer's only Fortean publication, as in 1957 he also started *Flying Saucers from Other Worlds* to further focus on UFOs and continue the Shaver Mysteries. It is because of these publications that John Keel essentially considers Palmer as "the man who invented flying saucers" in *Fortean Times* 41, Winter 1983.
60. Ashley, Michael. *Transformations: The Story of the Science-Fiction Magazines from 1950 to 1970*. London: Liverpool University Press, 2005: 16–17.
61. Knight, Damon. *Charles Fort—Prophet of the Unexplained: A Biography of the American Iconoclast Who Dared to Explain Centuries of Strange Occult Phenomena*. Point Pleasant, NY: New Saucerian Press, 2017: 203.
62. *Ibid*., 157.
63. Fort, Charles. *The Books of Charles Fort*. New York: Henry Holt and Company, 1941: 118.
64. Willis, Paul. "Brief Notes." *The INFO Journal: Science and the Unknown*. Arlington: International Fortean Organization, Spring 1968: 58.
65. Fort, Charles. *A Radical Corpuscle*. Newark: Moskowitz Private Printing, 1976.
66. Moskowitz, Sam. "Lo! The Poor Forteans." *Amazing Stories*. New York: Ziff-Davis, June 1965: 56.
67. *Ibid*., 57–58.
68. Shoemaker, Michael. "Re: Charles Fort Inquiry." Message to author. 17 November 2018. Email.
69. Knight, Damon. *The Futurians: The Story of the Science Fiction "Family" of the 30's that Produced Today's Top SF Writers and Editors*. New York: John Day, 1977: vii.
70. Liptack, Andrew. "The Futurians and the 1939 World Science Fiction Convention." *Kirkus Reviews*, Kirkus Media, 9 May 2013, www.kirkusreviews.com/features/futurians-and-1939-world-science-fiction-conventio/.
71. Knight, Damon. "Microscopic Moskowitz." *In Search of Wonder: Essays on Modern Science Fiction*. Chicago: Advent: Publishers, 2014: 105.
72. *Ibid*., 107.
73. Knight, Damon. "Anthologies." *In Search of Wonder: Essays on Modern Science Fiction*. Chicago: Advent:Publishers, 2014: 117.
74. *Ibid*., 2.
75. Milner, Andrew. "Science Fiction and the Literary Field." *Science Fiction Studies* 38, no. 3 (November 2011): 405.
76. *Ibid*.
77. Toronto, Richard. *War over Lemuria: Richard Shaver, Ray Palmer and the Strangest Chapter of 1940s Science Fiction*. Jefferson, NC: McFarland, 2013: 46.

Chapter 5

1. Clarke, Arthur C. *Astounding Days: A Science Fictional Autobiography*. New York: Bantam, 1989: 210.
2. McAleer, Neil. *Arthur C. Clarke: The Authorized Biography*. Chicago: Contemporary Books, 1992: 91.

3. *Ibid.*, 91.
4. Clarke, Arthur C. *Astounding Days: A Science Fictional Autobiography.* New York: Bantam, 1989: 114.
5. *Ibid.*, 115.
6. *Ibid.*, 114.
7. *Ibid.*
8. "Out of the Blue." Flynn, Charles and Michael Weigall, directors. *Arthur C. Clarke's Mysterious World,* season 1, episode 9, ITV, 4 Nov. 1980.
9. Clarke, Arthur C. *Childhood's End.* New York: Del Rey, 1953: vi.
10. *Ibid.*, vii.
11. *Ibid.*, 95.
12. *Ibid.*
13. Kripal, Jeffrey J. *Mutants & Mystics: Science Fiction, Superhero Comics, and the Paranormal.* Chicago: University of Chicago Press, 2015: 113.
14. *Ibid.*, 130.
15. Clarke, Arthur C. *2001: A Space Odyssey.* New York: Roc, 1968: 297.
16. Clarke, Arthur C. *Childhood's End.* New York: Del Rey, 1953: 177.
17. *Ibid.*, 95–96.
18. Kripal, Jeffrey J. *Mutants & Mystics: Science Fiction, Superhero Comics, and the Paranormal.* Chicago: University Of Chicago Press, 2015: 113.
19. Clarke, Arthur C. "Hazards of Prophecy: The Failure of Imagination." *Profiles of the Future.* New York: Harper & Row, 1958: 14.
20. *Ibid.*, 21.
21. Fort, Charles. *The Book of the Damned: The Collected Works of Charles Fort.* New York: Tarcher/Penguin. 2008: 1030–1031.
22. Clarke, Arthur C. "Space, the Unconquerable." *Profiles of the Future.* New York: Harper & Row, 1958: 113.
23. Clarke, Arthur C. *Astounding Days: A Science Fictional Autobiography.* New York: Bantam, 1989: 147.
24. Miller, P. Schuyler. "Book Reviews." *Astounding Stories,* Sep. 1949: 151.
25. Clarke, Arthur C. *Astounding Days: A Science Fictional Autobiography.* New York: Bantam, 1989: 24.
26. Note that this book does not examine the three sequels to *2001.* Clarke says that these novels are not so much narrative sequels as they are thematic sequels. This was perhaps because the advancement of technology made each successive work have inconsistencies. (Clarke, Arthur C. *2010: Odyssey Two.* New York: Del Rey, 1982: xv–xix.)
27. Vallee, Jacques. *Passport to Magonia: From Folklore to Flying Saucers.* Brisbane: Daily Grail Publishing, 2014: 35–36.
28. Clarke, Arthur C. *2001: A Space Odyssey.* New York: Roc, 1968: 281–282.
29. A side note of some Fortean interest: When the mysterious so-called "Men in Black" appear in various maybe-fiction texts, they are often wearing out-of-date clothing or driving cars that are significantly older models while looking brand new. Bowman also notes this type of phenomena in the hotel suite, finding four suits "made of material more like fur than like wool. It was also a little out of style; on Earth, no one had been wearing single-breasted suits for at least four years." These encounters are written about extensively in paranormal circles with many concluding that the Men in Black have extraterrestrial interests in mind or are in fact themselves extraterrestrials. This book makes no claim regarding this phenomenon, it merely acknowledges its existence (*ibid.*, 283).
30. *Ibid.*, 283.
31. *Ibid.*, 287.
32. Kripal, Jeffrey J. *Mutants & Mystics: Science Fiction, Superhero Comics, and the Paranormal.* Chicago: University Of Chicago Press, 2015: 113.
33. A copy of an antiquated book featuring Adamski's story fascinated a preteen me in my local library. It was not too long after that I was embarrassed for even giving a passing thought that the story might be anything more than what Clarke declares it as. As Clarke says later, everyone is stupid about *something.* Nevertheless, Adamski's book is a classic of its era, with long-haired blonde Venusians and their messages of love and peace throughout the galaxy.
34. Clarke, Arthur C. "More Last Words on UFOs." *Greetings, Carbon-Based Bipeds! Collected Essays 1934–1998.* New York: St. Martin's, 2001: 512–513.
35. *Ibid.*, 513.
36. Clarke, Arthur C. *Rendezvous with Rama.* New York: Bantam, 1973: 7.
37. *Ibid.*, 8.
38. *Ibid.*, 104.
39. *Ibid.*, 105.
40. *Ibid.*, 203–204.
41. *Ibid.*, 204.

42. *Ibid.*, 243.
43. Clarke, Arthur C. "The Possessed." *The Nine Billion Names of God: The Best Short Stories of Arthur C. Clarke.* New York: Signet, 1974: 122.
44. Clarke, Arthur C. "Dog Star." *The Nine Billion Names of God: The Best Short Stories of Arthur C. Clarke.* New York: Signet, 1974: 74–75.
45. Clarke, Arthur C. *Astounding Days: A Science Fictional Autobiography.* New York: Bantam, 1989: 116–117.
46. Kripal, Jeffrey J. *Authors of the Impossible: The Paranormal and the Sacred.* Chicago: University of Chicago Press, 2010: 1.
47. Clarke, Arthur C. *Astounding Days: A Science Fictional Autobiography.* New York: Bantam, 1989: 118.

Chapter 6

1. Dick, Philip K. *The Exegesis of Philip K Dick.* Boston: Houghton Mifflin Harcourt, 2011: 176–177.
2. Kripal, Jeffrey J. *Authors of the Impossible: The Paranormal and the Sacred.* Chicago: University of Chicago Press, 2010: 16.
3. Put in amphibian terms, the paradox inquires whether a frog trapped at the bottom of a cylinder can get out of the cylinder if every jump he makes is exactly half the height of the previous jump.
4. Dick, Philip K. "The Indefatigable Frog" in *Fantastic Story Magazine.* Kokomo, IN: Best Books, Inc., July 1953.
5. Dick, Tessa B. "Re: PKD and Fort." Message to author. 8 October 2018. Facebook message.
6. Steiger, Brad. "Philip K. Dick's Phylogenic Memory and the Divine Fire." *Alternate Perceptions Magazine.* Issue 118, November 2007. http://mysterious-america.com/philipdick-brads.html
7. Again, I reference INFO's Wikipedia entry which, for instance, lists Dick, Robert Heinlen, and Robert Anton Wilson as SF authors who were fans of Fort and in regular correspondence.
8. Kripal, Jeffrey J. *Mutants & Mystics: Science Fiction, Superhero Comics, and the Paranormal.* Chicago: University of Chicago Press, 2015: 271.
9. Dick, Philip K. *The Exegesis of Philip K. Dick.* Boston: Houghton Mifflin Harcourt, 2011: 855.
10. Kripal, Jeffrey J. *The Exegesis of Philip K. Dick.* Boston: Houghton Mifflin Harcourt, 2011. Annotation on page 855–856.
11. Keel, John A. *Disneyland of the Gods.* Seattle: New Saucerian Press, 1988: 174.
12. *Ibid.*, 144.
13. Bertrand, Frank C. "So I Don't Write About Heroes: An Interview with Philip K. Dick." *SF Eye.* Asheville, NC: 'Til You Go Blind Cooperative. Spring 1996, pp. 37–46.
14. *Ibid.* (Though Dick does not elaborate on how many amphetamines he was taking, if it was high usage, the drugs could certainly cause some forms of psychosis.)
15. Dick, Philip K. "How to Build a Universe That Doesn't Fall Apart Two Days Later." *Philip K. Dick: How to Build a Universe That Doesn't Fall Apart Two Days Later,* urbigenous.net/library/how_to_build.html. 1974. (This undelivered speech also includes Dick talking at length about how close he lives to Disneyland and thinks about its existence as "a living organism." Disneyland comes up time and time again in Forteana, notably in John Keel's *Disneyland of the Gods,* as a perfect example of a constructed reality shaped by external forces, a very Baudrillardian claim. To a Fortean, Disneyland is not all that different from our own world, shaped by some intangible force, invisible Imagineers.)
16. *Ibid.*
17. May, Andrew. *Pseudoscience and Science Fiction.* New York: Springer International Publishing, 2017: 52.
18. Whether intentional or unintentional, this is extremely reminiscent of the "Fortean Society."
19. Dick, Philip K. *VALIS.* New York: Mariner, 1981: 3.
20. *Ibid.*, 3.
21. *Ibid.*, 185.
22. Kripal, Jeffrey J. *Mutants & Mystics: Science Fiction, Superhero Comics, and the Paranormal.* Chicago: University of Chicago Press, 2015: 268–269.
23. *Ibid.*, 272.
24. *Ibid.*, 276.
25. *Ibid.*, 275.
26. Toronto, Richard. *War over Lemuria: Richard Shaver, Ray Palmer and the Strangest Chapter of 1940s Science Fiction.* Jefferson, NC: McFarland, 2013: 222.
27. Kripal, Jeffrey J. *Mutants & Mystics: Science Fiction, Superhero Comics, and the*

Paranormal. Chicago: University of Chicago Press, 2015: 6.
28. *Ibid.*, 269.
29. May, Andrew. *Pseudoscience and Science Fiction.* New York: Springer International Publishing, 2017: 53.
30. Dick, Philip K. *VALIS.* New York: Mariner, 1981.
31. *Ibid.*, 64.
32. *Ibid.*, 128.
33. *Ibid.*, 129.
34. Note again the fact that Strieber too was a fiction writer before he had encounters with alien intruders and subsequently wrote about this experience for his subsequent books. Dick seemed to be on a similar track before his death, unable to let his experience fade to the back of his mind.
35. Dick, Philip K. "Extracts from Philip K. Dick's essay 'If You Find This World Bad.'" Accessed February 25, 2018. http://empslocal.ex.ac.uk/people/staff/mrwatkin/PKDick.htm.

Chapter 7

1. Heinlein, Robert A. *Time Enough for Love: The Lives of Lazarus Long.* New York: Berkeley Books, 1973: 140.
2. Pappalardo, Joe. "Why 'Starship Troopers' Is the New 'The Art of War.'" *Popular Mechanics*, 5 Feb. 2015, www.popularmechanics.com/military/weapons/a13103/starship-troopers-is-the-new-the-art-of-war/. Accessed 5 Sep. 2018.
3. Webb, Stephen. *All the Wonder That Would Be: Exploring Past Notions of the Future.* New York: Springer International Publishing, 2017: 154.
4. *Ibid.*
5. *Ibid.*
6. Heinlein, Virginia. *Grumbles from the Grave.* New York: Del Rey, 1989: 6.
7. Patterson, William H., Jr. *Robert A. Heinlein: In Dialogue with his Century.* New York: Tor, 2010: 282.
8. Heinlein, Robert A. (as Anson McDonald). "Goldfish Bowl." *Astounding Science Fiction.* New York: Street and Smith, March 1942: 77.
9. Fort, Charles. *The Books of Charles Fort.* New York: Henry Holt and Company, 1941: 757.
10. *Ibid.*, 760.
11. Heinlein, Robert A. (as Anson McDonald). "Goldfish Bowl." *The Menace from Earth.* Chicago: Signet, 1962: 132.
12. *Ibid.*, 134.
13. Heinlein, Robert A. "The Year of the Jackpot." *The Menace from Earth.* Chicago: Signet, 1962: 7.
14. *Ibid.*
15. *Ibid.*, 18.
16. Heinlein, Robert A. *The Puppet Masters.* Chicago: Signet, 1951: 10.
17. Fort, Charles. *The Books of Charles Fort.* New York: Henry Holt and Company, 1941: 298.
18. *Ibid.*, 299.
19. Vallee, Jacques. *Messengers of Deception: UFO Contacts and Cults.* Brisbane: Daily Grail Publishing, 1979: 88.
20. *Ibid.*, 89.
21. *Ibid.*, 96.
22. *Ibid.*, 112.
23. *Ibid.*, 113.
24. Clareson, Thomas D., and Joe Sanders. *The Heritage of Heinlein: A Critical Reading of the Fiction.* Jefferson, NC: McFarland, 2014: 190.
25. *Ibid.*
26. Webb, Stephen. *All the Wonder That Would Be: Exploring Past Notions of the Future.* New York: Springer International Publishing, 2017: 155.
27. *Ibid.*
28. Heinlein, Robert A. "To Edgar D. Mitchell." 11 June 1974. The Heinlein Archives, Box 409, "Telepathy."
29. *Ibid.*
30. *Ibid.*

Chapter 8

1. Wilson, Robert Anton. *The New Inquisition: Irrational Rationalism and the Citadel of Science.* Phoenix: Falcon Press, 1986: 195.
2. Shea, Robert, and Robert Anton Wilson. *The Illuminatus! Trilogy.* New York: Dell Publishing, 1988. Inside cover.
3. *Ibid.*, 238–239.
4. *Ibid.*, 101.
5. *Ibid.*, 101–102
6. Keel, John A. *Operation Trojan Horse.* Lilburn, GA: IllumiNet Press, 1996: 194. (RAW might have also been fascinated by a similar encounter Malcolm X had with an MIB that Keel also references: "The late leader of a black militant group, reported a classic experience with a paraphysical 'man

in black' in his autobiography. He was serving a prison sentence at the time, and the entity materialized in his prison cell.")

7. Wilson, Robert Anton. *The New Inquisition: Irrational Rationalism and the Citadel of Science*. Phoenix: Falcon Press, 1986: 156.

8. Shea, Robert, and Robert Anton Wilson. *The Illuminatus! Trilogy*. New York: Dell Publishing, 1988: 274–275.

9. Fort, Charles. *The Books of Charles Fort*. New York: Henry Holt and Company, 1941: 678–679.

10. Shea, Robert and Robert Anton Wilson. *The Illuminatus! Trilogy*. New York: Dell Publishing, 1988: 238.

11. Wilson, Robert Anton. "The 23 Phenomenon" in *Fortean Times*. Issue 23, Autumn 1977: 34.

12. Nye, James. "Interview with Robert Anton Wilson." *Fortean Times*. Issue 79, February/March 1995. Reproduced on James Nye's blog at https://thefrogweb.wordpress.com/2014/11/23/raw/

13. Rickard, Robert. "Reviews and News." *Fortean Times*, Issue 17, August 1976: 27.

14. Wilson, Robert Anton. *The New Inquisition: Irrational Rationalism and the Citadel of Science*. Phoenix: Falcon Press, 1986: 144.

15. *Ibid*.

16. Wilson, Robert Anton. *Cosmic Trigger I: The Final Secret of the Illuminati*. Tempe: New Falcon Publications, 1977: v.

17. *Ibid.*, vi.

18. Davis, Erik. *High Weirdness: Drugs, Esoterica, and Visionary Experience in the Seventies*. London: Strange Attractor Press & The MIT Press, 2019: 263.

19. Fuller, R. Buckminster. "Introduction." *Charles Fort—Prophet of the Unexplained: A Biography of the American Iconoclast Who Dared to Explain Centuries of Strange Occult Phenomena*. Point Pleasant, NJ: New Saucerian Books, 2017: xv.

20. Wilson, Robert Anton. *The New Inquisition: Irrational Rationalism and the Citadel of Science*. Phoenix: Falcon Press, 1986: 3.

21. Wilson, Robert Anton. *Cosmic Trigger I: The Final Secret of the Illuminati*. Tempe: New Falcon Publications, 1977: 205.

22. Nye, James. "Interview with Robert Anton Wilson." *Fortean Times*. Issue 79, February/March 1995. Reproduced on James Nye's blog at https://thefrogweb.wordpress.com/2014/11/23/raw/

23. Keel, John A. *Disneyland of the Gods*. Point Pleasant, NJ: New Saucerian Books, 2016. Cover blurb by Robert Anton Wilson.

24. Vallee, Jacques. *Messengers of Deception: UFO Contacts and Cults*. Brisbane: Daily Grail Publishing, 2008. Back cover blurb by Robert Anton Wilson.

25. Wilson, Robert Anton. *Cosmic Trigger I: The Final Secret of the Illuminati*. Tempe: New Falcon Publications, 1977: 97.

26. Coleman, Loren. "23 Skidoo: Goodbye Robert Anton Wilson." Web blog post. *Cryptomundo*. January 11, 2007. Web August 13, 2018.

27. *Ibid*.

28. *Ibid*. (Supercheckers refers to the complex Chinese checkers-esque game which Charles Fort invented.)

29. Wilson, Robert Anton. *Cosmic Trigger I: The Final Secret of the Illuminati*. Tempe: New Falcon Publications, 1977: vi.

Chapter 9

1. Fort, Charles. *The Books of Charles Fort*. New York: Henry Holt and Company, 1941: 3.

2. Andrew May's *Pseudoscience and Science Fiction* (New York: Springer, 2017) helps to track more of these stray Fortean influences on SF with an in-depth focus on a variety of pulp SF over the last century. Among these are the highly prolific SF author and host of *Fortean TV*, Reverend Lionel Fanthorpe, whose vast catalog of fiction and maybe-fiction could be a wellspring for an entirely different book. Other "Fortean Footnotes" May explores include Colin Wilson and R.A. Lafferty, among others.

3. Gibson, William. "The Gernsback Continuum." *Burning Chrome*. New York: HarperCollins, 2003: 27–28.

4. *Ibid.*, 29.

5. *Ibid.*, 31

6. *Ibid.*, 36.

7. *Ibid.*, 30.

8. Gibson, William (GreatDismal). "@Elpico72 The Bar Hade was my affectionate approximation of a certain flavor of paranormal folk motif. Not from any actual source." 7 May 2010, 9:57 PM. Tweet.

9. Anomaly Archives. "William Gibson: Fortean!" Web blog post. *Anomaly Archives*. September 23, 2012. Web October 4, 2019.

(It is unclear if the reference to Fort's "three" books was a mistake on Gibson's part, or the author transcribing the speech. Fort released four books.)
10. Gibson, William. "Introduction." *Flying Saucers Are Real!—The UFO Library of Jack Womack*. Brooklyn: Anthology Editions, 2016: 7.
11. *Ibid.*
12. Davis, Hank. "Into Each Life, Some Periwinkles Must Fall." *Future Wars... and Other Punchlines.* Ed. Hank Davis. Riverdale, NY: Baen Books, 2015: 247
13. *Ibid.*, 251.
14. Drake, David. *Hammer's Slammers*. New York: Ace Books, 1979: 108.
15. Fort, Charles. *The Books of Charles Fort*. New York: Henry Holt and Company, 1941: 800–801.
16. *Ibid.*, 812.
17. King, Stephen. *Firestarter.* New York: Viking, 1980: 81.
18. Balliett, Blue. *Chasing Vermeer.* New York: Scholastic Press, 2004: 73.
19. *Ibid.*, v.
20. *Ibid.*, 256.
21. Gaydos, Stephen. "'Magnolia' Helmer Ribeted by Novelist's Frogs." *Vanity Fair.* February 7, 2000. http://variety.com/2000/film/news/magnolia-helmer-ribeted-by-novelist-s-frogs-1117776227/
22. Fort, Charles. *The Books of Charles Fort*. New York: Henry Holt and Company, 1941: 848.
23. Mr. X. "Letters to INFO." Message to author. 6 October 2018. Email. (Mr. X, Consulting Resologist, can be found at www.resologist.net)
24. Rennie, Gordon. *Necronauts.* Eastbourne, UK: Gardners Books, 2003: 18.
25. Lenkov, Peter M. *Fort: Prophet of the Unexplained.* Milwaukie, OR: Dark Horse Comics, 2002.
26. *Ibid.*, 10.
27. Kripal, Jeffrey J. *Mutants & Mystics: Science Fiction, Superhero Comics, and the Paranormal.* Chicago: University of Chicago Press, 2015: 114.

Chapter 10

1. Vallee, Jacques. *Passport to Magonia: From Folklore to Flying Saucers.* Brisbane: Daily Grail Publishing, 2014: 9.
2. Kripal, Jeffrey J. *The Secret Body: Erotic and Esoteric Currents in the History of Religion.* Chicago: University of Chicago Press, 2017: 9.
3. Vallee, Jacques. *Dimensions: A Casebook of Alien Contact.* San Antonio: Anomalist Books, 2013: 184–185.
4. *Ibid.*
5. Braun, Stephen. "The Strange Faith of Dr. Corder: He Believes That Aliens Walk Among Us and the Apocalypse Is Nigh. But Does That Mean He Isn't a Good Doctor?" *LA Times.* October 23, 1994. http://articles.latimes.com/1994-10-23/magazine/tm-53920_1_scott-corder
6. Dunn, Ragan. "They're Coming! Space alien invasion only 3 years away, says top UFO expert." *Weekly World News.* New York: American Media, 13 December 1988: 9.
7. Ress, Patricia Griffin. *Stranger than Fiction: The True Time Travel Adventures of Steven L. Gibbs, the Rainman of Time Travel.* Bloomington, IN: 1st Books Library, 2001: 6–7.
8. Rosales, Albert S. *Humanoid Encounters: The Others Amongst Us 1970–1974.* Denver: Triangulum Publishing, 2016: 123.
9. Edwards, Frank. *Flying Saucers—Serious Business!* New York: Bantam Books, 1966: 6.
10. Fort, Charles. *The Books of Charles Fort*. New York: Henry Holt and Company, 1941: 878.
11. Mezrich, Ben. *The 37th Parallel: The Secret Truth Behind America's UFO Highway.* New York: Atria Books, 2016: 205.
12. Gilland, Steve. "The Legend of Sinkhole Sam." *The Kansan,* 12 June 2010. https://www.thekansan.com/article/20100612/NEWS/306129943
13. *Ibid.*
14. Fort, Charles. *The Books of Charles Fort*. New York: Henry Holt and Company, 1941: 185.
15. *Ibid.*, 638.
16. *Ibid.*, 983.
17. Bord, Janet, and Colin Bord. *The Bigfoot Casebook.* New York: Granada, 1982: 111.
18. Stage, Wm. "Space Case." *Riverfront Times,* 5 Apr. 2000. https://www.riverfronttimes.com/stlouis/space-case/Content?oid=2474776
19. Templeton, David. "The Kecksburg Files." *The Pittsburgh Post-Gazette,* 9 September 1998. http://old.post-gazette.com/magazine/19980908ufo1.asp

20. Abrahams, Brad, director. *Love and Saucers*. Curator Pictures, 2017.

21. Denzler, Brenda. *The Lure of the Edge: Scientific Passions, Religious Beliefs, and the Pursuit of UFOs*. Berkeley: University of California Press, 2001: 159.

22. Cooper, Helene, Ralph Blumenthal, and Leslie Kean. "Glowing Auras and 'Black Money': The Pentagon's Mysterious UFO Program." *The New York Times*, 16 Dec. 2017, https://www.nytimes.com/2017/12/16/us/politics/pentagon-program-ufo-harry-reid.html.

23. *Ibid.*

Bibliography

Books

Almeida, Rafael Antunes. "UFOs, Ufologists, and Digital Media in Brazil." *Believing in Bits: Digital Media and the Supernatural.* Eds. Simone Natale and D.W. Pasulka. New York: Oxford University Press, 2019.

Andrews, Roy Chapman. *On the Trail of Ancient Man: A Narrative of the Field Work of the Central Asiatic Expeditions.* New York: The Knickerbocker Press, 1926.

Ashley, Michael. *Transformations : The Story of the Science-Fiction Magazines from 1950 to 1970.* London: Liverpool University Press, 2005.

Balliett, Blue. *Chasing Vermeer.* New York: Scholastic Press, 2004

Barker, Gray. *They Knew Too Much About Flying Saucers.* New York: University Books, 1956.

Bauer, Henry H. *Science or Pseudoscience: Magnetic Healing, Psychic Phenomena, and Other Heterodoxies.* Chicago: University of Illinois Press, 2001.

Beckley, Timothy Green. *The Matrix Control System of Philip K. Dick and the Paranormal Synchronicities of Timothy Green Beckley.* New Brunswick, NJ: Inner Light Global Communications, 2017.

Bord, Janet, and Colin Bord. *The Bigfoot Casebook.* New York: Granada, 1982.

Bowler, Peter J. *Evolution: The History of an Idea.* Berkeley: University of California Press, 2003.

Brown, Bridget. *They Know Us Better Than We Know Ourselves: The History and Politics of Alien Abduction.* New York: New York University Press, 2007.

Brunwald, Jan Harold. *Too Good to be True: The Colossal Book of Urban Legends.* New York: W.W. Norton & Co., 1999

Carrére Emmanuel. *I Am Alive and You Are Dead: A Journey into the Mind of Philip K. Dick.* New York: Metropolitan Books, 1993.

Churchward, James. *The Lost Continent of MU.* New York: Paperback Library, 1970.

Clancy, Susan. *Abducted: How People Come to Believe They Were Kidnapped by Aliens.* Cambridge: Harvard University Press, 2005.

Clareson, Thomas D. and Joe Sanders. *The Heritage of Heinlein: A Critical Reading of the Fiction.* Jefferson, NC: McFarland, 2014.

Clarke, Arthur C. *Astounding Days: A Science Fictional Autobiography.* New York: Bantam, 1989.

_____. *Childhood's End.* New York: Del Rey, 1953. Page vi.

_____. "Dog Star." *The Nine Billion Names of God: The Best Short Stories of Arthur C. Clarke.* New York: Signet, 1974.

_____. "Hazards of Prophecy: The Failure of Imagination." *Profiles of the Future.* New York: Harper & Row, 1958.

_____. "More Last Words on UFOs." *Greetings, Carbon-Based Bipeds! Collected Essays 1934–1998.* New York: St. Martin's, 2001.

_____. "The Possessed." *The Nine Billion Names of God: The Best Short Stories of Arthur C. Clarke.* New York: Signet, 1974. Page 122.

_____. *Rendezvous with Rama.* New York: Bantam, 1973.

_____. "Space, the Unconquerable." *Profiles of the Future.* New York: Harper & Row, 1958.

_____. *2001: A Space Odyssey*. New York: Roc, 1968.
_____. *2010: Odyssey Two*. New York: Del Rey, 1982.
Conroy, Ed. *Report on Communion: The Facts Behind the Most Controversial True Story of All Time*. New York: Avon Books, 1989.
Corliss, William R. *Handbook of Unusual Natural Phenomena*. Glen Arm, MD: The Sourcebook Project, 1977.
Croce, Paul Jerome. "Science and Religion." *Encyclopedia of American Cultural and Intellectual History*. New York: Scribner's, 1999.
Davis, Erik. *High Weirdness: Drugs, Esoterica, and Visionary Experience in the Seventies*. London: Strange Attractor Press & The MIT Press, 2019.
Davis, Hank. "Into Each Life, Some Periwinkles Must Fall." *Future Wars… and Other Punchlines*. Ed. Hank Davis. Riverdale, NY: Baen Books, 2015.
Denzler, Brenda. *The Lure of the Edge: Scientific Passions, Religious Beliefs, and the Pursuit of UFOs*. Berkeley: University of California Press, 2001.
Dick, Philip K. *The Exegesis of Philip K. Dick*. Boston: Houghton Mifflin Harcourt, 2011.
_____. *VALIS*. New York: Mariner, 1981.
Dick, Tessa B. "Introduction." *Flying Saucer to the Center of Your Mind: Selected Writings of John A. Keel*. Seattle: Metadisc Books, 2013.
Dolan, Richard M. *UFOs and the National Security State: Chronology of a Cover-up 1941–1973*. Charlottesville: Hampton Roads Publishing Co., 2002.
Drake, David. *Hammer's Slammers*. New York: Ace Books, 1979.
Edwards, Frank. *Flying Saucers—Serious Business!* New York: Bantam Books, 1966.
Feindt, Carl W. *UFOs and Water: Physical Effects of UFOs on Water Through Accounts by Eyewitnesses*. Bloomington: Xlibris Corporation, 2010.
Fisher, Mark. *The Weird and the Eerie*. London: Repeater Books, 2016.
Fort, Charles. *The Book of the Damned: The Collected Works of Charles Fort*. New York: Tarcher/Perigree, 2008.
_____. *The Books of Charles Fort*. New York: Henry Holt and Company, 1941.
_____. *A Radical Corpuscle*. Newark: Moskowitz Private Printing, 1976
Fuller, R. Buckminster. "Introduction." *Charles Fort—Prophet of the Unexplained: A Biography of the American Iconoclast Who Dared to Explain Centuries of Strange Occult Phenomena*. Point Pleasant, NJ: New Saucerian Books, 2017.
Gardner, Martin. *Fads and Fallacies in the Name of Science: The Curious Theories of Modern Pseudoscientists and the Strange, Amusing and Alarming Cults That Surround Them. A Study in Human Gullibility*. New York: Dover Publications, 1952.
Gibson, William. "The Gernsback Continuum." *Burning Chrome*. New York: HarperCollins, 2003.
_____. "Introduction." *Flying Saucers Are Real!—The UFO Library of Jack Womack*. Brooklyn: Anthology Editions, 2016.
Gould, Rupert T. *Oddities*. New York: Paperback Library, 1965.
Gross, Loren E. *Charles Fort, The Fortean Society, and Unidentified Flying Objects*. Fremont, CA: Privately published, 1976.
Hansen, George P. *The Trickster and the Paranormal*. Bloomington: Xlibris Corporation, 2001.
Harvey, Doug. "Hole Story." *Aspects of Mel's Hole: Artists Respond to a Paranormal Land Event Occurring in Radiospace*. Ed. Doug Harvey. Santa Ana: Grand Central Press, 2008.
Heinlein, Robert A. "Goldfish Bowl." *The Menace from Earth*. Chicago: Signet, 1962.
_____. "Project Nightmare." *The Menace from Earth*. Chicago: Signet, 1962.
_____. *The Puppet Masters*. Chicago: Signet, 1951.
_____. "The Year of the Jackpot." *The Menace from Earth*. Chicago: Signet, 1962.
Heinlein, Virginia. *Grumbles from the Grave*. New York: Del Rey, 1989.
Herbert, Frank. "Sandworms of Dune." *The Maker of Dune: Insights of a Master of Science Fiction*. New York: Berkeley Books, 1987.
Howe, Linda Moulton. *Glimpses of Other Realities, Volume 1: Facts and Eyewitnesses*. Huntington Valley, PA: LMH Productions, 1993.
Hynek, J. Allen, and Jacques Vallee. *The Edge of Reality: A Progress Report on Unidentified Flying Objects*. Chicago: Henry Regnery Company, 1975.
Jeffrey, Adi-Kent Thomas. *Parallel Universe*. New York: Warner Books, 1977.
Josiffe, Christopher. *Gef! The Strange Tale of*

an *Extra-Special Talking Mongoose*. London: Strange Attractor Press, 2017.
Jung, Carl Gustav. *Flying Saucers: A Modern Myth of Things Seen in the Skies*. New York: Routledge, 2002.
Keel, John A. *Disneyland of the Gods*. Seattle: New Saucerian Press, 1988.
_____. *The Mothman Prophecies*. New York: Tor, 2002.
_____. *Operation Trojan Horse*. Lilburn, GA: IllumiNet Press, 1996.
Kelleher, Colm A., and George Knapp. *Hunt for the Skinwalker: Science Confronts the Unexplained at a Remote Ranch in Utah*. New York: Pocket Books, 2005.
Keyes, Daniel. *The Minds of Billy Milligan*. New York: Bantam, 1981.
Keyhoe, Donald. *The Flying Saucers are Real*. New York: Fawcett, 1950.
Kinsella, Michael. *Legend-Tripping Online: Supernatural Folklore and the Search for Ong's Hat*. Jackson: University Press of Mississippi, 2011.
Knight, Damon. "Anthologies." In *Search of Wonder: Essays on Modern Science Fiction*. Chicago: Advent Publishers, 2014.
_____. *Charles Fort—Prophet of the Unexplained: A Biography of the American Iconoclast Who Dared to Explain Centuries of Strange Occult Phenomena*. Point Pleasant, NJ: New Saucerian Press, 2017.
_____. "Critics." In *Search of Wonder: Essays on Modern Science Fiction*. Chicago: Advent:Publishers, 2014.
_____. *The Futurians: The Story of the Science Fiction "Family" of the 30's that Produced Today's Top SF Writers and Editors*. New York: John Day, 1977.
_____. "Microscopic Moskowitz." In *Search of Wonder: Essays on Modern Science Fiction*. Chicago: Advent:Publishers, 2014.
Knight, Peter. *Conspiracy Theories in American History: An Encyclopedia*. Santa Barbara: ABC-CLIO Inc., 2003.
Konda, Thomas Milan. *Conspiracies of Conspiracies: How Delusions Have Overrun America*. Chicago: University of Chicago Press, 2019.
Kripal, Jeffrey J. *Authors of the Impossible: The Paranormal and the Sacred*. Chicago: University of Chicago Press, 2010.
_____. *Esalen: America and the Religion of No Religion*. Chicago: University of Chicago Press, 2007.
_____. *The Flip: Epiphanies of Mind and the Future of Knowledge*. New York: Bellevue Literary Press, 2019.
_____. *Mutants & Mystics: Science Fiction, Superhero Comics, and the Paranormal*. Chicago: University of Chicago Press, 2015.
_____. *The Secret Body: Erotic and Esoteric Currents in the History of Religion*. Chicago: University of Chicago Press, 2017.
LaChance, Steven, and Laura Long-Helbig. *The Uninvited: The True Story of the Union Screaming House*. Woodbury, NY: Llewellyn Publications, 2008.
Leiber, Fritz. *H.P. Lovecraft: A Symposium*. Folcroft Library Editions, 1972. Sponsored by the Los Angeles Science Fantasy Society.
Leiber, Fritz, and Bernard C. Gilford. *You're All Alone / The Liquid Man*. Medford, OR: Armchair Fiction, 2010.
Lepselter, Susan. *The Resonance of Unseen Things: Poetics, Power, Captivity, and UFOs in the American Uncanny*. Ann Arbor: University of Michigan Press, 2016.
Matheny, Joseph. *The Incunabula Papers: Ong's Hat and Other Gateways to New Dimensions*. Self-published, 1999.
May, Andrew. *Pseudoscience and Science Fiction*. New York: Springer International Publishing, 2017.
McAleer, Neil. *Arthur C. Clarke: The Authorized Biography*. Chicago: Contemporary Books, 1992.
Mezrich, Ben. *The 37th Parallel: The Secret Truth Behind America's UFO Highway*. New York: Atria Books, 2016.
Miller, R. Dewitt. *Impossible—Yet it Happened!* New York: Ace Books, 1947.
Morehouse, David. *Psychic Warrior*. New York: St. Martin's Press, 1996.
Moretti, Nick. *The Bell Witch Anthology*. North Charleston, SC: Booksurge Publishing, 2008.
Moskowitz, Sam. *Seekers of Tomorrow: Masters of Modern Science Fiction*. New York: The World Publishing Company, 1966.
Moss, Stephanie. "*Dracula* and *The Blair Witch Project*: The Problem with Scientific Empiricism." *Nothing That Is: Millennial Cinema and the Blair Witch Controversies*. Eds. Sarah L. Higley and Jeffrey Andrew Weinstock. Detroit: Wayne State University Press, 2004.
Natale, Simone, and D.W. Pasulka. "Introduction." *Believing in Bits: Digital Media*

and the Supernatural. Eds. Simone Natale and D.W. Pasulka. New York: Oxford University Press, 2019.

Nichols, Preston B., and Peter Moon. *The Montauk Project: Experiments in Time*. Westbury, NY: Sky Books, 1992.

O'Brien, Barbara. *Operators and Things: The Inner Life of a Schizophrenic*. Los Angeles: Silver Birch Press, 2011.

Pasulka, D.W. *American Cosmic: UFOs, Religion, Technology*. New York: Oxford University Press, 2019.

Patterson, William H., Jr. *Robert A. Heinlein: In Dialogue with his Century*. New York: Tor, 2010.

Phillips, Graham, and Martin Keatman. *The Green Stone*. London: Panther Books, 1983.

Putnam, Robert. *Bowling Alone: The Collapse and Revival of American Communities*. New York: Simon & Schuster, 2000.

Radway, Janice. *Reading the Romance: Women, Patriarchy, and Popular Literature*. Chapel Hill: University of North Carolina Press, 1991.

Redfern, Nick. *The Slenderman Mysteries: An Internet Urban Legend Comes to Life*. Newburyport, MA: New Page Books, 2017.

Regal, Brian. *Pseudoscience: A Critical Encyclopedia*. Santa Barbara: ABC-CLIO, 2009.

Ress, Patricia Griffin. *Stranger than Fiction: The True Time Travel Adventures of Steven L. Gibbs, the Rainman of Time Travel*. Bloomington: 1st Books Library, 2001.

Rickels, Laurence A. *I Think I Am: Philip K. Dick*. Minneapolis: University of Minnesota Press, 2010.

Roberts, Anthony, and Geoff Gilbertson. *The Dark Gods*. London: Rider/Hutchinson, 1980.

Rogo, D. Scott, and Raymond Bayless. *Phone Calls from the Dead*. New York: Berkley Books, 1979.

Rosales, Albert S. *Humanoid Encounters: The Others Amongst Us 1970–1974*. Denver: Triangulum Publishing, 2016.

Roth, Christopher F. "Ufology as Anthropology: Race, Extraterrestrials, and the Occult." *E.T. Culture: Anthropology in Outerspaces*. Ed. Debora Battaglia. Durham, NC: Duke University Press, 2005.

Schweitzer, Darrell. *Windows of the Imagination: Essays on Fantastic Literature*. Berkeley Heights, CA: Wildside Press, 1999.

Shaver, Richard S. *The Shaver Mystery, Book One*. Medford, OR: Armchair Fiction, 2011.

Shea, Robert, and Robert Anton Wilson. *The Illuminatus! Trilogy*. New York: Dell Publishing, 1988.

Slemen, Thomas. *Strange but True: Mysterious and Bizarre People*. New York: Barnes and Noble, 1998.

Steinmeyer, Jim. *Charles Fort: The Man Who Invented the Supernatural*. New York: Tarcher/Penguin, 2008.

_____. "Introduction." *The Book of the Damned: The Collected Works of Charles Fort*. New York: Tarcher/Perigree, 2008.

Strieber, Whitley. *Communion: A True Story*. New York: Avon Books, 1987.

Strieber, Whitley and Jeffrey J. Kripal. *The Super Natural: Why the Unexplained Is Real*. New York: Tarcher/Perigree, 2016.

Sutin, Lawrence. *Divine Invasions: A Life of Philip K. Dick*. New York: Da Capo Press, 2005.

Suvin, Darko. *Metamorphoses of Science Fiction: On the Poetics and History of a Literary Genre*. New Haven, CT: Yale University Press, 1979.

Toronto, Richard. *War over Lemuria: Richard Shaver, Ray Palmer and the Strangest Chapter of 1940s Science Fiction*. Jefferson, NC: McFarland, 2013.

Tucker, Brian. "An Awfully Deep Hole." *Aspects of Mel's Hole: Artists Respond to a Paranormal Land Event Occurring in Radiospace*. Ed. Doug Harvey. Santa Ana: Grand Central Press, 2008.

Tyson, Donald. *The Dream World of H.P. Lovecraft: His Life, His Demons, His Universe*. Woodbury, NY: Llewellyn Publications, 2010.

Vallee, Jacques. *Confrontations: A Scientist's Search for Alien Contact*. New York: Ballantine Books, 1990.

_____. *Dimensions: A Casebook of Alien Contact*. San Antonio: Anomalist Books, 2013.

_____. *Messengers of Deception: UFO Contacts and Cults*. Brisbane: Daily Grail Publishing, 1979.

_____. *Passport to Magonia: From Folklore to Flying Saucers*. Brisbane: Daily Grail Publishing. 2014.

_____. *UFOs: The Psychic Solution* (originally published as *The Invisible College*). Frogmore, Hertfordshire: Panther Books, 1975.

Vida-Spence, Judith E. "What's Missing?" *Aspects of Mel's Hole: Artists Respond to a Paranormal Land Event Occurring in Radiospace*. Ed. Doug Harvey. Santa Ana: Grand Central Press, 2008.

Wargo, Eric. *Time Loops: Precognition, Retrocausation, and the Unconscious*. San Antonio: Anomalist Books, 2018.

Webb, Stephen. *All the Wonder That Would Be: Exploring Past Notions of the Future*. New York: Springer International Publishing, 2017.

Webster, Ken. *The Vertical Plane: The Mystery of the Dodleston Messages—A Bizarre Record of Communication Through Time*. London: Grafton, 1989.

Wells, H.G. *The Time Machine*. New York: Airmont, 1895

———. *The War of the Worlds*. London: Houghton Mifflin Harcourt, 1898.

Wetzel, George T. *Collected Essays on H.P. Lovecraft and Others*. Rockville: Wildside Press, 2015.

Wilkins, Hubert, and Harold M. Sherman. *Thoughts through Space: A Remarkable Adventure in the Realm of the Mind*. New York: Creative Age Press, 1942.

Wilson, Colin. *The Directory of Possibilities*. New York: Rutledge Press, 1981.

———. *The Strength to Dream: Literature and the Imagination*. London: Abacus, 1976.

Wilson, Robert Anton. *Cosmic Trigger I: The Final Secret of the Illuminati*. Tempe: New Falcon Publications, 1977.

———. *The New Inquisition: Irrational Rationalism and the Citadel of Science*. Phoenix: Falcon Press, 1986.

Magazines

Alexander, Jack. "UFO Expert Warns Earthlings: Space aliens will invade if we lay one finger on 'em!" *Weekly World News*. New York: American Media, 2 March 1993.

Arnold, Kenneth. "The Saucers Still Patrol Our Skies." *Amazing Stories*. New York: Ziff-Davis, October 1957.

Campbell, John W. "Review of *The Books of Charles Fort*." *Astounding Science Fiction*. New York: Street & Smith, August 1941.

deFord, Miriam Allen. "Slips Take Over." *The Magazine of Fantasy and Science Fiction*. New York: Mercury Press, September 1964.

Dick, Philip K. "The Indefatigable Frog." *Fantastic Story*. Kokomo, IN: Best Books, 1953.

Dunn, Ragan. "They're Coming!: Space alien invasion only 3 years away, says top UFO expert." *Weekly World News*. New York: American Media, 13 December 1988.

Foster, Mike. "Batboy led US troops to Saddam... Gotcha!" *Weekly World News*. New York: American Media, 13 January 2004.

Gernsback, Hugo. "Foreword to *The Space Visitors*." *Air Wonder Stories*. Mt. Morris, MI: Stellar Publishing Corporation, March 1930.

Hamilton, Edmond. "The Earth-Owners." *Weird Tales*. Indianapolis: Popular Fiction Publishing, August 1931.

Heinlein, Robert A. (as Anson McDonald). "Goldfish Bowl." *Astounding Science Fiction*. New York: Street and Smith, March 1942.

Herbert, Frank. "Rat Race." *Astounding Science Fiction*. New York: Street and Smith, July 1955.

Holloway, James. "H.P. Lovecraft and the Horror of History." *Fortean Times*, Issue 369. London: Dennis Publishing, August 2018.

Johnson, Robert Barbour. "Charles Fort: His Objectives Fade in the West." *IF: Worlds of Science Fiction*. Buffalo: Quinn Publishing Company, July 1952.

Keel, John A. *The Lunarite*. Issue 1, 1946. Scan at http://www.johnkeel.com/?p=48

———. "Was PKD a Flake?" *Philip K. Dick Society Newsletter #15* (ed. Paul Williams). Philip K. Dick Society, 1987.

Kidd, Ian James. "From Dominants to the Damned: Fort and Philosophy." *Fortean Times*, Issue 388. London: Dennis Publishing, January 2020.

Langford, Dave. "SF Books of the Damned." *Fortean Times Weird Year 1996*. London: John Brown Publishing, 1996.

May, Andrew. "Fanthorpe's Fortean Fiction." *Fortean Times*. London: Dennis Publishing, February 2013.

Miller, P. Schuyler. "Book Reviews." *Astounding Stories*. New York: Street and Smith, September 1949.

Moskowitz, Sam. "Lo! The Poor Forteans." *Amazing Stories*. New York: Ziff-Davis, June 1965.

Norkova, Julie. "Hell is Other Planets."

Analog Science Fiction and Fact. Norwalk: Dell Magazines, January/February 2018.
Palmer, Raymond A. "Is the Government Hiding Saucer Facts?" *Amazing Stories.* New York: Ziff-Davis, October 1957.
Rickard, Bob. "Reviews and News." *Fortean Times*, Issue 17, August 1976.
Rogers, Margaret. "I Have Been in the Caves." *Amazing Stories.* Chicago: Ziff-Davis, January 1947.
Russell, Eric Frank. "The Creeping Coffins of Barbados" in *Fantastic.* New York: Ziff-Davis, April 1958.
_____. "Sinister Barrier." *Unknown.* New York: Street & Smith, March 1939.
Shaeffer, Robert. "The 'Transformation' of Whitley Strieber." *BASIS*, the Bay Area Skeptics Newsletter. November 1988. http://www.debunker.com/texts/strieber.html
Shaver, Richard S. "Historical Aspect of the Saucers." *Amazing Stories.* New York: Ziff-Davis, October 1957.
_____. "I Remember Lemuria!" *Amazing Stories.* Chicago: Ziff-Davis, March 1945.
_____. "A Witch in the Night." *The Hidden World.* Mundelein, IL: Palmer Publications, Spring 1961.
Sherman, Harold M. "The Green Man." *Amazing Stories.* Chicago: Ziff-Davis Publishing, October 1946.
Sutton, David. *Fortean Times.* London: Dennis Publishing, June 2013. Issue 302.
Thayer, Tiffany. *Doubt* 61. New York: The Fortean Society, 1931.
Tremaine, F. Orlin, editor. "Table of Contents." *Astounding Stories.* New York: Street and Smith, April 1934.
Willis, Paul. "Brief Notes" in *The INFO Journal: Science and the Unknown.* Vol. 1, No. 3. Arlington: International Fortean Organization, Spring 1968.
_____. "Editorial" in *The INFO Journal: Science and the Unknown.* Vol. 4, No. 4. Arlington: International Fortean Organization, March 1976. Inside cover.
_____. "Obituary" in *The INFO Journal: Science and the Unknown.* Vol. 4, No. 3. Arlington: International Fortean Organization, May 1975.
Wilson, Robert Anton. "The 23 Phenomenon." *Fortean Times.* Issue 23, Autumn 1977.

Journals

Boeche, Ray W. "Where's Steve McQueen When You Need Him?" *Journal of the Fortean Research Center* 1, no. 1 (April 1986): pp. 5–6.
Clark, John. "Small, Vulnerable ETs: The Green Children of Woolpit." *Science Fiction Studies* 33, no. 2 (July 2006): pp. 209–229.
Gavin, Michael. "Real Robinson Crusoe." *Eighteenth-Century Fiction* 25, no. 2 (Winter 2012–13): pp. 301–325.
Keel, John A. "The Flying Saucer Subculture." *The Journal of Popular Culture* 8, no. 4 (Spring 1975): pp. 871–896.
Milner, Andrew. "Science Fiction and the Literary Field." *Science Fiction Studies* 38, no. 3 (November 2011): pp. 393–411.
Nodelman, Perry. "The Cognitive Estrangement of Darko Suvin." *Children's Literature Association Quarterly* 5, no. 4 (Winter 1981): pp. 24–27.
Palmer, Christopher. "Postmodernism and the Birth of the Author in Philip K. Dick's Valis." *Science Fiction Studies* 18, no. 3 (November 1991): pp. 330–342.
Partington, John S. "The Death of the Static: H.G. Wells and the Kinetic Utopia." *Utopian Studies* 11, no. 2 (2000): pp. 96–111.
Suvin, Darko. "On the Poetics of the Science Fiction Genre." *College English* 34, no. 3 (December 1972): pp. 372–382.
Tausk, Victor. "On the Origin of the 'Influencing Machine' in Schizophrenia." *Journal of Psychotherapy Practice and Research* 1, no. 2 (Spring 1992): pp. 184–206.

Comic Books

Fox, Gardner. *Showcase* #61. New York: National Periodical Publications, 1966.
Lenkov, Peter M. *Fort: Prophet of the Unexplained.* Milwaukie: Dark Horse Comics, 2002.
Rennie, Gordon. *Necronauts.* Eastbourne: Gardners Books, 2003.

Interviews

Bertrand, Frank C. "So I Don't Write About Heroes: An Interview with Philip K. Dick." *SF Eye*. Asheville, NC: 'Til You Go Blind Cooperative, Spring 1996.
Nye, James. "Interview with Robert Anton

Wilson." *Fortean Times*, Issue 79. February/March 1995. Reproduced on James Nye's blog at https://thefrogweb.wordpress.com/2014/11/23/raw/

Letters

Heinlein, Robert A. "To Edgar D. Mitchell." 11 June 1974. The Heinlein Archives, Box 409, "Telepathy."

Lovecraft, H.P. "To Fritz Leiber 9 November 1936." *Selected Letters V: 1934–1937*. Sauk City, WI: Arkham House, 1976.

_____. "To Fritz Leiber 15 November 1936." *Selected Letters V: 1934–1937*. Sauk City, WI: Arkham House, 1976.

Letters in Magazines

Rogers, Margaret (as D.C. Rogers). "Action for Mrs. Rogers!" *Amazing Stories*. December 1946. Chicago: Ziff-Davis, 1946.

_____. "Wow! Don't Stop Here!" *Amazing Stories*. September 1946. Chicago: Ziff-Davis, 1946. **Emails**

Dick, Tessa B. "Re: PKD and Fort." Message to author. 8 October 2018. Facebook message.

Drake, David. "Re: Various INFO Issues." Message to author. 14 November 2018. Email.

Mr. X. "Letters to INFO." Message to author. 6 October 2018. Email.

Rock, Ben. "Re: Blair Witch and Forteana." Message to author. 10 July 2019. Facebook message.

Shoemaker, Michael. "Re: Charles Fort Inquiry." Message to author. 17 November 2018. Email.

Websites

Anomaly Archives. "William Gibson: Fortean!" Web blog post. *Anomaly Archives*. September 23, 2012. Web October 4, 2019.

Baratta, Anthony. "WonderCon 2008: Day 2—Part 1!" at *Comingsoon.net*. 24 February 2008. https://www.comingsoon.net/movies/features/42310-wondercon-2008-day-2-part-1#0DgyWWXeljPO0PzR.99

Brice-Sadler, Michael. "Half a million people signed up to storm Area 51. What happens if they actually show?" *The Washington Post*. 12 July 2019. https://beta.washingtonpost.com/national-security/2019/07/13/half-million-people-signed-up-storm-area-what-happens-if-they-actually-show-up/.

Britt, Ryan. "Meet the UFO Expert Who Doesn't Believe in Aliens." *Inverse*, Full Stack Media Inc., 13 September 2016, https://www.inverse.com/article/20857-ufos-flying-saucers-jack-womack.

Coleman, Loren. "Mothman Illustrator Frazetta Dies." Web blog post. *Cryptomundo*. 10 May 2010. Accessed on 13 July 2019. https://cryptomundo.com/cryptozoo-news/frazetta-obit/.

_____. "23 Skidoo: Goodbye Robert Anton Wilson." Web blog post. *Cryptomundo*. January 11th, 2007. Accessed August 13, 2018. https://cryptomundo.com/cryptozoo-news/23-skidoo-raw/.

Dick, Philip K. "Extracts from Philip K. Dick's essay 'If You Find This World Bad.'" Accessed February 25, 2018. http://empslocal.ex.ac.uk/people/staff/mrwatkin/PKDick.htm.

_____. "How to Build a Universe That Doesn't Fall Apart Two Days Later." *Philip K. Dick: How to Build a Universe That Doesn't Fall Apart Two Days Later*, urbigenous.net/library/how_to_build.html. 1974.

Gilland, Steve. "The Legend of Sinkhole Sam." *The Kansan*, 12 June 2010, https://www.thekansan.com/article/20100612/NEWS/306129943.

"International Fortean Organization." *Wikipedia*, Wikimedia Foundation, 5 Sept. 2018, en.wikipedia.org/wiki/International_Fortean_Organization.

Johnston, Mike. "Getting to the Bottom of Mel's Hole." *The Kittitas County Daily Record*. 31 March 2012. Accessed 15 July 2019. https://www.dailyrecordnews.com/news/getting-to-the-bottom-of-mel-s-hole/article_d72b6a68-7ac2-11e1-b3ce-001a4bcf887a.html

Keel, John A. "The Man Who Invented Flying Saucers." *Fortean Times*. No. 41, Winter 1983. Accessed 14 July 2019. http://www.thejinn.net/man_who_invented_flying_saucers.htm

Liptack, Andrew. "The Futurians and the 1939 World Science Fiction Convention." *Kirkus Reviews*, Kirkus Media, 9 May 2013, www.kirkusreviews.com/features/futurians-and-1939-world-science-fiction-conventio/.

Lovecraft, H.P. "The Descendant." *"The Descendant" by H. P. Lovecraft*, www.hplovecraft.com/writings/texts/fiction/de.aspx.

Nickell, Joe. "Charles Fort: Purveyor of the Unprobed." *Skeptical Briefs*, Vol. 18.3. Amherst: Committee for Skeptical Inquiry, Winter 2008/2009. https://skepticalinquirer.org/newsletter/charles_fort_purveyor_of_the_unprobed/

Pappalardo, Joe. "Why 'Starship Troopers' Is the New 'The Art of War.'" *Popular Mechanics*, 5 Feb. 2015, www.popularmechanics.com/military/weapons/a13103/starship-troopers-is-the-new-the-art-of-war/. Accessed 5 Sep. 2018.

Raynes, Brett. "Tim Beckley Reports on the Matrix and the Strange Universe of Philip K. Dick." *AP Magazine*, June 2017, www.apmagazine.info/index.php/index.php?option=com_content&view=article&id=984.

Rickard, Bob. Reply to "Help Finding a Source About INFO." Forteana.org forums, 24 May 2019. https://forums.forteana.org/index.php?threads/help-finding-a-source-about-info.64640/

Senkowski, Ernst. *Instrumental Transcommunication*. (Translated from German) http://www.worlditc.org/c_07_senki_f_38.12.11.htm Originally published 1995.

Steiger, Brad. "Philip K. Dick's Phylogenic Memory and the Divine Fire." *Alternate Perceptions Magazine*. Issue #118, November 2007. http://mysterious-america.com/-philipdick-brads.html

Womack, Jack. "Jack Womack: Going, Going, Gone." Forum post at Inkwell.vue. 1 August 2001. https://people.well.com/conf/inkwell.vue/topics/118/Jack-Womack-Going-Going-Gone-page01.html#post23

_____. "Jack Womack: Going, Going, Gone." Forum post at Inkwell.vue. 2 August 2001. https://people.well.com/conf/inkwell.vue/topics/118/Jack-Womack-Going-Going-Gone-page02.html#post27

Newspapers

Braun, Stephen. "The Strange Faith of Dr. Corder: He Believes That Aliens Walk Among Us and the Apocalypse Is Nigh. But Does That Mean He Isn't a Good Doctor?" *LA Times*. October 23, 1994. http://articles.latimes.com/1994-10-23/magazine/tm-53920_1_scott-corder

Cooper, Helene, Ralph Blumenthal and Leslie Kean. "Glowing Auras and 'Black Money': The Pentagon's Mysterious UFO Program." *The New York Times*, 16 December 2017, https://www.nytimes.com/2017/12/16/us/politics/pentagon-program-ufo-harry-reid.html.

Heitman, Danny. "Fiction as Authentic as Fact." *The Wall Street Journal*. New York: News Corp, 11 January 2013. https://www.wsj.com/articles/SB10001424127887323936804578227971298012486

Jonas, Gerald. "Arthur C. Clarke, Author Who Saw Science Fiction Become Real, Dies at 90." *The New York Times*, 18 March 2008, www.nytimes.com/2008/03/19/books/19clarke.html.

Stage, Wm. "Space Case." *Riverfront Times*, 5 April 2000. https://www.riverfronttimes.com/stlouis/space-case/Content?oid=2474776

Templeton, David. "The Kecksburg Files." *The Pittsburgh Post-Gazette*. 9 September 1998. http://old.post-gazette.com/magazine/19980908ufo1.asp

Miscellaneous

Abrahams, Brad, director. *Love and Saucers*. Curator Pictures, 2017.

Gibson, William (GreatDismal). "@Elpico72 The Bar Hade was my affectionate approximation of a certain flavor of paranormal folk motif. Not from any actual source." 7 May 2010, 9:57 PM. Tweet.

Grundy, Benjamin, and Aaron Wright. "17.05." *Mysterious Universe*, season 17, episode 5, 2017. https://mysteriousuniverse.org/2017/02/17-05-mu-podcast/

Menger, Howard. *Authentic Music from Another Planet*, Slate Enterprises, 1957. LP record.

"Out of the Blue." Flynn, Charles and Michael Weigall, directors. *Arthur C. Clarke's Mysterious World*, season 1, episode 9, ITV, 4 November 1980.

Stivelman, Alan, director. *Witness of Another World*. Humano Films SA, 2018

Index

The Illuminatus Trilogy 131–135, 153
"The Indefatigable Frog" 112
influencing machine 86
Institute of Noetic Sciences (IONS) 125, 128–129
International Fortean Organization (INFO) 14, 50–54, 69, 71, 93, 114, 120, 128, 160n120

Johnson, Robert Barbour 78
The Journal of the Fortean Research Center 31, 52

Keel, John A. 9, 15, 30, 41–43, 47, 50, 55–56, 96, 100, 113–114, 133, 137
Keyhoe, Donald 47, 141
King, Stephen 142–143
Knight, Damon 6, 15–16, 47, 54, 93–96, 160n116

Lazar, Bob 31
Leary, Timothy 131, 138
Leiber, Fritz 52, 62–63, 70–72; letters to H.P. Lovecraft 62–63, 70
Lo! 12, 13, 16–17, 20, 25–26, 35, 47–48, 49, 63, 66, 69, 75–76, 89, 90, 98, 113, 122, 133–134, 142, 143
Lovecraft, Howard Phillips 60–63, 66, 67, 70–71, 145

Magnolia (1999 film) 144
A Maze of Death 115
Mel's Hole 44–45
Menger, Howard 33
Messengers of Deception 41, 48, 57, 76, 90, 126–127, 137
Miller, R. Dewitt 18–20
Milligan, Billy 86–87
Mines, Samuel 17
Mr. X 52, 144
Mitchell, Edgar 128–129
Monism 15, 117
Moskowitz, Sam 66–67, 70, 89–90, 93–95
The Mothman Prophecies 30, 41–42, 47, 56

The New Inquisition 133, 135, 136–137
New Lands 12, 15, 35, 66, 68

O'Brien, Barbara 20, 85–86
Ong's Hat 37–38

Palmer, Raymond A. 29, 54, 74–75, 79–85, 87–93, 99, 113, 146
Passport to Magonia 5–6, 48
"The Possessed" 108
"Project Nightmare" 125
The Puppet Masters 73, 125–127, 134

"A Radical Corpuscle" 13, 15, 72, 94, 100, 118
"Rat Race" 72–73
Rendezvous with Rama 106–108

The Report from Iron Mountain 57
Rock, Ben 39
Rogers, Margaret 83–86
Russell, Eric Frank 14, 17, 59, 60, 63–67, 69, 73, 90, 98, 102–103, 113, 121, 123, 124

A Scanner Darkly 114
Shaver, Richard S. 7, 20, 29, 32, 45, 54, 55–56, 75, 78, 80–89, 90, 91–92, 93, 94, 113, 116, 117, 153
Shea, Robert 131–134, 153
Sherman, Harold M. 74–77
Shipley, Maynard 69, 162n42
Shoemaker, Michael 53, 69, 94–95
Sinister Barrier 63–67, 69, 90, 102–103, 113
Sitchin, Zecharia 35–36
Skinwalker legend 31
"The Space Visitors" 67
Starship Troopers 120
Steiger, Brad 112–114
Strieber, Whitley 27, 29, 32–33, 43, 47–48, 57, 118, 137
Suvin, Darko 20, 23, 37, 51

Thayer, Tiffany 14, 65, 94, 136
The Time Machine 9–10, 80
truth-fiction 20, 37, 55, 79, 80
2001: A Space Odyssey 1–2, 100–106, 107, 118, 122, 123, 153

Unknown (magazine) 63–65, 90, 113

VALIS 15, 102, 112–119
Vallee, Jacques 5–6, 18, 21, 34–35, 41, 48–49, 56–57, 74, 76, 90, 100, 103–105, 123, 126–127, 137, 147–148, 153
The Vertical Plane 39–41
Vulcan's Hammer 86

The War of the Worlds 9–10, 47
Weekly World News 32, 148
Wells, H.G. 5–6, 9–10, 13, 14, 16, 47, 60, 61, 73, 102, 106, 107, 111
Who Goes There? 89–90
Wild Talents 12, 16, 49–50, 68–69, 77, 125, 129, 143, 144, 149
Willis brothers (Ron and Paul) 14, 52–54, 69
Wilson, Colin 63, 168n2
Wilson, Robert Anton 24, 32, 52, 116, 125, 131–138
Womack, Jack 25–26, 141

X and Y (proposed books) 11, 123
The X-Files 52, 55, 141, 150

"The Year of the Jackpot" 124–125
"You're All Alone" 71–72

Index

Ace Books 19–20, 25, 85, 140–141
Adamski, George 75–77
agnosticism 11, 50, 135–138
Algonquin Roundtable 14, 66
Amazing Stories 29, 55, 75–76, 79–89, 94–96
Ancient Aliens (TV series) 36, 39
Anubis (SF fanzine) 52–54
Arnold, Kenneth 47–48, 80, 88, 146, 164n59
Asimov, Isaac 68, 96
Astounding Stories (*Analog Science Fiction*) 16, 18, 63, 65, 83, 85, 89–98, 113, 121–122

Balliett, Blue 143–144
The Blair Witch Project 23, 38–39
Blish, James 53
The Book of the Damned 11–12, 14, 16, 20, 49, 66–67, 123, 125–126, 140–141
Browne, Howard 81, 87–89

"The Call of Cthulu" 60–61
Campbell, John W. 59, 70, 83, 89–96, 108, 121–122
Childhood's End 97, 99–103, 107, 109, 111, 118
Clarke, Arthur C. 32–33, 46, 90, 93, 96, 97–111, 117–118, 122–123, 128, 138, 153
Coast to Coast AM 38, 43–44
comic books 65, 79, 145–146
Corliss, William R. 46
cosmic pessimism 10–11, 60–61, 63, 102, 106–107
Cosmic Trigger 135–138
cryptozoology 32, 46–47, 51, 72–74

Däniken, Erich Von 35–36
Davis, Hank 141–142
Dean Drive 91–92
deFord, Miriam Allen 68–69
Dick, Philip K. 15, 24, 32, 52, 56, 57–58, 86, 93, 96, 102, 111–119, 128, 134–136; *Exegesis of* 113, 116–118
Dick, Tessa 112
"Dog Star" 108–109
Doubt (magazine)
Drake, David 52, 141–142, 160n116
Dreadful Sanctuary 65, 73

"The Dreams in the Witch-House" 61
Dreiser, Theodore 1, 10–14, 16, 66
Dune 72, 73–74

"The Earth Owners" 67, 71
Edwards, Frank 25, 143, 149–150
Eye in the Sky 115

Fairman, Paul W. 87–89
Fanthorpe, Lionel 168n2
Farmer, Phillip José 92
FATE Magazine 54, 87–88, 93, 133
Filing, Anna 16
Fortean Society 13–14, 51–52, 54, 63, 69, 94, 136
Fortean Times 31, 39, 53, 62, 134–135
Frazetta, Frank 56
"From Beyond" 60
Fuller, R. Buckminster 93, 136, 138
Futurians 6, 93–96, 97, 113

Gardner, Martin 15, 28, 35, 135
Gardner, Thomas S. 67, 81
Gibson, William 116, 139–141
Gnosticism 115, 117
The Golden Man 128
"Goldfish Bowl" 107, 121–125
Gould, Rupert T. 18–19, 65
"The Green Man" 74–76

Hamilton, Edmond 14, 66–68, 71, 124
Hancock, Graham 35–36
Hecht, Ben 14
Heinlein, Robert A. 52–53, 69, 71, 107, 120–130, 134; interest in no "World as Myth" 121, 127–128
Herbert, Frank 72–74, 107
"Herbert West—Reanimator" 60
Hieronymus machine 91–92
Hoffmann, E.T.A. 5
Holzer, Hans 19–20
Hubbard, L. Ron 90–92
Huxley, T.H. 10–11, 60
Hynek, J. Allen 48–49, 103–104

www.ingramcontent.com/pod-product-compliance
Lightning Source LLC
Chambersburg PA
CBHW021356300426
44114CB00012B/1250